Language, Literature and
the Learner

APPLIED LINGUISTICS AND LANGUAGE STUDY

General Editor
Professor Christopher N. Candlin, Macquarie University, Sydney

For a complete list of books in this series see pages v and vi

Language, Literature and the Learner

Creative Classroom Practice

Edited by

**Ronald Carter
and
John McRae**

Longman

London and New York

Pearson Education Limited
Edinburgh Gate
Harlow, Essex CM20 2JE
United Kingdom
and Associated Companies throughout the world

Published in the United States of America
by Pearson Education Inc, New York

First Published 1996
Second impression 1999

ISBN 0 582 293235 Ppr

British Library Cataloguing-in-Publication Data

A catalogue record for this book is
available from the British Library

Library of Congress Cataloging-in-Publication Data

Language, literature, and the learner : creative classroom practice/
    edited by Ronald Carter and John McRae.
        p.   cm. — (Applied linguistics and language study)
    Includes bibliographical references and index.
        ISBN 0–582–29323–5
        1. Philology—Study and teaching (Secondary) I. Carter, Ronald.
    II. McRae, John. III. Series.
    P51.L3534   1996
    407'.1'2—dc20   96–33278
                                                              CIP

Set by 8H in 10/12pt New Baskerville

Printed and bound by Antony Rowe Ltd, Eastbourne
Transferred to digital print on demand, 2003

APPLIED LINGUISTICS AND LANGUAGE STUDY

GENERAL EDITOR

PROFESSOR CHRISTOPHER N. CANDLIN

Macquarie University, Sydney

Contents

Contributors

Ronald Carter is Professor of Modern English Language in the Department of English Studies, University of Nottingham.

Guy Cook is Reader in Applied Linguistics in the Department of English for Speakers of Other Languages, University of London.

Alan Durant is Professor and Head of the School of English, Cultural and Communication Studies, Middlesex University.

Anthony Jennings lectures at the University of Rome III.

Alan Maley is Senior Fellow in the Department of English Language and Literature at the National University of Singapore.

Mao Sihui is Associate Professor of English Language and Literature in the Department of English, Guangzdong University of Foreign Studies, Guangzhou, China.

Michael McCarthy is Reader in Applied Linguistics and Director of the Centre for English Language Education, Department of English Studies, University of Nottingham.

John McRae is Special Professor in the Department of English Studies at the University of Nottingham.

Mick Short is Senior Lecturer in the Department of Linguistics and Modern English Language, Lancaster University.

Barbara Sinclair is lecturer in TESOL in the Faculty of Education, University of Nottingham.

Malachi Edwin Vethamani is lecturer in TESOL and literatures in English in the Department of Languages at the Universiti Pertanian, Kuala Lumpur, Malaysia.

Anita Weston lectures at the University of Rome, La Sapienza.

General Editor's Preface

It is somewhat more difficult than usual to provide a General Editors' Preface to this collection, for the straightforward reason that the Editors themselves have gone to some very useful and insightful lengths in their own Introduction and through the abstracts prefacing each paper, to provide the reader with an extensive framework for engaging with the book. By these means, and through the choice of papers itself, they convincingly argue their case for constructing a pedagogy for language and literature teaching where both disciplines interact and help define each other's relevance for what Ron Carter calls in his paper the 'language and literature classroom'. They do so both in terms of recommending a varied and differentiated subject-matter and in terms of motivating alternative pedagogic modes. Given this scoping of the book, what I would like to argue here, then, is a related but slightly different case for the relevance now and importance of this collection, a case which in keeping with the tenor of this most recent contribution to the *Applied Linguistics and Language Study Series,* is focused on and warranted by the classroom and its curriculum.

About twenty years or so ago now, and imbued by much the same set of goals and issues as in this collection, my colleague Michael Breen and myself asked ourselves the Ward Goodenough anthropological question of how you would recognise a 'communicative classroom' if you ever found yourself in one, and the answer that we came up with, as you might expect, rather depended on how one had learned to construct the classroom in the first place, either as a teacher, or as a learner, or as both. In the event, we chose to construct and recognise it as a site where in relation to language and language learning and teaching, the relationships among a number of participating persons, positions, topics, subject-matters, processes, orientations, roles, values, and ideologies were held not to be fixed, and their nature or preeminence taken for granted, but rather to be in a state of constant, creative and usefully exploratory struggle. Framing this creativity and defining the activities of this classroom was the search (never-ending, of course) for meaning. In fact, we deliberately constructed and crafted our model classroom as a communicative site rich in meaning potential, governed and characterised by two operational metaphors, each mutually reinforcing of the other, that of the *laboratory* and that of the *observatory*. A site where language learning work of all kinds was to be jointly and differentiatedly done, as in a laboratory, but also a site where the subject-matter and the raw material resource for such creative and adaptive work would desirably come from learners' *own* expeditions and researches: observing the real world of communication outside the classroom walls, inquiring into the available rescenscions and catalogues of the discourses of that world, and, equally importantly, exploring the imaginary and reflective world of the learners' own experiences and minds. One could take the metaphors further, we thought, by pointing out how this observational work would always be refracted through the prism of the learners' knowledges and experiences activated in the classroom laboratory, and, that promoting and guiding that process was, perhaps, the main pedagogic challenge facing the language teacher. Such a classroom would then be a site where, drawing on rather than resisting the obvious asymmetries and variabilities of participant knowledge, experience, communicative repertoires, perceptions of relevance and personal affective engagement, collective and collaborative work on language and learning could be enabled to thrive. A site, too, where the mutual involvement of teachers and learners at different classroom moments in shared and changing participant roles and practices was to be positively encouraged. Indeed, in a now well-known paper, Michael Breen subsequently even likened the experience of this exploration to that of the ethnographer's coral garden, transposing that creative metaphor for a culture, where grasping the significance of the form of products and artefacts, both made and modelled, presupposed a sympathetic appreciation of the artisanship of their creation. So, that classroom was a world worth exploring and a world worth explaining. The prior questions were, how to engender it and how to document its goings-on?

It is here that another reminiscence is in order and becomes relevant. Somewhat prior to the above, I had been (and still to some extent am) involved in what might now bid fair to be reckoned the longest-lasting reported-on program of informal, collective, teacher professional development linked to curriculum development and reform, in the modern history of second/foreign language education, one associated with the teaching of English (and other languages) in the German (and now much much widely geographically drawn) secondary school system. The relevant issue here is that the main considerations of that program, then as now, were the means by which the classroom described loosely above could be operationalised. How could the metaphors of this classroom and its meaning potential be realised in practice?

Insofar as there can ever be one particular stimulus to any initiative of such a kind, a couple of small English language classroom teacher texts called *Encounters*, written in the late 1970s by team members Martin Seletzky and Mitch Legutke, (among many others developed over the years by the ever renewing program team members, it must be said) offered one significant means to such a realisation. What these particular books did was to take very seriously what was and continues to my mind really to be the guiding principle of communicative language teaching, (a precept, somewhat improbably you might think in this pedagogic context, actively canvassed by us at the time through the writings of the German sociologist Juergen Habermas, notably, I recall, in an article in *Die Deutsche Schule*), a principle which focused on the central importance to the promoting of communicative competence of the restoring to/creating within the learner the right and the means and the awareness of personal capacity to make her or his own meanings from and with texts – guided, of course, by the curriculum and facilitated by the teacher.

The books in question were about language in literature and literature in language. Not, however, narrowly in either case since they were as much if not more about discourse as they were about form, as much if not more about everyday creativity in language as they were about the polished forms of the pedagogically approved (and largely metropolitan) canon, and as their title announced, centrally about personally considered and collaboratively discussed and negotiated encounters with texts. Making that connection among language, language learning and language teaching through the creative exploitation in the classroom of the meaning potential of all three, was quite radical at the time. It was so, because it broke the conventions: that literature was to be regarded pedagogically as something separate from language, and without question from separate from *language* learning, that schoolchildren, especially in a foreign language, could not be relied upon to create imaginative texts which were literature-like at very least, that they could not be entrusted with exploiting their communicative competence to make their own meanings and offer them for further exploration and appraisal by their peers, even if that was ultimately the only worthwhile, tenable and indeed utilitarian goal of the entire process of language schooling.

What these books did (though we didn't make quite that leap at the time) was to set out in embryo a curricular framework for language education which had not language and not literature at its basis, but *creativity*. In short, to make the connection that enhancing communicative *capacity* (a better term than *competence*, as Widdowson rightly noted ten years ago) was at heart a matter of developing learners' creative abilities, enabling them to be realised in communicative action through engagement with texts, and continually to test the boundaries of learners' abilities and knowledge by posing them the challenge of meaning-making tasks.

Now, such a focus on creativity poses a number of challenges: its principles need defining, its cultural relativity needs acknowledging, its scope in terms of social as well as aesthetic practices needs mapping, and above all in that classroom site, its pedagogic value needs arguing. What we felt sure about (though maybe we would not have been able to put it that way then), as Ron Carter and John McRea now make very clear in the underlying philosophy of this collection, is that creativity involved a connectionist rather than a linear and serialist form of meaning-making practice, a process of continual problem-sensing and problem-posing, drawing variably on a range of members' resources. It was a chicken-and-egg matter really whether the classroom practice we wanted (for other social reasons) to engender made us look to these books for ways of working with imaginative texts, or vice-versa; the main point was to establish the linkage and to keep three balls in the classroom air at once: describing texts, interpreting their value and explaining their personal, social and historical significance. More than that, however, such a linkage allowed two further feats, the one connecting creativity with *culture* and the other connecting the principles and practices of creativity with the *curriculum* as a whole. Culture proved less of a problem than curriculum. After all, it is reasonably commonplace to look at culture in terms of the trio of artefacts, behaviours and values, and all three can be treated descriptively and separately as nominalised objects (products/actions/beliefs), treated interpretively as processes (acts of producing/behaving/valuing) or explained as practices and products whose normative conventionality or potentially transf rming unconventionality implies a connection with historically specific and socially structured context and symbolic processes. Of course, culture is at once all three, and expanding on Brian Street's aphorism when he called culture 'a verb' we may say that in addition to a morphology and a grammar governing its conventions, it has also tense, aspect, voice, mood and, above all, it has modality. Seen from this semiotic perspective, the job of studying culture should not so much be a devilling for some fixed inheritance of shared meanings abstracted from experience, but rather of proposing candidate and context-sensitive explanations for creative and active symbolisation and meaning-making. Just so for language learning and language teaching. The links between culture, language and communicative capacity thus become clear, as does the need in such cultural exploration for the mediating power of imaginative texts, whatever their source. Halliday's comment is here very apt:

> ... because all our linguistic acts as adults are mediated by the ideational and interpersonal systems which are at the centre of the language system we create for ourselves, every act is not only linguistic; a use of the potential of the language system, but it is also social and cultural, an expression of who we are and what we give value to.

So, creative language use is characteristic of all human communication, not some special and exclusive authorial act enshrined in some privileged texts, and, as significantly, such linguistic creativity is not just a expression of personal identity but also at once a reflection and an act of maintenance (or the reverse) of an increasingly contested social order. In short, communication implies a drawing on members' resources to co-construct the production and reception of messages whose nature and purposefulness within a culture are always diverse, again always co-constructed and set within the bounds of imaginable (but not uninfringeable) convention.

The question remains: what about the link to curriculum? Can such creativity become a curricular act? You might not think so by looking around you, now as then. After all, for many learners and teachers, curricula act to constrain, they suppress. You would be wrong, though, to infer from that unfortunate if common experience the existence of some general and fundamentally contravening principle. Any creativity, after all, presupposes a frame. The achievement comes from the flexibility of the curriculum to encourage (not just *permit*) intentional pattern-breaking within the frame, promote the testing of its boundaries and support the regular and constant pattern-forming and transforming of its conventionalities. We know language works like that, we assert that culture may do so also, the question for us then as now is can curricula stand the strain? As I said at the outset about the classroom, it depends on how you construct the curriculum. One way which would be in harmony with what has been written above, (though not yet especially creative) would be to begin by distinguishing within the curriculum three 'levels' (though the word is too hard and fast for complete comfort). Overarching would be a set of curriculum guidelines and principles for language learning and teaching, imbued by a set of precepts, values, and ideologies, very important among which would be that of creativity (in the senses drawn on earlier in this Preface and throughout the papers in this collection). Intermediate, and governed by such principles, would be the curriculum documents that act as resources for learning in the classroom: the books, the data, the resources, the tasks, if you like, the objects and artefacts of the culture of the curriculum. Again, many of the papers in this collection admirably suggest something of their shape and nature. At the point most intimate to the classroom site are the procedures and processes of classroom action: what is done and accomplished in the social context of learning and teaching. This is potentially the engine from which, governed by those overarching principles and resourced by those curriculum artefacts, the necessary power for language learning work of the laboratory and the observatory can be creatively provided. Again, there are papers here which have such a process focus. But still, where does that leave the question of *curriculum* creativity? Achieving that requires communication, but of a distinctive kind. What is needed here is an institutional system, a governance if you like, where the activities and processes of learning and teaching can act to influence, and indeed guarantee, the viability, authenticity, and relevance of the curriculum resources, but also and at a higher 'level' provide a continuing monitor of, and where necessary a challenge to, the continuing credibility of the curriculum guidelines. With such a creative system in place, the curriculum achieves the wherewithal for its continuing renewal, it has the means of realising its own meaning potential as an educational process.

What it requires, at base, is an infusion at all 'levels' of the principles, knowledge and practices governing creative and imaginative language use. It is in this way, then, that we saw in our minds one way in which *creativity, classrooms, culture, communicative capacity*, and the language educational *curriculum* itself, could achieve some harmonious integration. Where teachers and learners could influence this process was, chiefly, in terms of choices of resources and in terms of classroom actions. To support them in this task, what they needed were helpful resources which gave priority to creative uses of language and which, drawing on both canonical and everyday imaginative discourses, showed how they could exploit the communicative repertoires of their learners, and through the experience of that successful action, to influence the ways in which the overarching principles could themselves be redefined. This is the 'slightly different case' I have wanted to argue in respect of the value of *Language, Literature and the Learner*. Had they been available at that time, the papers in this book would have offered just such a resource for classroom action and curriculum change. The pleasure and significance of these papers now lies not only in their intrinsic value, but also because the intellectual climate in which they will now be received is at last entirely appropriate and conducive to their utility. The issue that still remains, however, in language education is not whether classroom action, curriculum resources and curriculum principles have access to a common language, but whether that language and the circumstances of its use are adequate, responsive and creative enough to allow the 'levels' of the curriculum to communicate.

Professor Christopher N Candlin
General Editor
Macquarie University, Sydney
Australia

Publisher's acknowledgements

We are grateful to the following for permission to reproduce copyright material:

IDV, Harlow, for the Cinzano advertisement on page 159; Carlin Dick and The British Council for Figures 10.1 and 10.2 from 'British Cultural Studies as a multidimensional subject' pp. 17–20, *British Studies Now Anthology* edited by Nick Wadham-Smith, The British Council 1995; the author, Eric Amman for his haiku poem 'quietly dozing'; The Bookmark, Inc for an extract from the article 'May Day Eve' by Nick Joaquin from *Philippine Contemporary Literature* (1970); Cambridge University Press for the poem 'Still Life' by Alan Duff from *The Inward Ear* by Alan Maley and Alan Duff (1989); Faber and Faber Ltd for extracts from the play *Woman in Mind* by Alan Ayckbourn (1986); HarperCollins Publishers, for the imprint Flamingo, for extracts from *By Grand Central Station I Sat Down and Wept* by Elizabeth Smart; the author, Philip Jayaretnam for an extract from 'Making Coffee' from *Skoob Pacifica Anthology No. 1: S.E. Asia Writes Back!* (Skoob Books, 1993) Copyright Jayaretnam (his latest novel is *Abraham's Promise* (Times Editions Ltd 1995; University of Hawaii Press, 1995); Macmillan General Books, for the imprint Papermac, for the poem 'Heredity' from *The Complete Poems of Thomas Hardy*; the author, Gerda Mayer for her poem 'Well Caught' © Gerda Mayer (first published in *Samphire*, 1975 and *The Knockabout Show*, Chatto Poets for the Young, Chatto & Windus, 1978); Penguin Books Ltd/the author's agent on behalf of Paul Theroux for an adapted extract from *The Kingdom By The Sea* by Paul Theroux (Hamish Hamilton, 1983) copyright © Paul Theroux 1983; Random House UK Ltd on behalf of the Estate of the Author and Harcourt Brace & Company for an adapted extract from *To the Lighthouse* by Virginia Woolf (Chatto & Windus) copyright 1927 by Harcourt Brace & Company and renewed 1954 by Leonard Woolf; Simon & Schuster for an adapted extract from *Earthly Powers* by Anthony Burgess. Copyright © 1980 by Anthony Burgess; The Estate of Virginia Woolf for an extract from *To the Lighthouse – the original holograph draft*, transcribed and edited by Susan Dick (University of Toronto Press, 1982) © The Estate of Virginia Woolf, 1941.

We have unfortunately been unable to trace the copyright holder of the poems 'The Wall' by Abdul Ghafar Ibrahim and 'Offerings' by Hilary Tham and would appreciate any information which would enable us to do so.

Editors' acknowledgements

The editors of this book wish to acknowledge, as they do with many of their projects, the invaluable help and support provided by Jeremy Hunter on the writing and editing of the book.

The book is dedicated to Jane Carter and to Jeremy Hunter.

Introduction

About this book

The essays in this book originated in three international seminars
hosted in the English Studies department at the University of
Nottingham during the years 1990–1994. The seminars were all
devoted to the teaching of literature in the second or foreign language classroom and explicitly addressed the interface between
language and literature teaching, with particular reference to
English in the secondary school and, more generally, to intermediate and upper-intermediate learners. Participants attended from
over thirty different countries; many are teachers or teacher-trainers
and it is inevitable therefore that issues related to the appropriate
preparation of teachers for the integrated language and literature
classroom were a prominent feature of discussions and have entered
into a number of the papers collected in this volume. Although
issues of practice can never be theory-free, the focus of the seminars
and of the papers in this collection is practical, classroom-based and
methodology-sensitive; in this respect the collection is a companion
volume to Carter, Walker and Brumfit (eds. 1989) – a volume which
also grew out of seminars organised by the British Council.[1]

The book also complements Short (ed. 1989) which is another
volume of collected papers addressed to the integration of language
and literature, although it is concerned principally with the teaching of *stylistics* and with more advanced and university-level students.
Language, Literature and the Learner aims to be a book which does not
neglect why we do it, but it is mainly concerned to demonstrate how
we do it. It is a resource manual for the practising teacher.

It is not our aim in this introduction to write a survey of the
field. Such overviews exist elsewhere and in his opening paper

Ronald Carter devotes some space to reviewing recent and current developments in the field. We do, however, feel obliged to provide a framework within which the papers can be read. Collections of papers by diverse hands can often be no more than collections of papers by diverse hands; our aim is to argue that there are distinctive and coherent practical language-based approaches to the teaching of literature, that the Nottingham seminars underlined such coherence, and that the papers which have grown organically from the seminars can be read as part of a unified and coordinated perspective.

Literature for study; literature as resource

Maley (1989) and, by extension, in this volume, makes a valuable distinction between the *study* of literature and the *use* of literature as a resource for language learning. The study of literature involves an approach to texts as aesthetically patterned artefacts; using literature as a linguistic resource involves starting from the fact that literature is language in use and can therefore be exploited for language-learning purposes. The study of literature also involves, Maley points out, a considerable baggage of metalanguage, critical concepts, knowledge of conventions and the like, which for second-language learners presupposes a prior engagement with the study of literature in a first language. It does not automatically lead to a consideration of the role of language in literature. Needless to say, the two different approaches stem from different traditions and imply different methodologies. These different traditions, which are not necessarily mutually exclusive, are represented by the contributions to this book; there is, however, an emphasis on literature as a resource in the classroom for language growth and development and on language as a point of entry (McRae 1991) to greater literary understanding and appreciation.

Literature teaching as product; literature teaching as process

Product-based teaching

In spite of numerous advantages, the analytical and study techniques associated with approaches to the *study* of literature are *product-centred.* The best work has tended to focus on the text as holistic, as something which is intact and even sacrosanct; the related pedagogies have been concerned with the development of skills for reading the text as an object of study. Consequently, techniques are presented for the student to acquire, with the underlying assumption that they are learned by practice rather in the manner of an apprentice in the company of the expert practitioner. In many respects, this runs counter to current language-teaching theory and practice which is more concerned with process and with texts which, if pedagogically required, can be extended, re-written, lexically or grammatically altered, or literally 'cut up' in order to develop appropriate capacities in the student. It also runs counter to recent developments in literary theory which argue that texts are not completely fixed or stable entities.

More product- and teacher-centred still are methods of teaching literature which take the text as a body of knowledge which has to be transmitted to the student in the form of 'background' to be remembered and conveniently recalled when the situation, usually in the form of examinations, requires it. Such methods of presenting literature are directed towards a development of knowledge *about* literature rather than knowledge *of* literature (see Carter and Long 1991, ch. 1). There is normally little concern with how to use knowledge to read literature for oneself or to learn how to make one's own meanings. Like the text itself, the meanings are, as it were, pre-given. They are stable and in place. The outcome for students is that they learn to rely on authorities outside themselves, either in the form of the teacher or in the form of histories of literature or books of literary criticism, which are often simply memorised for narrowly instrumental purposes. Students with good memories do well under such a system. The really successful are possibly those who would in any case develop the necessary literary competence whether they had a teacher or not. Needless to say, such methods do not bear any systematic relation to the development of linguistic skills in students and those teaching literature in this way would probably be opposed to any notion that literature and language study might be integrated.

The above description of product-centred teaching is inevitably a little caricatured. We have to recognise that literature is always more than language and that appreciation and enjoyment of literature transcend the development of linguistic capacities. We shall return to these issues subsequently. But it is important to explain the context within which more process-based methodologies for literature teaching have evolved.

Process-based teaching

Several of the papers in this collection explore the role of literary texts in the language classroom and, in particular, as a resource for language development. Fundamentally, it involves the teacher coming down from the pedestal or lectern and involves a class-room treatment of literature which does not view literature as a sacrosanct object for reverential, product-centred study. A process-centred pedagogy for literature means that literary texts do not have special status in the classroom. Methodologically, this has at least the following implications:

- strategies drawn from the EFL classroom will be applied, if necessary in an adapted way, to the teaching of literary texts. This means that a whole range of standard procedures such as cloze, re-writing, prediction activities, role-playing are deployed in the literature lesson; or, to put it in another way, literary texts are treated in the language lesson in ways which may not be radically different from the ways in which any other kind of text is treated.
- texts are manipulated in order to activate student response. A text can be 'cut up' and students asked to re-arrange it; it can be dramatised even if it is not overtly a dramatic text (see McCarthy, this volume).
- the orientation is away from teacher-centredness towards language-based, student-centred activities which aim to involve students with the text, to develop their perceptions of it and to help them explore and express those perceptions. Comparison with other texts and other media can lead to such student-centredness, as Guy Cook, Mao Sihui and Anthony Jennings suggest in their contributions to the volume.
- the channel of communication between teacher and student will cease to be exclusively one-way; there will be a proportion of group and pair work appropriate to the nature of the activities which will in turn be those appropriate to the particular text (see, in particular, Durant, in this volume). It is not assumed that there is only one way in which such reading can be organised and a main overall aim is to encourage greater

self-sufficiency among students and correspondingly less reliance on the teacher as a source of knowledge. Greater learner autonomy, as Barbara Sinclair points out (chapter 8), entails strategies for learners who have begun to work out themselves their own preferred modes of reading.

Teaching literature; teaching literature as language

A consistent argument advanced by teachers of literature with no marked linguistic interests is that such language-based and process-oriented approaches to the teaching of literature are reductive. That is, in so far as they succeed, they succeed only by reducing the text to its language and consequently fail to recognise that literary texts are holistic artefacts, are situated within cultural traditions, are historically shaped and grow out of the lived experiences of the writer. Literary texts are therefore so much more than their language. Studying literature as language may in some educational contexts be a necessary condition for the development of literary competence but such practices are by no means a sufficient condition. Full appreciation of literature requires an extensive, detailed and disciplined study which acknowledges that product-based teaching, which in turns draws on historical, socio-cultural and biographical information about texts, is a key component in any approach to the teaching of literature as literature.

We accept that arguments for language-based approaches (e.g. Carter, Walker and Brumfit 1989; Carter and Long 1991) may have allowed commitments to student-centred and process-based methodologies to undervalue the part that more information-based, teacher-directed and holistic approaches play in the study of literature. Indeed it has not always been sufficiently underlined that process and product, literature for study and literature for resource, teacher-centred and student-centred are not mutually inimical but can and should rather complement each other as necessary continuities in the development of learning to read literature. In the previous two sections we have, of course, deliberately reinforced divisions so that readers have a clear framework with which to consider the papers in this volume in particular and the teaching of literature in general. Before proceeding to explore further differences, distinctions, and continuities, we should say explicitly that none of the contributors to this volume sees the teaching of literature and the teaching of literature as language as disconnected pedagogic practices.

Contributors generally argue that teaching literary texts should result in literary experiences and that the work undertaken on the language of the texts should not simply be an end in itself but should also service literary goals. A basic element in this literary experience could be said to be the way in which literary texts do not so much *refer* to experiences as *represent* them (McRae 1991). This representation of experience, be it emotional, intellectual or imaginative, occurs in and through linguistic and formal elements in the text and by a process of mimesis which allows correlations between form and meaning to be highlighted in such a way that the reader activates the process. The literary experience is not then a direct one, though readers may be able to relate it to actual experience; it is essentially an indirect representational one which readers have to activate. To relate to this experience, readers are normally required to suspend disbelief and participate imaginatively in the world created by the text; and the way words are used encourages this imaginative involvement and enhances its pleasure. It is important that something of the nature of this representation of experience is conveyed in the lesson, whether it be termed a literature or a language lesson.

Other significant points are that literary texts provide authentic, unsimplified material (though this is not to say that simplified texts may not have a place in certain contexts). Such materials construct experiences or 'content' in a non-trivial way which gives voice to complexities and subtleties not always present in other types of text. A further feature of literary texts is that ambiguities and indeterminacies in experience are preserved, thus providing many natural opportunities for discussion and for resolution of differing interpretations. As Anita Weston (this volume) points out, literary texts generate many questions about what means what and how things come to mean what they mean.

It is probably preferable therefore to regard the positions articulated in the different papers in this volume as operating along a continuum. Along this continuum, individual positions inevitably exhibit tendencies towards either literature for study or literature as resource, towards either product- or process-based methodologies, towards either literature as language or literature as literature before it is literature as language. We repeat, however, that an orientation to the practical classroom-based interfaces between language and literature remains a dominant paradigm.

Literatures in English; Englishes in literature

Literature in English has been an academic subject for only a little over one hundred years. For much of that time, the discipline has attracted controversy: who's in and who's out of the canon (from Saintsbury to Leavis to, most recently, Harold Bloom); high culture versus low or popular culture; re-thinking '-isms' (feminism, new historicism, etc.) and minority discourses (Scottish, Irish, Welsh writings, gay voices, immigrant writing, etc.); as well as the welter of critical approaches which have burgeoned – reader response, structuralism, deconstruction, and language-based and stylistic approaches calling on discourse analysis, speech act theory, etc.

Critics create canons; canons and critics co-exist. As critical approaches – philosophical, lingusitic, and historical – have expanded, so have the canons. Few would now consider what used to be called 'Commonwealth Literature' marginal (see Rushdie 1983/1991). Indeed, few would now even dare to call it Commonwealth writing; there are many new Englishes all over the world, from far more nations than were ever British colonies. The recent label 'post-colonial' has also been found inadequate by many critics, such that now, perhaps, 'new literatures in English' is the most appropriate term to cover this exciting and ever-expanding field.

The canon of English literature is continually expanding too. A few years ago, such names as Aphra Behn or Charlotte Smith would hardly have been mentioned in a history of English literature. Now, thanks to feminist criticism, it would be unthinkable to leave them out.

At any stage on the continuum of the language/literature interface, language-based approaches to text serve one cardinal purpose: they tell us what the text *is*, what it *says* and how it *works*. Whether this is seen as an aid to language learning, to text awareness, or to the wider study of literature, a focus on the processes of the language will take the reader to the linguistic heart of the text. This is as true for a literary text as it is for any cultural text: the language may be verbal, visual, even vocal (see pp. 21–2 and note 3, p. 184).

In this ever-expanding universe of discourse, English is no longer the language of a few islands off the north-west coast of Europe. It is the first or second language of many millions: 'world English' and 'new Englishes' have emerged alongside 'standard English' (see Wilkinson 1994). It is no longer possible to speak dismissively of local varieties as being in some way inferior or deviant. Over the past twenty years or so, there has been a far-reaching and welcome revaluation of the range of Englishes.

In pedagogic terms, *any* English is a resource, whatever 'standard' is the learner's target language. Varieties abound, even within local Englishes: Glasgow Scots English is different from Edinburgh Scots English (as the novels of James Kelman and the recently successful writer Irvine Welsh illustrate); WASP [White Anglo-Saxon Protestant] American English is different from black American street English (see Labov 1969; Pinker 1994); Calcutta Indian English is different from Madras Indian English. Social factors, cultural factors, linguistic factors, all combine to make the range endless.

How Englishes work, how texts work and how different readers in different contexts receive these texts: this is the heart of the interface approach. It suggests ways of getting into texts without prejudging – *before* critical opinions, received ideas, or historical background are brought into play (see chapter 12).

In its pedagogic applications, stylistics has been accused of tending towards the simplistic. In demythologising literary texts, in moving towards literature with a small 'l', this is a risk. However, it would be highly unrealistic to ignore the historical and critical applications of the work. Literature, history and criticism have always gone together, and, in teaching, the one approach which unites rather than divides is an approach which focuses on language. How *any* text works is the first tenet of interface work: Caedmon or Culler, Layamon or Lacan. The historical, social, cultural, critical, psychological and philosophical aspects of language and literature study all necessarily *derive from* and *reflect back* to linguistic parameters.

The field is wide open. There are more Englishes and more literatures now than ever before. We need tools to work in the field: the language focus should not limit our studies; rather it should be the key which opens up the fullest possible study of all the interfaces between language and its representational expressions.

Conclusion: the structure of the book

Language, Literature and the Learner – as a collection of papers devoted to the teaching of literature in non-native speaker language-learning contexts – is an extension of, but is different in crucial ways from, previous collections in the late 1980s:

  (i) This volume aims to be broader and more eclectic in scope. As a whole it tries to be alert to criticisms made concerning interfaces between language and literature teaching and explicitly opens up debate in key areas.
 (ii) Contributions are less defensive and less concerned to establish clear-cut positions.
(iii) The volume has a particular commitment to practical, classroom-based exemplification. Some papers deliberately do not explicitly address theoretical issues.
 (iv) Familiar methodological strategies and procedures are illustrated but are refined and extended in the light of continuing reflection on their use and usefulness.
  (v) In keeping with a concern with more intermediate levels of learner language competence, there is less blanket emphasis on stylistics (but see the valuable *practical* stylistic approach adopted by Short in this volume). There is a related recognition that, in relation to the teaching of literature, stylistics can be all the richer if students are first prepared by a thorough practice in more language-based approaches.
 (vi) There is a greater emphasis on the creation of literary experiences both by analogy with, or in and through, other media or by experiencing the text in its socio-cultural and historical context.
(vii) An effort to situate the teaching of literature within developing practices in the teaching of English as a foreign language – for example, practices of learner training – is continued.
(viii) A concern continues with continuities between a wide range of texts in terms of the notion of literariness; a concern continues to question the nature of canonicity in the selection of texts for teaching and testing.
 (ix) The extension of the texts available for work at the interface. English literature and English language are now

recognised to be sites of contestation rather than as unproblematic hegemonies. It is increasingly preferable to talk in terms of English literatures and languages.

Ronald Carter and John McRae
Department of English Studies,
University of Nottingham, 1996

Note

1   Parts of this introduction link with and draw on the introduction to Carter, Walker and Brumfit (eds. 1989).

1

Look both ways before crossing: developments in the language and literature classroom

Ronald Carter argues in this paper that creativity is pervasive in language use: in idioms and everyday metaphor; in jokes; in advertising and newspaper headlines; and in the highly patterned instances of canonical literary texts. This paper illustrates and analyses such use and suggests that language learners should be given greater opportunities to experience, interpret and use language in its more creative aspects.

Such approaches require pedagogies which are more process-based and which involve greater language awareness on the part of teachers and learners. Such language awareness can also be a point of entry for learners into cultural awareness, both with a small 'c' and a large 'C'. It can be an essential prerequisite for the development of literature teaching in and through English. Issues for theoretical consideration are debated in the paper and there is an extensively worked-out classroom-based illustration. Both theoretical and practical issues are explored in relation to a review of recent developments in the field, and the paper is therefore usefully positioned as the first in this volume.

1.1 Looking back

The past ten years or so of activity in the field of literature teaching in ELT have witnessed some clear trends and tendencies. The past five years have witnessed a veritable explosion of publications – books, journal articles, teaching materials – as well as a high proportion of conferences, colloquia, and seminars devoted to the teaching of literature. The majority of activities have been at the interface of language and literature teaching. Indeed, if one main trend is to be discerned, it is that of a shift of balance. The balance has moved away from the teaching of literature *per se* and towards the teaching of literature at the interface with language teaching. Likewise, discussion of the kinds of text used in the EFL/ESL classroom now only rarely takes place without reference to literary texts and to how they might be integrated with more familiar language teaching materials.

1.2 Language-based approaches

In the early 1980s language-based approaches tended to be almost indistinguishable from stylistics. The place of stylistics in ELT as a distinct activity will be explored subsequently, but from the mid-1980s – with the publication of McRae and Boardman's *Reading Between the Lines* (1984) – language-based approaches became more distinctive and definitive in their own right. Language-based approaches are essentially integrative. They seek to **integrate** language and literature study. They also offer approaches to literary texts which are accessible not just to more advanced students but to a wider range of students, from lower to upper intermediate levels.

Here is a concrete example of language-based approaches:

Students are given a sentence. They are told that the sentence is a complete poem and, working in pairs or small groups, that they have to re-construct this sentence as a poem. They must also give particular attention to the relationship between form and meaning; in other words, the way the words are disposed on the page should be connected with the subject matter or theme(s) encoded by the sentence.

40 – Love
middle aged couple playing tennis when the game ends and they go home the net will still be between them.

At an appropriate point students are then introduced to the text as written by the contemporary British poet, Roger McGough.

40 –	LOVE
middle	aged
couple	playing
ten	nis
when	the
game	ends

and	they
go	home
the	net
will	still
be	be
tween	them

What principles and what particular pedagogic strategies are exemplified by this example of a language-based approach to this poem? Two main principles can be isolated:

1.   Activity-principle
Students actively participate in making the poem mean. They do not simply respond to an already complete artefact; they are involved in its construction. It is not simply a finished product, a given for them to react to. It is presented as a process.

2.   Process-principle
Students are more likely to appreciate and understand texts if they experience them directly as part of a process of meaning-creation. Strategies such as this exercise in re-writing also place the responsibility for meaning-making on the students, usually working in pairs or in a small group. Interpretation becomes their own, as much the student's property as the teacher's, though the teacher's role in assisting such processes obviously has to be active and purposeful.

This is, then, what is generally understood when it is said that language-based approaches are **student-centred**, **activity-based** and **process-oriented**.

Strategies such as those of re-writing are, of course, not especially original (see Pope 1995). Language-based approaches involve numerous techniques and procedures which are familiar, even over familiar, in teaching English as a foreign language. They include: prediction exercises; cloze exercises; ranking tasks; active comprehension techniques; producing and acting out the text and so on. These techniques are tried and tested and do have the advantage of being familiar to teachers even though they are normally suitably modified, particularly in the case of poetry, to bring out characteristics which are peculiar to literary texts. Language-based approaches are also selected by teachers in order to support the development in students of interpretive and inferencing skills, particularly interpretation of the relations between forms and meanings.

For example, in the case of the poem 40 – Love, one aim of the activity of re-writing is to enhance understanding and appreciation of the analogy between a game of tennis and the monotonous regularity of a marriage which, with the partners in their forties, has lost much excitement and originality in the relationship. The very oppositions and balances in the structure of the poem compel us to reflect on the nature of 'love' in middle age. The act of reconstructing the poem can be a way of writing one's way into this kind of reading.

1.3 Stylistic approaches

It would, of course, be naive to suggest that there are no limitations or disadvantages to language-based approaches. The disadvantages are to some extent shared with stylistics and it is to the issues of stylistics and the teaching of literature that attention can now be given. Such a move recognises an important continuum between language-based approaches and stylistics, the former providing as it were a pre-stylistic basis for subsequently more systematic and rigorous scrutiny of language (for illustrations see Carter and Long 1987, and for further discussion see Carter and Long 1991). An example of a stylistic approach can be illustrated by the following text, which is the first stanza from a poem by the American poet e e cummings:

> yes is a pleasant country
> If's wintry
> (my lovely)
> Let's open the year.

The poem uses very simple language. But the poem is ungrammatical and it is also semantically deviant. We don't open years; conjunctions do not normally appear in subject position. How can yes be a country, and so on? But I have watched with fascination how groups of students in many parts of the world, sometimes discussing in English or in their mother tongue – according to level – can begin to unpick its meanings, begin to interpret it, begin to make it make sense, by exploring the language as a starting point.

Most groups end up with a reading which takes its cue from the brackets '(my lovely)'. It is read as a love poem or an interchange between lovers. The speaker is trying to persuade his or her lover to say **yes**, to be affirmative and positive – to make yes not deviant but normal. To keep saying **if** imposes conditions (if is a conditional) – it makes the response cold and unpleasant. The speaker is appealing for a new start – for a new beginning to a new year. Let's move (metaphorically) from a cold to a warm country. Saying yes is warm; saying **if** is cold.

This kind of discussion of this kind of text is rooted in the development of language awareness; and careful analysis of the linguistic choices shows how rules are broken for creative purposes (for a pedagogically-driven account of language awareness, see Van Lier 1995). Stylistic analysis helps to foster interpretive skills and to encourage reading between the lines of what is said. Stylistic analysis can also help teach the confidence to make sense of language input which isn't always – in real communicative contexts – neat, clear and immediately comprehensible. This is seen as a major advantage of stylistics. Students keep working at the language, making inferences, extracting all the possible clues to meaning. They have to do this and do it in this way because the text is almost all they have to go on. It can provide a solid basis for interpretation. The process of analysis is also **retrievable**. By an explicit step-by-step analysis of the language you can also show others how you've reached a particular interpretation (see Widdowson 1975).

The past decade has also witnessed a wealth of publications devoted to stylistic analysis and some devoted to the teaching of stylistics in EFL/ESL contexts. Stylistics made several significant advances during the 1980s and, in so far as stylistics is parasitic upon linguistics, it is perhaps inevitable that we should record a significant move towards **discourse stylistics** during the last few years. This operates under the direct influence of work in pragmatics, discourse analysis and text linguistics, and this work continues to provide the field of stylistics with increasingly sophisticated means of discussing both longer stretches of text and, indeed, longer texts.

The advantages of stylistics can be listed as follows:

(i) stylistics provides students with a **method** of scrutinising texts, a 'way in' to a text, opening up starting points for fuller interpretation. The method is detailed, explicit and retrievable – that is, it shows how you reach or begin to reach an interpretation. From a teaching point of view, students

learn to open a text not by osmosis but explicitly and consciously. A pedagogically sensitive stylistics can give students
increased confidence in reading and interpretation.

(ii) basing interpretation on systematic verbal analysis reaffirms
the centrality of **language** as **the** aesthetic medium of **literature**.

(iii) non-native students possess the kind of conscious, systematic
knowledge about the language which provides the best basis
for stylistic analysis. In many respects, therefore, non-native
students are often better at stylistic analysis than native
speakers.

During the 1980s there were marked tendencies to over-
confidence on the part of stylisticians. This led to some disadvantages in stylistics for the teaching of literature in EFL/ESL:

(a) an over-determination of the text. An assumption that there is
one central meaning to a text and that, if only you analyse the
language of the text in enough detail, that meaning will be
located and located objectively. Much recent work in literary
theory has shown the dangers of assuming objectivity (e.g.
Birch 1989).

(b) it is an approach to texts best suited to advanced study. There
has been a tendency to assume stylistics can operate at all
levels. It is important that language-based approaches should
provide a basis from which stylistic analysis can develop.

(c) a failure to appreciate properly the concerns of literary critics
and integrate fully with those concerns. Stylisticians may have
tended to read rather too exclusively as linguists. Thus, questions of point of view, author/reader relations and historical
and cultural knowledge have tended to take second place to
the analysis of language, as if language were no more than a
neutral system rather than a site of conflicting ideologies and
points of view, interacting with socio-cultural contexts. In
other words, during the 1980s stylistics tended to be too **innocent** as a critical and reading practice. Language is not and
cannot be neutral.

(d) emphasis on poetry and short stories to the exclusion of other
genres. There have been few examples of stylistics applied to
complete novels. Short stories by Hemingway and short lyric
poems by Dylan Thomas and Wallace Stevens have predomin-
ated.

(e) a further difficulty is an attention to words on the page which appears not to recognise that texts are historically determined and are produced in specific historical contexts. Many teachers of literature quite properly stress the importance of historical understanding on the part of students and complain of the tendency in stylistics to reduce all texts to an ahistorical level of language. This is also, it should be noted, a particular disadvantage of language-based approaches.

1.4   Looking forward

Let us now turn from the past to the future. There are many possible developments to outline. Three main trends can be isolated which are likely to be influential in the teaching of literature, mainly in EFL contexts.

1.4.1   *Literature with a small 'l'*

In two important respects, work at the interface of language and literature *has* responded to developments in contemporary literary theory. Firstly, it has responded to the challenges against canonicity embracing a central notion that canons are not just there but are rather naturalised within academic communities. There are alternative ways of examining texts than from within a chronological line from Beowulf to Virginia Woolf or from Caedmon to Angela Carter. There are many texts which in some English departments are excluded from this kind of assembly: for example, much contemporary literature, writing by women or from different ethnic groups as well as literatures written in English in different parts of the world.

Secondly, and connected with challenges to a single literary canon of great works, is the selection for analysis and interpretation of texts not normally considered to be literary. This is what McRae has termed literature with a small 'l' (McRae 1991; Carter 1995; McCarthy and Carter 1994). It includes advertisements, jokes, puns, newspaper headlines, examples of verbal play: all these are texts which use language in ways which could be said to be literary or have elements of literariness inherent in them. The language used in such texts does not simply **refer** to activities, entities and events in the external world; it displays and creatively patterns its discourse in such a way as to invite readers to interpret how it **represents** that world. In many recent language-based textbooks, canonical and non-canonical texts are arranged alongside each other and they are subjected to the same pedagogic procedures.

It is likely that many more textbooks exist which do not privilege a particular canon and which make all texts and their associated rhetorics available for critical scrutiny (see Gower 1986). It is often said that such an approach demeans literary language; instead, however, it can be argued that such practices underline the referential and representational **continuities** across all texts and enhance respect for the creativity of much ordinary everyday language use.

One set of examples must suffice. The names assigned to hair salons often reveal degrees of creativity and inventiveness which we ignore or dismiss at our peril as non-literary or merely functional. Names such as:

Headlines
Head Start
Cut 'n' Dried
Way Ahead
Shampers
Klippers

play with language form, and ambiguities of sound and meaning, in ways which students can be taught to appreciate. It does not, of course, preclude progression to the denser and more highly patterned used of language found in much canonical literature. Indeed, such a focus can actively prepare students for it. Here is another example:

Mind you, it's a car for the 90's.

The interpretive processing of this advertisement involves a recognition of multiple ambiguities in the word 'nineties' – an effort encouraged by a spoken discourse marker ('mind you'), which subtly serves to make you, the reader, part of an ongoing discourse, involving you in a personal engagement with the meanings of the text (see Cook 1992; Carter and Nash 1990).

1.4.2   *Creativity and everyday English*

The above examples serve to isolate a literariness present in everyday instances of language. The examples are of more **deliberately** constructed language, for specific purposes of selling a product. There is a certain craftedness and rhetoricity in the language used.

Yet much research into so-called ordinary, everyday language use is revealing that creativity is even more pervasive and endemic than may previously have been thought possible. It also reveals that it is a spontaneous, ongoing part of conversational exchanges (see Tannen 1989). Here are some examples from a corpus of casual, naturalistic, unscripted conversational English collected in the English Studies Department at Nottingham University:

B Yes, he must have a bob or two.
A Whatever he does, he makes money out it. Just like that.
B Bob's your uncle.
A He's quite a lot of money erm tied up in property and things like that. He's got a finger in all kinds of pies and houses and things. A couple in Bristol, one in Cleveland I think.

B I don't know but she seems to have picked up all kinds of lame ducks and traumas along the way.
A That that's her vocation.
B Perhaps it is. She should have been a counsellor.
A Yeah but the trouble with her is she puts all her socialist carts before the horses.

The speakers here play with words and echoes of words and associations within and across turn-boundaries. In so doing, 'fixed' expressions become less fixed, idioms which our dictionaries tell us are immutable become creatively transmuted and extended, and key words in key phrases are a source for puns and verbal play. It is not surprising, therefore, that advertisers exploit such patterns and creative deviations from them. Here is a recent advertisement from a British airline, Virgin Atlantic, which promotes new, wider and more comfortable seating by playing on the fixed binomial expression 'aches and pains'.

Relief from aches on planes

Another example:

The one and Tobleronly

plays on the phonology of the fixed phrase 'one and only' to suggest the uniqueness of a Swiss chocolate bar (Toblerone).

These examples are some of the many kinds of linguistic creativity that one finds in a corpus of everyday conversation and in our everyday encounters with language. They have in common with literary language that language is being made to 'stick out' from its context of use. Casual conversation is classically marked by a high degree of automatic and unconscious routine language use, but, now and again, speakers make their language draw attention to itself in some way, displacing it from its immediate context, a phenomenon Widdowson (1975) has argued to be a fundamental characteristic of poetic language. It can be argued therefore that to use in the language class only those types of dialogue that are transparent and transactional, and devoid of richness, cultural reference and creativity, is to misrepresent what speakers actually do and simultaneously to lose an opportunity for interesting language awareness work of the kind which can be an ideal precursor to enhanced literary awareness (for a related argument, see Carter and McCarthy 1995).

1.4.3 *Language awareness/cultural awareness*

One implication of the recognition of creativity and literariness in everyday language is that courses in cultural studies can be re-shaped. We will continue to need courses and books called Modern American Life; Britain Today; British Culture and Institutions. But such information-driven programmes rarely develop the skills necessary for cultural interpretation and analysis, for one set of encyclopaedic knowledge often only leads to another set, and facts of this kind are often easily forgotten. Instead, it is important to help students practise skills by which cultural knowledge and awareness can be developed and to root the development of such skills both in an engagement with the everyday language and in creative, process-oriented, activity-based methodologies which give responsibility to learners for working out for themselves meanings and significations (see Van Lier 1995).

For example, what can we learn about English culture from the following idioms and fixed phrases, all of which involve some reference to foreign, in this case mainly European, nations?

Dutch courage
to go Dutch
double-Dutch
Dutch cap
If that's true, then I'm a Dutchman
Dutch-auction

It's all Greek to me
Beware of Greeks bearing gifts

French leave
French letter
French kiss
French lessons

French fries	cuisine
French bread	chaise-longue
French dressing	meringue
French windows	souffle
French polish	mousse
French beans	croissant

In fact, we learn not only a lot of useful and widely used phrases, but also something about British insularity and distrust of foreigners, to the point where the British can be interpreted as believing almost all of them to be untrustworthy, inauthentic and ignorant. They also reveal attitudes towards other languages than English, an accompanying feeling of linguistic superiority and a suspicion that foreigners engage in sexual practices that we dare not even name, except by giving them a foreign name. Such linguistic formulations may also be not unconnected with a history of wars against the French and the Dutch, in particular, in a good number of which the English were defeated. Certainly during the French occupation of England in the eleventh, twelfth and thirteenth centuries, most of the terms in the lexicon for interior decoration and for food and food preparation took over the English language in the way that the French people took over the central running of national and local households. The equation of the word **French** and of words of French origin with this central aspect of daily life has remained a largely unchanged aspect of English culture to the present day.

Other examples could, of course, be enumerated, but a discovery-based language awareness component in ELT programmes could do much simultaneously to develop sensitivity to language and to enhance cultural understanding. And who is to say that such skills are not an essential part of reading all cultural features and products whether that culture be rather in the manner argued earlier for literature, or constructed with a small or a large 'c'? (see Brown 1990; McCarthy 1990; McCarthy and Carter 1994).

1.4.4 Theoretical conclusions

The following main conclusions might be drawn from the above discussion:

1. Creativity is not exclusive but is inclusive in a wide range of discourses. It is more common and routine in language use than is sometimes supposed. We need to explore ways of helping all learners – and not just advanced learners – better to engage with such uses.
2. In so doing, we can also lay a basis for literary awareness of a more conventional kind. Indeed, literature with a small 'l' may be studied both as a preliminary step towards and alongside more canonical literary study. Related pedagogic practices involve a more integrated approach to language and literature study.
3. Literary awareness of this kind can develop from ongoing work in reading and discourse studies (e.g. Davies 1995; Nunan 1994) and from the rapidly growing language awareness movement. A crucial component in such language and literary awareness is the fostering of interpretive and analytical skills.
4. Literary texts are difficult to define and, indeed, at least one main defining feature is that they resist easy classification and definition. In this paper, however, the argument has led to a definition of literary discourse as *culturally-rooted language which is purposefully patterned and representational, which actively promotes a process of interpretation and which encourages a pleasurable interaction with and negotiation of its meanings.* The teaching of literature needs to be at least sensitive to such a definition and constantly to develop classroom procedures which foster awareness of and response to such discourse practices.
5. Language and literature have been kept distinct in many curricula in many parts of the world and often for good reason; but much of mutual benefit can be learned from our better understanding of the **continuities** between the study of the language and the study of its literatures.

1.5 Looking both ways: a classroom-based conclusion

The following example is drawn from a workbook (Zyngier 1994a) written specifically for Brazilian university students of English with little previous experience of close reading of texts. The material allows an extended, practical, classroom-based exploration of the theoretical position concerning integrated language and literature teaching argued for in this paper. To what extent does this sample of a 1½-hr workshop allow the emergence of 'literature as patterned, representational, pleasurably interpersonal discourse for negotiated interpretation' and to what extent is the teaching approach sensitive both to such a definition and to principles of process-based, activity-centred methodology which encourages an enhanced language awareness and a developing learner autonomy? To what extent does the material look both ways (to literary and language development) before crossing?

Example 1.1 What is a literary text? Checking literariness

1. Complete this passage with the most common words that come to your mind:

> When many faces I can . . . . ., I'm lost in multiplicity. And . . . . .
> my identity, I ask in . . . . ., ... is me? The I that hides in flesh
> and . . . . . is blind and . . . . . when not alone.

> When many voices can be . . . . ., crescendo, ... word on
> word, I cannot . . . . . the voice that . . . . ., in solitude when . . . . .
> falls. For only there is wholeness found beyond the range of
> sight and . . . . ., the integrated . . . . . is free to come and . . . . .,
> to hear and . . . . .

2. How do you feel when you are lost in a crowd? Is your experience different from the description in the text?
3. Now go to the end of the Unit. Read Passage 1. Check your options above and compare them to the author's choices. How different or similar were your answers?
4. Compare:

> For only there is wholeness found – beyond the range of sight
> and sound . . . . .

> to

> For only there is wholeness found
> Beyond the range of sight and sound.

(a) Which is more poetic?
(b) Why?

5. Check the words that have been used to describe the author's experience.
   (a) What is being observed?
   (b) Do the words used introduce a different way of appreciating the object under observation?
6. Now, consider this title: 'The Arrival of the Bee Box'. What do you expect?
7. Describe a bee box. Complete:

   Bee boxes are ....
   ....
   ....

8. How can you get a bee box?
9. Read the poem: The poem 'The Arrival of the Bee Box' can be found in *Ariel* by Sylvia Plath (Faber, 1968), p. 63.
10. How did the poet get a bee box?
11. Look at your description in no. 7. Compare it to the poet's description.
12. Group all the words or expressions related to

    BEE   **BOX**

13. Can you build a relationship between the two groups above?
14. Write down some of the expressions or descriptions you consider very unexpected.
15. Based on the relationship you have found between the bees and the box, how can you explain the last line of the poem?

Remember

- When you read, you carry out a 'dialogue' with the text.
- The text provokes a response from you.
- The text determines the nature of the discourse and in particular what freedom you have to construct your interpretation.
- You must find justification for your reaction in the language of the text.
- Different from a dialogue, you are in complete control of your reading. You can stop, go back, skip, review, etc. at any moment.
- In a literary text there must be a very delicate balance between *confirmation and frustration*.
- The text points forwards. It gives you clues. You should be able to identify the signs.

Passage 1

Lost in a Crowd

When many faces I can see – I'm lost in multiplicity. And losing my identity, I ask in terror, Where is me? The I that hides in flesh and bone – is blind and deaf when not alone.

When many voices can be heard – crescendo, rising word on word – I cannot hear the voice that calls – in solitude when silence falls. For only there is wholeness found – beyond the range of sight and sound – the integrated self is free – to come and go, to hear and see.

It can be argued, from the point of view of teaching the text as a holistic literary artefact, that the approach is unduly reductive. There is no social or historical information provided; there is little or no reference to an established, largely American, tradition of 'confessional' poetry nor to other poems by the writer; crucial biographical information about Sylvia Plath, in particular her suicidal proclivities, is elided. The teaching is weighted towards 'process' in such a way that without the insertion of such product-based facts, any interpretation can but be at best attenuated.

It can also be argued that the approach provides a way into the text, activating a student's involvement and questioning to a point where such 'information' can be released without unduly determining a reading response; and that, without the provision of such basic points of entry, students can easily be left outside the text, revering the text but mystified by it, dependent on the teacher's rather than on their own developing interpretation, looking only one way at a literary artefact without recognising its continuities with ordinary language use or with the language choices they themselves can produce. The extent to which teachers choose to look both ways, and to encourage their students to do the same, may be a factor in determining how many students cross the road to linguistic and literary competence.

2

Representational language learning: from language awareness to text awareness

JOHN McRAE

The author reviews the fundamental importance of underlining the difference between *referential* and *representational* materials in any language teaching/learning context. The implications of that difference in relation to text and to materials used in language classes is explored. This will give teachers the opportunity to reflect on the kind of materials they use, and the appropriacy of the content to the language-learning pay-off, or to the teaching aim of any text work.

The paper proceeds to examine the development of language awareness, leading on to text awareness, and indeed to cultural awareness – all are seen as part of the ongoing process of helping language learners become better, more aware readers of any kind of text. Various strategies are outlined to help set these patterns of awareness in motion. Developing the learner's ability to read, think, and interpret text of any kind is seen as the heart of the question.

There follows a discussion of how an apparatus relates to a text, and how a text can be exploited in class. Various stages are suggested, with many possible alternative directions for class and further work – these might usefully be referred to in relation to texts and methods outlined in other articles throughout the book. Question-types and kinds of activities are examined, in relation to teaching and learning aims, and to the development of thinking skills in the learner.

The article concludes with a wide-ranging A to Z of the main issues and questions which will concern teachers working with representational materials.

2.1 Introduction

Since the early 1980s there has been a strong theoretical undercurrent advocating the use of literature in language teaching.

Widdowson (1975; 1984) raised the fundamental issues and these have been developed, examined, and amplified, most significantly in Brumfit and Carter (1986), Carter and Long (1991), Duff and Maley (1991), McRae (1991) and Widdowson (1992).

The key concept in the application of literary materials to language teaching is that of referential materials and representational materials. Referential language, and therefore referential materials, remain close to what they mean in a dictionary sense: reductively speaking, one word has one meaning, one grammatical construction is right and another wrong, the words mean what they say, no more and no less. At this stage of language use, any text or communication is on one level only: purely informational, or at the level of basic interpersonal communication.

It is worth stressing immediately that an emphasis on representational language learning does not detract in any way from the basic importance of referential language learning: it is fundamental to any learner's knowledge about language and of a language system that rules, structures and grammar be acquired and that the way the language operates be understood in an ongoing way.

Where representational language learning differs from purely referential language learning is that the rules are questioned, played around with, and put to different uses as part of that ongoing process of language acquisition. It is something of a truism that 'rules are made to be broken' but in language teaching there has often been an insistence on mere correctness of form (accuracy) to the detriment of fluency; the pendulum has then been known to swing in the other direction, with fluency privileged above accuracy. Communicative language teaching has come in for a great deal of criticism because of this ambivalence, hence talk of a 'return to grammar' as part of the swings and roundabouts of language-teaching fashions and fads.

Representational language teaching is neither fashion nor fad. Above all it is not a ploy to bring Literature into the language classroom – there is a great difference between literature in the language-teaching context and Literature as an institutional discipline, or as the subject of specialist study. Literature with a small 'l' is a suitable shorthand way of describing the approach, although it falls short of being a definition of it (see McRae 1991).

2.2   Representational teaching and learning; some theoretical considerations

It takes imagination to learn a language. This is the basic tenet underlying representational language teaching. The use of characters, cartoons, stories, images, songs, and video all attest to language teachers' attempts to appeal to the learner's imagination, and are all in their way moves towards representational teaching and learning. But most language-teaching/learning materials, especially beyond the primary level, have a hidden agenda that is targeting fluency, accuracy, or some combination of the two, rather than building linguistic competence allied to the ability to think in the target language and work freely within its language system.

Every language teacher is aware that learners like to know what the learning pay-off is, what is being learned in any particular lesson. And that pay-off is usually conceived on a referential basis, whether functional, notional, or communicative in the widest senses of these terms. How useful the learning pay-off might be to a learner's perceived needs is, of course, an open question. English for Special Purposes in particular makes demands on the teacher according to the learner's needs (airline pilots, computer programmers, sales persons, doctors, research scientists, etc.) with the result that the teacher is frequently caught between non-specialist awareness/ignorance and referential language expertise which the learner may consider inappropriate or redundant.

This is where knowledge about language (KAL) becomes of paramount importance. The extreme case of the specialist learner is not widely different from the more usual teenage or young adult learner. The necessity of imaginative engagement with the target language, and the concomitant development of language awareness in a contrastive way between native and target language become crucial precisely at the point where the language learning process begins to become more than an exercise in learning and applying rules. In a plurilingual context (India, Malaysia, many of the former Soviet states, for example) the resource of more than one known language is all the more useful in the contrastive teaching of language awareness.

The acquisition of vocabulary which goes beyond the merely synonymic is frequently the turning-point in this process. Students not infrequently ask why there should be more than one word to express 'the same' idea; having already learned one word, why do they have to learn others? This limited attitude would be like learning to drive without ever changing out of first gear. English has a greater word-hoard than any other language, and this is to be seen as a resource rather than as a deterrent to learning.

Language is richness and variety, not the monotone of singularity of vision and intent. As such it is language itself that demands a more representational approach to learning and teaching. For as soon as language begins to mean, it begins to expand its meaning, to make demands on its users, whether speakers, listeners, readers or writers. And as soon as this happens, questions of interpretation, of shades of meaning, of reaction and response are brought into play. Imagination begins to operate, even within the limited language knowledge of a learner at an early stage, as any parent of a small child knows. The move is from reference to preference: the learner begins to prefer one meaning rather than another, to go beyond the merely referential into personal preference and choice.

The child's imagination is, of course, a wondrous resource, but by the time institutions and scholastic pressures have taken over, the learning potential of that resource has very often been crushed: language learning is one of the few subjects where imagination must be rediscovered and developed as a resource in learning, as it would be in art or music.

It is a subject with a unique range of possible learning strategies and structures, from the rule-bound to the completely free play of fantasy. Either extreme would be dangerous and counter-productive. A balance which allows for both knowledge about language and knowledge of language, which encourages an awareness of the language system and how it works at the same time as showing the range of flexibility the system allows for (and indeed encourages) will be a productive educational balance. The mere understanding of what is read or heard is little more than construing lumpen meaning out of foreign words and phrases. The development of language competence in a learner has to allow for imaginative interaction, for an element of creativity, and for an affective element of subjective, personal development, all of which go well beyond the limitations of referential language.

A purely referential text is rare: the contents listed on a tin of soup, the instructions how to operate a piece of machinery, the health warning on a cigarette packet, the information in a holiday brochure. But even these texts are not neutral. Instructions can be simple or complex, easy to understand or not. Holiday brochures often conceal more than they reveal. Health warnings can be couched in stronger or weaker language: 'Smoking may damage your health' is a different meaning from 'Smoking causes cancer.'

A health warning is just as much a text as a flight manual, and it requires the reader to exercise some discretion and judgement, to go through some evaluative procedures as regards how and why the message is being communicated, in short to process the text in terms of language, content, effect and impact. Failure to do this will not, of course, necessarily be fatal in the case of a cigarette packet. But it might be in the case of an instruction manual – so the more referential the instruction manual is, with less scope for imaginative interpretation (and misinterpretation) the better. Referentiality is necessary. But as soon as degrees of referentiality come into play there is a move towards interpretative space. It is at that point that the awareness of what single words and phrases can do or be made to do, within one language system or contrastively between two or more language systems, becomes more than language awareness. There is an immediate and vital necessity for text awareness.

Carter and Nash (1990) call this Seeing Through Language, and to a considerable extent that is what every language learner must do. Language, especially in the hands of other people, is not necessarily to be trusted. As soon as the purely referential level is passed, areas of risk are opened up. And we are still a very long way from Literature.

A philosophy of language teaching which incorporates examples of text of any kind that demonstrate how language works within the rules and beyond the rules will expose learners to the representational possibilities of all language, including the acquisition of a new awareness of their native language. As a way of teaching language it is to be encouraged from as early a stage as possible. It is not a separate stage, a higher level, or a luxury.

Representational language is all around us: it is language in use in a way that second-language acquisition theorists often ignore. It involves discussion, reflection, and consideration of meaning, rather than the mere construing or the unthinking acceptance of meaning. It involves shades of meaning, understanding of point of view, and notions of where language is coming from. It contains elements of intentionality and elements of uncertainty. Often it does not allow for 100% 'correct' answers. As such, some teachers (but fewer learners) have been known to fight shy of representational language-learning techniques, preferring to stay safely within the realm of the known, the fixed, the secure. As things stand in language teaching now, this is no longer possible. In a few years' time it is to be expected that all language-learning materials will incorporate representational materials as part of the awareness-building processes within language acquisition.

We are now on the threshold of a new phase in the history of language teaching, and it has to be seen as a major step forward: language as text, and text as the representation of thought, ideas, intentions, ideology, and world-view. This does not mean 'out with the old, on with the new.' Language-teaching methodologies have developed sufficiently now to be flexible, to incorporate new thinking and new areas of study without losing the basic hard-won tried and tested techniques which the past twenty years have built up. What is now required is the fuller integration of text into teaching, the mixing of representational with referential, the development of language awareness concurrently with knowledge about language. This will allow the experience of what has been done and can be done with language to become part of the wider language frame of reference that students acquire.

2.3   Texts and apparatus

Exposure to as wide a range of texts as possible, with as wide a range of apparatus as possible, is the way in to representational language study. Texts can be as short as a word or a phrase – in context or out of context. As Ron Carter shows in the previous chapter, the shortest advertising slogans or shop names can present levels of linguistic rule-bending that are a useful part of the learner's introduction to representational language and the awareness of what is being done with, to and by language.

'Travellin' style' is the slogan of a bus company. It would normally therefore be read, as opposed to heard as discourse. But there is an obvious play on words between 'travellin' style' and 'travel in style' which renders the phrase differently in terms of sound, lexis and grammar: this is an example of wordsplay, the playing with words which allows for plurality of meaning even on a very simple level. A learner need not analyse every single such example in detail, but the awareness that a gerund, sounded as if spoken with the elision of the final consonant, is morphologically transformed into two lexical items, creating a different verb form (imperative) with a preposition, is a major step forward in the realisation of how English works.   ·

All the learner is asked to do is to work comparatively, contrasting two phrases, evaluating their impact and the way their meanings are achieved. Once introduced into such a way of reading or approaching text, many learners never look back: a certain outlook on language and learning has already been acquired through just this initial exposure. For others the game is a waste of time – some learners never want to go beyond the purely referential level, or think they don't. But these are very often the learners who get most deeply involved in questions of interpretation when faced with representational texts whose meaning is wide open to interpretation.

What is being considered is how language works, and what it is doing. McRae (1991, pp. 95–96) examines in detail the areas where study can usefully be applied. The checklist includes lexis, syntax, cohesion, phonology, graphology, semantics, dialect, register, period, function. Morphology is not included, but as the example given above demonstrates, it most certainly could be. Style also is deliberately omitted from the list, as it implies a higher level of engagement with texts and textual analysis. The teaching and learning process has to focus on aspects of text, and on textual production and reception, seeing through, seeing round, and seeing into the workings of the texts themselves.

The longer a piece of text, the more can be done with it, and the more open the whole process can become. Very often the apparatus that accompanies such texts will raise questions of reaction, response, and opinion. The 'answer' (in the Teacher's Book perhaps) will very often have to be 'open response'. This is not ducking the issue. Rather it is offering the opportunity for language production, interaction and debate.

Language production is one of the main aims of the language teacher: controlled open response to language and the issues language raises is far and away the most fruitful teaching/learning resource available, if the teacher is willing to take advantage of it. Teacher resistance, often perfectly comprehensible (see McRae 1991, p. 9), is usually due to the lack of measurable learning pay-off. But in this context language learning is moving beyond the traditional four skills of listening, speaking, reading, and writing to the deployment of the indispensable but often ignored or taken-for-granted fifth skill, thinking.

This involves going beyond the mechanics of grammar practice, beyond the repetitions of reinforcement, into areas of individual reaction and response which are firmly grounded in the language of the lesson and the level at which teacher and learner are working. At the same time the learner is invited to stretch beyond the limitations of level, to expand lexical and structural competence, to experiment with the target language in affective and practical ways.

This involves conceptualising, and it involves, sooner or later, working with ideas. So there is a danger of abstraction. But it can be kept to a minimum if the focus is kept on language, especially in the initial stages. Once the learner is accustomed to questioning and exploring the language itself, the move on to the plane of ideas is a natural one. Neither teachers nor learners need to be philosophers, applied linguists, discourse analysts or literary critics.

Perhaps even more worth stressing is the fact that teachers of Literature should not disparage an approach that privileges language. There is no mystery or mystique, no need to fear stylistics or any of the fashionable trends and '-isms' of recent critical theory. Language is open to all. The language/literature interface is probably the richest vein of learning potential for learners at all levels of language, and indeed of Literature study. The present volume is addressed to teachers throughout the spectrum in the hope that they might be encouraged to expand their own horizons and range of competence in whatever directions they feel possible.

Since 1984 there have been many publications in the language teaching field which have put together representational materials in ways suitable for integration into language and/or literature courses. Teachers have worked through these or dipped in to them according to the requirements of learners, the curriculum, the syllabus, the last ten minutes of the last lesson of the week, or whatever.

What is needed now is an approach which takes that process of integration further. Where Literature was considered appropriate only for upper-intermediate learners and above, it is now recognised that language awareness and text awareness have to be encouraged and developed from the earliest stages of language learning. Work done for the primary sector has encouraged the use of story-telling and later the reading of stories in highly motivating ways (see Ellis and Brewster 1991). Secondary school reading and adult reading have not caught up with these imaginative ways of working.

Text selection and level is the heart of the problem. But as Cook (1992) has shown, and as a few textbooks demonstrate, even the shortest advertising slogan, one-liner, headline or joke can help the student into an awareness of what the language is doing, its effects, and its impact. Any text that comes to hand can be turned to good use. What is important is how and why it is used, such that representational materials become part of the language learning process in a more and more systematic and regular way.

I will now address the question of practical materials preparation, not with the intention of prescribing materials, or selecting text examples – I have already done that in several books. Rather the intention here is to set down some of the guiding principles in representational language teaching and learning which will enable the teacher to work with representational materials of various kinds, and which will give the students the enabling language and confidence to work with these materials whilst at the same time developing their linguistic competence in the target language, as well as their language and text awareness in L1 and L2.

There is no such thing as an infallible methodology. The teacher's greatest resource is the eternal trio: students, classroom and teacher. Anything offered as a methodology is only a set of ideas which have been tried out and found to work in some contexts (and not to fail in others!)

Above all, it is important that the teacher know what is being learned with the materials used: there is no point in taking a piece of text into class just because you like it. The bottom line always has to be the learning achieved. So the question must be asked, 'What will my students get from this text?' The answer can be at many levels: a few minutes' enjoyment might be the minimum answer; whatever the case, some learning has to be achieved, some difference reached in students' perceptions of the language, the text, or even the world, between the time before the text was presented to them (the time of innocence) and the time when the text has been used (the time of experience).

How much use can be made of any text is variable, as we will see. But it is vital that the students see and appreciate what was intended in the teacher's using a particular piece of text or material. Whether or not it worked can then be evaluated. No teacher always has a successful lesson, and some element of risk is usually not a bad thing. But, with a spirit of collaboration between teacher and students, even a piece of text that does not work as the teacher intended can be instructive to teacher and learner together.

In order that a text achieve some learning purpose, some degree of apparatus is vital. At the most minimal level this can be a question such as 'How do you like this?' or 'What do you think of this?' But there is the danger of lazy teaching here. The guidelines and ideas which follow are intended to help teachers and learners round, through, and over some of the many traps that lie in wait for them on the road from lazy teaching to successful learning.

When an apparatus is prepared, the first element will be a pre-reading (or pre-listening) question or stimulus. It is important not to spend too long on this: the text is the main object of the study, and a warm-up activity that goes on too long can be distracting, taxing, and counter-productive. Too often the warm-up activity is more fun than the text – this makes the text itself a waste of time, and is a disservice to all concerned. A good teacher/class rapport means that warm-up can be kept to a minimum, and hands-on work maximised.

The pre-question or stimulus should always start from what the students will understand. No matter how long or complex the text, a pre-reading question can be formulated to give the students confidence in what they do know rather than allowing them to be distracted by what they do not know. It is important, therefore, never to start with difficulties or things the students will not understand. These must be kept back until students have the confidence to face them. The focus should be on what strikes them, what they find memorable or identifiable. Students should not be asked to do too much – better a brief pre-question with fuller follow-up than a multiple-part question, especially in the earliest stages. The pre-question/stimulus can be used to lead where the teacher wants to go, towards the teaching aim. Of course, very often the best lessons are those where the class takes the teacher somewhere unexpected. As long as things do not get out of control, the teacher should consider this positive, a sign of creative learning and interpretative autonomy.

Once the text has been presented, the directions in which the lesson can go are literally innumerable. It has to be remembered that there are stages in language learning, and that the old-fashioned notion that Literature is a reserved province for upper-intermediate-level learners and above still holds in many people's minds. So teaching aims should be defined in relation to levels as regards the learners' own development: at the earliest level the focus will be on language – what is happening, how it is different from what learners have already acquired or learned, how familiar/unfamiliar is this particular example of language use, why is something being done with language in this way, who is doing it and to what effect?

From that stage will develop a growing language awareness, which becomes the second stage in representational learning development. The samples of language used can be longer, and gradually more complex, with a greater variety of sources, registers, dialects, etc. Learners' first acquaintance with register and dialect will very often come from exposure to text from songs and rap music: this is linguistic variety as a very useful resource, memorable, identifiable, and immensely useful as contrastive language use in relation to the referential language students are studying and acquiring.

As confidence in handling texts grows, the third stage, text awareness will be reached. By this time learners are building up a reading frame of reference, which is vitally important as a continuing source of information and comparison: texts must always be related to other texts, and judged or evaluated contrastively, even at the most subjective level of students preferring one text rather than another. The enabling language which helps them express judgements, and discuss, justify, challenge, interrupt, criticise, contradict, is at this stage a fundamental part of language acquisition: already beyond the purely referential, it has become the language of choice and of processes of evaluation and selection.

What can be addressed in order to help develop text awareness are such things as 'addresser/addressee' – who is speaking, and to whom? What effect is desired? (e.g. in an advertisement the addressee is being urged usually to buy a product). This can be achieved in a variety of ways, which learners can be encouraged to identify: persuasion, seduction, logic, rhetoric, blackmail, intimidation, competitiveness, peer pressure, and so on. Most of these concepts can be expressed even at low levels of language competence.

Similarly, how a text works can be examined – what does it presume about the reader, what does the reader share with the text/author, and what is unshared or new, what is the text attempting to do in terms of conveying information, tring to convince or exhort, confirming or challenging what the reader thinks? Newspaper headlines giving different points of view on the same subject can be very useful here, as can focusing on the use of active or passive forms changing the status of the text and the point of view. All of these are possible learning-focus areas.

Attention must be given to verbal or visual elements, to the morphology involved in punning wordplay, to the sounds evoked or exploited, to what is new to students as well as to what is known, to what is apparent in a text and what may be hidden, to cultural references (which will very often be unfamiliar). All of these, at the simplest, non-technical level, are areas of text curiosity which can be exploited. Of course, the teacher has to avoid explaining too much, standing in front of the text. 'What do you think it might refer to?' is always a more useful stimulus than teacher-talking input. Thus the process becomes one of involving the student in the ramifications of the text, or some of them, developing skills in inference and implicature, cultural recognition, questions of social status, register and point of view, all of which slowly build into textual awareness through language awareness and knowledge of the language and the ideas, culture, politics, sensibilities, and language users it represents.

These are all areas which anodyne, purely referential language teaching has tended to shrink from. But most language learners are sentient thinking beings, with intellectual curiosity much greater than their level of knowledge of the target language. Representational language learning allows closer and closer involvement with the target culture, mindframe and language, while not seeking to impose historical, literary or cultural studies as such. Language is the way in to whatever areas of experience the learner wishes to explore, simply because language is the most readily accessible manifestation and expression of culture, society and experience.

It will be noticeable that no mention has yet been made of question-types. This is because, at the earliest stages, comprehension is not the most vital part of language awareness. Obviously it assumes greater importance as texts studied become longer and more complex. To a great extent the language awareness work done at the early stages is a preparation for the reading of longer texts of any type.

Carter and Long's taxonomy of question-types (Carter and Long 1991, pp. 36–42) usefully delineates several levels of question: those which help in the understanding of the text, that is questions of comprehension and clarification (wh- questions are usual here); those which can be considered low-order questions, examining literal, referential levels of meaning, the propositional content of the text (questions on individual lexical items or paragraph cohesion can be considered of this kind). These two types are very closely related. Then come the higher-order questions, which move beyond the referential or propositional level and on to response and interpretation, evaluation, and comparison with other texts. These questions involve inference, the evoking of the reader's own experiential baggage, cultural awareness, maturity, reading frame of reference, and so on. Thus they lead to the kind of open response which has already been mentioned. Comprehension questions tend to be closed in nature. That is to say, there is a right or a wrong answer, to be found explicitly or through inference. Open questions tend not to have a 'correct' answer.

This may very well be as far as most language learners go with representational materials. Many learners do not read widely outside the classroom or outside their special area of interest. So this whole area of text awareness is often pre-literary, in that it does not necessarily involve any actual literary texts. But there is nothing to be afraid of in introducing some elements of literariness into contrastive text awareness work, between songs, short poems, and short passages of prose, for instance.

What is being examined is not the literariness of the text, but the way the various kinds of text work (or do not work), and the criteria of interest and validity to learners' experience remain what they always were. This is where a collection of materials can be useful, perhaps thematically bringing together surprising combinations of text-type and period, as well as genre and style. The regular use of such a collection of materials has another great advantage in this context – it helps avoid the danger of arbitrariness in the use of texts, giving a selection that can be the basis for the teacher and the students to bring in additional textual material.

From text awareness, the move to literature is almost an imperceptible one, in that 'literariness' is almost impossible to categorise and define, as Carter and Long's 'clines of literariness' very usefully demonstrate (see Carter and Long 1991, p. 101 ff.)

As the texts used become longer and possibly more literary, in that they consist of writing that is in some way ideational rather than simply containing wordplay or breaking the rules, the greater the range of areas that can be explored within the context of language development and text awareness. Of course there will be grey areas here which overlap with Literature teaching, but it must be part of the teacher's aim to demystify, to accentuate the linguistic potential of the texts, rather than to heavy up the academic input.

In any apparatus it is worth bearing in mind that every question must lead to an answer, whether the answer be factual (contained in the text as information), conjectural (perhaps implied or suggested in the text, or to be deduced from it), or opinion-based and possibly to be reached only through reflection, discussion, argument, or further reading.

Especially in the earliest stages it is important that students be reassured of what kind of answer is expected. Prompts inviting opinions ('in your opinion . . .' or 'what do you think . . .?') will indicate the higher-level expectation in the question. All questions should lead somewhere: this may seem too obvious to be worth stating, but an apparatus often contains hanging questions which are there just because they can be asked, and do not take the learner on beyond the answer. If a question is worth asking it should lead further. Thus a low-level question about a lexical item and its meaning, context, or connotations can lead on to an awareness-type question about the lexical choice, alternative lexical possibilities, why the writer chose that word in preference to others, and so on. In this way the low-level question is developed, and exploited with wider reference to what the text is for and how it achieves its aims.

Of course many questions simply help to clarify something in the text, and as such cannot be greatly expanded upon. But it is important to seek clarification only of areas of interest which can later give opportunities for further exploitation. The teacher must bear in mind that it is hardly ever possible to clarify every single concept in a text, or to examine every single new lexical item.

Above all, questions and the apparatus in general must be clear. If necessary the questions should be simplified, not the text. A text is only as difficult as what the learner is asked to do with it.

The teacher should not be afraid of not knowing the 'correct' answer in a representational context. Over and above the 'open response' idea, what the teacher has to do is referee, marshal the various arguments that emerge, suggest other points of view if only one emerges, stimulate rather than close discussion, help learners summarise in order to retain the points discussed, review, recycle, and monitor. The teacher cannot be the fount and origin of all knowledge. So, knowing where to send students to seek information, to develop research skills, becomes a vital part of the teacher's role and of the learner's development, both in class and autonomously.

Learners are therefore being encouraged not to learn and repeat examples of language, but to develop their own thinking skills, and to acquire the language, and thereupon to organise the language and ideas into presentable spoken or written forms. It is never monochrome language, but rather language that reflects multiplicity of point of view, the possibility of several interpretations, a moving beyond the referentiality of facts and data – which, of course, still retain their primary significance, but as part of language learning rather than as the be-all and end-all.

2.4   A practical A to Z

As teachers and learners move on in representational language study, both will acquire some tricks and techniques to facilitate the processes of reading and evaluating texts. What follows is a series of do's and don'ts, reminders, suggestions and tricks, easy ways round some problem areas. Any such list is incomplete, and individual teachers will be able to add to it from their own experience: all further contributions welcome!

active and passive: awareness of how the active and passive voices are manipulated often gives a useful insight into how language is being used, or point of view changed. By extension, the reversal of a subject/verb/object relationship can be very revealing. A good example is found in Wordsworth's *Daffodils*, where the speaking 'I' is the active viewer of all around until the final verse when the daffodils he has seen become the subject as 'they flash upon that inward eye' and he becomes acted upon rather than acting. The trick is used by writers of everything from advertising copy to political speeches – as well as Romantic poetry.

answers: open or closed, factual or conjectural, are not always definitive. Students should be encouraged to have preferred answers, to evaluate possible answers, to reject as well as to accept answers. There are always more questions than answers, as the saying goes.

apparatus: it should not always be necessary to do all the tasks in the apparatus – some can be skipped, and students should be encouraged to know when they want to skip; phase and mix high-order and low-order questions; do not follow the same pattern in the apparatus for every text; give some texts very little apparatus; encourage the readers to suggest further apparatus if necessary – why should the teacher always supply all the apparatus?

argument: arguing and discussing are useful in working with representational materials. An argument should not become a free-for-all, however. Structured discussion and debate, group work to reach agreed opinions, and balanced monitoring of divergent views are required. The teacher will often have to act as referee. People also change their minds as a result of later reading or further reflection.

author: not always the authority. Roland Barthes suggested that we are living with 'The Death of the Author' and that every reader can rewrite the original author's texts in his or her own way. An author cannot insist on an interpretation; a reader can; other readers can too.

autonomy: learner autonomy has to be one of the teacher's aims at all times. The teacher's supportive role is as an enabler and confidence-builder, indicating ways towards autonomy and self-evaluation.

background: if too much background information is needed, a text should not be used. Background can be the subject of further investigation and research. It should not get in the way.

beginning and end: one of the clearest ways of helping students find something to say about a text is to compare the very beginning and the very end – the first and last sentences of a prose text, the first and last lines of a poem. Any text will contain movement, in the sense that something will have happened between the beginning and the end, and very often the highly specific comparison of beginning and ending can help focus on this. Famous poems like *Dover Beach* or *Daffodils* can be handled just as usefully in this way as short extracts in prose. It is also a very useful clue into an unseen text that students might have to comment on.

cohesion and time: the most obvious kinds of cohesion are often signalled temporally: then, afterwards, later, or before . . . and so on. But students can often miss temporal cohesion signalled in the changing tenses of the verb – from past to present, from past to present perfect, for example. In Browning's *Porphyria's Lover*, for example, applying the beginning and end technique outlined above, a comparison of the first line, 'The rain set early in tonight' and the last line, 'And still God has not said a word' shows, among other things, a shift from past to present perfect, implying perhaps some element of continuation.

confidence: the object of any teacher/learner relationship must be to give the learner confidence. Be positive rather than negative, even with opinions which might be wrong – the ability to justify an opinion is a paramount learning aim. Reading confidence and confidence in handling texts of any kind is built up through trust that the teacher is providing appropriate textual material, and that the apparatus is designed with a view to enhancing and building up this confidence towards greater and greater learner autonomy. Teacher confidence is therefore vital too.

consolidation and reinforcement: at some stage(s) it is advisable to take time to recap, rethink, review, and evaluate what has been read during one lesson, or over a period of time. This helps establish more firmly a reading frame of reference, to which learners can continue to refer as the course goes on. A reading diary is a major aid in this.

curiosity: is the reader's curiosity aroused? The reader must use curiosity to probe into such areas as: what he/she wants to know, how the author communicates and how the communication works; questions of character, motivation, intention, point of view, place, plot, attitudes, tone, language, new information. It is very rare that a text will not be able to meet some of the reader's curiosity, as long as that curiosity is focused: target reader curiosity into specific areas of study such as those outlined above.

diary: a reading diary or notebook, especially to document the reading of and the reaction and response to longer texts, is a constantly useful document. Favourite lines, quotations and ideas can be preserved here too, and become a useful resource for future writing and discussion.

ease: what is easy, what is difficult? Does the author make it easy for the reader to follow the lines of the argument? Or is there an element of deliberate mystification? Very often it is not the reader's fault that a text contains knots and difficulties. It is part of reading confidence to be able to judge whether or not a text is worth reading despite the difficulties encountered. If the reader wants to give up on a text, that's fine, as long as reasons can be given. Perhaps some readers will accept a text and others reject it because of the very same knots and problems.

English: what kind of English is being used? Dialect, British English, American English, or one of the many local Englishes? Is it modern or archaic, simple or complex, technical and specialised or simple, rich in lexis or full of commonly used vocabulary? Thus language use is seen as variety and richness rather than as deviation in any negative sense, although very often it will imply some deviation from the norms of the language system. But any language system involves spoken as well as written language, native-speaker and non-native-speaker modes: all such frames of reference and ranges of preference give an endless range of Englishes. Questions of register, tone, sound, class, social status, addresser/addressee all come into play as soon as the reader starts thinking about which English is used in a text and the possible reasons why. A key question is 'What would you have written?' This invites the learner to compare his/her own English with the English used, and therefore to evaluate (positively or negatively) the effects the text achieves.

expansion, or further interest: readers should be encouraged to read on, possibly on the same subject area, in the same author or period, for contrasts, additional information or enjoyment, to go into the context, to find quotations, or just to go on reading. Similarly expansion out from the texts read can lead into other areas of interest, to texts which students find for themselves or

want to introduce to the rest of the class. Reading in students'
own language(s) is to be encouraged too; newspapers might present the same story in quite a different way in students' L1; all
cultures have similar songs or love poetry, ways of forbidding
things, ways of selling things – compare and contrast at all times.

expectations: it is vital, as part of the process of reading, that the
reader be aware of his/her expectations and how the text plays
with them. Often an expectation gap between what the reader
anticipates and what actually happens is what allows for successful effects of humour, surprise, etc. Prediction activities and
questions such as 'what do you think is going to happen next?'
alert readers to their own expectations, and therefore to the
effects gained.

history: the study of the history of literature is somewhere beyond
the scope of using representational materials in language learning. It is however clearly more helpful to the learner to start
from the text and the processes of the text in any study of literature, rather than to start with a list of names, dates, and facts to
which it might be very difficult to relate. Working out from a
sample text, the student will be better able to relate the text to
the historical context, the period, and to the ideas, issues, and
the place in history of the text and the writer concerned. (See
Carter and McRae, *The Penguin Guide to English Literature*, 1996,
and *The Routledge History of Literature in English*, 1997.)

ideas: look for specific words and phrases which take the text
beyond the referential and towards the realm of ideas. The language of ideas need not be complex!

imagination: to be encouraged, appealed to, but not overused.
Samuel Beckett wrote a short novel whose title will repay some
consideration: *Imagination Dead Imagine.*

interpretation: George Eliot wrote, 'All meanings, we know,
depend on the key of interpretation.' This is the essence of representational language teaching and study. Students learn to
read, interpret, negotiate, and discuss meaning, developing language skills all the time, the five skills, including the thinking
skill.

irony: often the most difficult element for learners to grasp. Play
up to this by challenging and provoking when an affirmation is
read: with Chaucer's 'he was a verray, parfitt, gentil knight' for
example, the knight was in fact not true, perfect, or gentle: the
affirmation can be read as an ironic challenge to point of view.

Ambrose Bierce's *The Enlarged Devil's Dictionary* is very useful here, as it gives subversive dictionary definitions, and thereby questions even the validity of what is often the student's ultimate refuge. Irony is a mode of questioning, and definitions like Bierce's are an appropriate way into the kind of questioning that representational teaching encourages.

jokes: often a good way into wordplay and how language can be played with. Compare how jokes work in students' L1. There is no danger in having a laugh – being serious is no substitute for being a good teacher.

language-based approaches: everything in this book places the emphasis first on language, leading to interpretation, on how a text works in terms of process rather than as product. This is not an end in itself, rather it is an enabling process, allowing the reader to go as far as he or she wants into any text with a solid basis of linguistic security and understanding.

lateral thinking: discussion about a text need not be limited to what the text says. Invite physical descriptions of characters who are not actually described; 'What kind of ear-rings would she wear?' is a fun question about a female character; find colours, smells, sounds; is it a fast or a slow text; what senses are involved; what is going on in the next room? Is the author laughing at us as we talk about the text? Or is the author likely to be happy about what we are saying?

literature: can have a small 'l' as well as a large 'L'.

meaning: flexible.

misreading: always possible. Failure to understand cohesion, rather than lack of lexical knowledge, is the most common cause of misreading. If misreadings occur it is usually useful to try to see (and show) why they happened: because something has not been noticed, or has been disregarded? Or because of interference from L1 or from another context? Or just a plain ordinary mistaken reading?

motivation: every reading and re-reading should be motivated. Teachers often spend a long time motivating the first reading, but forget to motivate, with specific reading aims, or apparatus, the second, third, and further readings. This can lead to unfocused reading – the best motivation is always that the student has something specific to look for or check up on, possibly to correct or clarify a previous reading, or because the earlier reading has led to this new questioning.

nonsense: useful as representational reading, especially for how language works, its effects in terms of sound and sense, and the relief of not having to work out 'proper' meanings.

one-liners: whether quotations or invented lines, these can be useful in terms of establishing context, who might have been speaking and to whom, or simply because they are memorable. Why are some lines more memorable and quotable than others? Students should be encouraged to build up a quotation hoard of their own.

point of view: one of the fundamentals: who is speaking, and to whom? Is it the author, an implied author, a character, an unidentified voice, an invisible third person narrator? Who is 'I'? Whose is the voice in an advertisement? Would it be different with another voice? Would it work? Does the point of view shift during the text? Imagine a video camera as a means of shifting point of view, especially in a descriptive text.

positive or negative: a useful question to get discussion going about a text – is it positive or negative? Usually there will be two opinions at least. Can be applied also to single lexical items in the evaluation of meaning and connotations. Should always lead on to another question, perhaps 'how can you tell?' or perhaps along the lines of 'why are there two answers to the question?'

prediction: immensely useful in the context of 'what do you think is going to happen?' Also reverse or pre-prediction, focusing on what might have happened before the extract or text begins.

premises: it is not always easy for the learner to understand the premises and assumptions behind what a writer says. What is shared, what unshared between author and reader? Which premises are necessary to the understanding of the text, and which only contributory? As with vocabulary, students have to learn to decide how much it is worth finding out, and how much can be taken on trust.

pronouns: inexpert readers often do not notice simple words they already know, and worry over unfamiliar words. Yet it is often the simplest words that are the most dangerous. 'You' is the classic example – when an author uses 'you', the question has to be asked 'who is you?' If it is the reader, why is the author addressing him/her – complicity, trying to involve us in shared assumptions? There is usually a reason, and it will have something to do with point of view, of trying to create a sense of oneness with the reader. Advertisers use 'you' and politicians 'us' all the time. The aware reader will watch out for pronoun manipulation, and will begin to see through some rhetorical strategies of language use.

quotations: useful as learning hooks and memory aids.

sounds: most texts have sounds, either explicitly or implicitly. Explore them adverbially, as in 'he said, angrily', or in terms of speed, alliteration, vowel sounds, harsh sounds, smooth sounds, the kind of voice that should ideally read the text (especially useful with advertisements).

testing and evaluation: the frequently quoted words of Jonathan Culler (1977) can usefully be repeated here: 'our examinations are not designed merely to check whether [the student] has read and remembered certain books but to test his or her progress as a reader of literature'; whether of literature or of any other kind of text, this progress must be the teacher's and the learner's main aim. How this is tested or evaluated is a subject which deserves wider exploration than is possible here. McRae (1991) offers the following very broad outlines:

The evaluation of student performance in this kind of testing situation will take account of linguistic capabilities (fluency, accuracy, self-correction, etc.):

- the ability to make connections and cross-references;
- the ability to quote and summarise constructively;
- the ability to balance arguments and reach conclusions;
- the ability to take subjective standpoints and relate them to objective criteria;
- the ability to contextualise;

and many others, depending on individual situations. Flexibility is of the essence, and there is no such thing as a perfect answer or an ideal candidate.

Marks will be awarded according to the criteria established locally, as dictated by syllabus requirements and so on. It is to be stressed that marks are awarded, not subtracted. This is not, like dictation perhaps, a test whereby a perfect standard is set up and all imperfections result in lost marks. The examination or test should give the student the opportunity to show

- what has been learned,
- how that learning has been applied, and
- how that learning can be expressed.

(See also Carter and Long 1991; Brumfit ed. 1991)

title: it is very often a good idea not to give the title of a text when it is presented, inviting readers to suggest possible titles at a later stage, and to evaluate the original title in relation to their own assumptions and conclusions about the text.

together: the putting together of unexpected combinations of texts is one of the joys of representational teaching and learning. A recent song and a few lines from Shakespeare, a newspaper report and a passage from a novel, two texts from completely different periods. By putting texts together they illuminate each other as well as reflecting the shared concerns of writers through the centuries and in different countries and cultures. An endless resource.

top ten: invite students to grade texts in order of preference, with clearly stated reasons. (It shouldn't be easy.) This brings some subjective, and later objective elements of critical judgement into play, and encourages evaluation of what is read. Taking note of other people's judgements can be useful here (colleagues, the teacher – even critics, at higher levels).

trivia: just as useful as serious material, in a balanced programme.

verification: ties in closely with evaluation. Constant reference to what has been read and discussed, and the encouragement of written work about it, will build up learner competence in balancing arguments, expressing opinions and preferences, summarising what has been read, drawing conclusions, and so on. This might well become the basis for the process of evaluation at the end of a course of study.

vocabulary: usually adduced by learners (and teachers) as the main drawback to encouraging reading. Start to eliminate this feeling at as early a stage as possible, with short texts, by having students decide which one word (or two at most) they really need to know in order to feel comfortable with the text. This begins to create a sense of autonomy, as well as encouraging group and class collaboration. Vocabulary confidence is a vital part of reading competence, and depends on the learner rather than the teacher identifying vocabulary needs. A vocabulary notebook is, of course, useful, but learners must be aware of how much vocabulary they wish to consider passive, and how much active. Using quotations as memory aids is to be encouraged here. The evaluation of lexical choice and the discussion of why one word is used rather than another which the learner

might use, is a vital awareness-raising exercise in the appreciation of lexical variety.

what is the text about?: sometimes a useful question in order to
show that the text is not about one single thing. Often, however,
unanswerable without going into a wide range of topics and
ideas.

2.5   Conclusion

Finally some don'ts:
DON'T

- ask every possible question;
- stand in front of the text; or kill it; (or kill the students);
- apologise;
- explain;
- impose an interpretation;
- forget your teaching aims (syllabus/curriculum);
- always ask for written follow-up work;
- patronise reader, author, or text;
- force things;
- let your own feelings (positive or negative) interfere, although
  naturally they can be brought in;
- tell. Show rather than tell;
- always use texts you know. Be prepared to take risks, and share
  the risk-taking with students;
- be afraid of texts or of yourself (unfamiliarity, ignorance, etc.)
  or of students' reactions;
- waste time;
- over-prepare. It is often worse than under-preparing;
- rush; or plod;
- pretend you know all the answers;
- forget to wrap up, underlining what has been achieved, even
  though some things might have to be left hanging;
- threaten exams;
- try to do everything yourself. Consult colleagues; collaborate,
  especially with students;
- be too tricksy, technical, or showy; don't hog the lesson:
  remember teacher talking time;
- worry if not everybody participates all the time;
- use jargon.

Many teachers will find such a list superfluous, if not downright rude. But we are all guilty of moments of misjudgement when we are teaching, and can always learn how to do it a little better. For teachers who already work with representational materials, either at a pre-literary level or beyond, there will be no need to encourage them further. For the majority who might be tempted, I will end with a one-liner which is guaranteed to get some reaction. As with so many of the best quotations in English it is from Oscar Wilde: 'I can resist everything except temptation.'

3

Stylistics 'upside down': using stylistic analysis in the teaching of language and literature

MICK SHORT

The author argues that stylistic analysis is a useful means for relatively inexperienced or unsophisticated students to arrive at possible meanings of texts, especially those students with little or no linguistic knowledge who may nevertheless be enthusiastic readers of English literature.

Mick Short reviews in turn the approaches used in a course (at Lancaster University) on *Language and Style*, in relation to Poetry, Fictional Prose, and Drama. Interpretation of texts is shown to be dependent on an understanding of such linguistic features as deviation, lexical choice, point of view and turn-taking – all of which contribute to meaning.

Practical examples are given and discussed, outlining ways in which students are prepared – or 'softened up' – as they learn to read texts interactively and systematically. This 'bottom-up' or 'upside down' approach to the discipline of stylistic analysis is exemplified, advocated, and defended by the author. In particular, the use of checksheets, which offer enabling metalanguage at the same time as introducing students to an approach which may be both new and unappealing to them, is examined. Feedback is often suggested as the basis for seminar activities, and self-assessment.

3.1 Introduction

In this paper[1] I will argue that stylistic analysis, which until now has largely been thought of as an analytical tool to support or test interpretative hypotheses already arrived at by sophisticated interpreters of literary texts, can also be used by less sophisticated readers who happen to have been trained in the methodology to help them puzzle out meaning when they get stuck. I believe that what I suggest applies to a wide range of language and literature

41

students, both native- and non-native-speaking. This is because a number of the issues discussed have general educational application, and so, with local modifications, can be used in a variety of educational contexts. However, to teach stylistics successfully to less sophisticated students means finding new, and more accessible, ways to teach it, and so I go on to explore ways in which this might be done, using my experience over the last few years, teaching stylistics on a course called *Language and Style* to first-year, native-speaking, English undergraduates who have little or no experience of language work. In a sense, much of what I will say is not new. Many of the teaching techniques we use are already established in the teaching of language and literature to non-native speakers of English (see, for example, Brumfit and Carter 1986, Carter and Long 1987, Carter, Walker and Brumfit 1989, Lazar 1993, Short 1988, Widdowson 1975, 1992), and others besides us have also begun to experiment with them in teaching native-speaking students (see Durant and Fabb 1990, Montgomery *et al.* 1992). But the extensive use of what we call checksheets in teaching is, I think, new (although the one Geoffrey Leech and I produced for chapter 3 of Leech and Short 1981 has been used all round the world), and I would also claim novelty for the combination of the elements in the way I suggest below.

3.2   My argument summarised

(a) Stylistics is usually thought of as an analytical technique to help support or test already-formed interpretative hypotheses. But 'turned upside down' it can be of considerable use to learners (and indeed the stylistic critic) when there is a puzzle over meaning.

(b) Clearly you cannot teach stylistics to everyone. Some will not be able to cope with the specialised vocabulary or analytical approach. But where the 'lower' limit *is* for stylistics is not clear, and the educational and age levels where stylistics can be appropriate is probably lower than most assume.

(c) In order to teach stylistics 'down the levels', however, we need to be prepared to make our terminology more transparent and to find teaching techniques to help students over the initial hurdles, when the approach seems strange and difficult. Teaching techniques usually associated with English language teaching to non-native students of English are often helpful for this purpose, in teaching both native- and non-native-speaking students.

(d) The sorts of techniques mentioned under (c) above can, by and large, be described as 'softening up' techniques, aimed at getting students interested in doing analytical work in its various aspects. But, as with analytical work in any other subject, students do eventually have to cope with the grind of learning techniques and applying them in analysis. Once they have been 'softened up', the careful use of checksheets is particularly helpful. Checksheets also have the added advantage of encouraging students to be more systematic analytically, another skill which it is important for them to acquire.

3.3   The *Language and Style* course and its students

I will not describe the structure and philosophy of the course in any detail here.[2] That has already been done in Breen and Short (1988) and Short and Breen (1988). However, some brief remarks about my students and the course they take will help the reader understand the context of what follows. Most of our students come to university assuming that the study of English means the study of English literature. Particularly in our first-year group (which will include at one extreme those intending to major in English, and at the other extreme those who are merely doing it as a makeweight third subject in our three-subject Part I), we are faced with many students who know very little about their own language, and appear to think that doing English means to curl up by the fire and read a novel, prior to having a cosy and informal chat about it. Many are highly resistant to studying poetry, because it is 'difficult', and, by and large, novels and stories are much preferred to plays. Moreover, for the last thirty years, English language as a focus of study in its own right has been largely ignored in UK schools. Language study was equated with English grammar, and deemed to be boring and irrelevant; and English teachers began to rely on students' experience of other modern languages to provide them with some basic grammatical knowledge to use in text description. But, as the teaching of modern languages itself became less grammar-based and more 'communicative', that grammar 'safety net' also disappeared. The consequence is that many of our students, when they arrive at university, have some difficulty in identifying which are the nouns, verbs, adjectives and adverbs in a sentence, let alone coping with anything more sophisticated. The advent of the new English Language A-level syllabi, which include a wide range of aspects of language study and sometimes even include some elementary stylistics, does mean that more students are arriving at university with a somewhat more sophisticated knowledge of English language than before, but the majority have still not taken an A-level English Language course, and are more or less *tabula rasa* in terms of explicit knowledge about language.

Our task, then, is to take relatively sophisticated readers of English literature, who have little if any knowledge of English language, and persuade them that the close scrutiny and analysis of the language of the texts they read will be interesting and rewarding. Moreover, many of those students are not just ignorant of their own language. They are also highly resistant to learning about it, sometimes because their traditional literature-trained teachers have tended to disparage language study as hard and boring.

We used to think that, as the students lacked language knowledge, the best thing was to give it to them in preparation for doing stylistic analysis proper towards the end of the year. Hence they imbibed units on grammar, phonetics, varieties of English and so on, before arriving at the part of the course which was of most interest to them. The problem was that many of them had switched off long before they got to the stylistics unit, and so had little language knowledge to apply to literary texts when invited to do so. Now, we start with the primary assumption that we must keep them interested in what they are doing. So, we start with literary texts and literary problems each week, and 'drip feed' linguistic knowledge to them, as and when it is relevant for some task or discussion. This helps to increase their feeling that the language knowledge is relevant to their needs, and, although they arrive at the end of the year with an incomplete knowledge of the language areas they are introduced to, by and large they perform better in their assessable work and are more interested in what they do. The examples of work seen below should be contextualised within this general framework.

3.4   The structure of the remainder of this paper

In essence, I will run through the basic argument, which I have summarised in section 3.2 above, three times: once in relation to each of the three literary genres. I do this to show that what I am talking about applies not just to poetry (because poems are typically short and self-contained, stylisticians tend to take most of their examples from this genre) but to all three genres. The *Language and Style* course, incidentally, looks at all three genres in turn, introducing techniques of language analysis that have most interpretative benefit for the relevant genre (although we are careful to point out that analytical techniques introduced in relation to one genre are also usually applicable to the other genres, and indeed the analysis of any text – literary or non-literary).

For poetry, fictional prose, and drama in turn, I will pick one example of how 'stylistics upside down' can be used to help in interpretative matters. I will then present (a) one or more examples of 'softening-up' work in the same area, derived largely from English language teaching work, and (b) a checksheet to help students become more knowledgeable and more sophisticated in that area.

3.5   Poetry

Although in my own research I use stylistic analysis mainly to flesh out and back up interpretations that I have already arrived at through the largely intuitive process of careful reading, I sometimes find that performing the analysis makes me alter my interpretation. The alteration may be radical, or it may be a matter of refinement or detail. The analysis makes me be more careful about the argument I can put forward, and so helps me to perceive misconstruals in my original interpretative hypotheses. This experience has also led me to use stylistic analysis when I feel I have not completely understood something I have read. What happens in this case is that I scan the text for significant foregroundings and patterns, and use what I know about how these factors constrain textual meaning (in conjunction with (a) what I have managed to understand, and (b) the overall assumption of textual interpretative unity) to try out readings until I get something that works. Below, I examine how such a strategy might work with part of a poem by Roger McGough which exhibits foregrounding through both deviation and parallelism.

3.5.1   *Deviation, parallelism, and interpretation*

Consider the situation where someone reads the poem below and
has some difficulty in understanding lines 9–14:

Comeclose and Sleepnow

1	it is afterwards
	and you talk on tiptoe
	happy to be part
	of the darkness
5	lips becoming limp
	a prelude to tiredness.
	Comeclose and Sleepnow
	for in the morning
	when a policeman
10	disguised as the sun
	creeps into the room
	and your mother
	disguised as birds
	calls from the trees
15	you will put on a dress of guilt
	and shoes with broken high ideals
	and refusing coffee
	run
	alltheway
20	home

The first thing we can notice about lines 9–14 is that the two
coordinated subordinate clauses exhibit extensive parallelism.
They both have the structure Subject – Verb – Adverbial.
Moreover, the Subject NP of each clause consists of a determiner
and headword followed by a relative clause with the structure 'dis-
guised as X'. If we apply what I like to call the 'parallelism rule',
we will search for ways of making the parallel structures either
parallel or opposite in meaning. Many stylisticians have pointed to
this semantic reading tendency when parallel structures are
observed. Secondly we can note a semantic deviation in both
Subject NPs in terms of the relation between the headword and
the post-modifying relative clause (which, in effect, is also another
parallel). Policemen cannot literally disguise themselves as the
sun, and a mother cannot sensibly disguise herself as birds. Hence
our interpretation of these lines will have to be 'non-literal', taking account of both the semantic deviations and the parallelisms.

We can see from the rest of the text that the poem appears to be a free direct representation (Leech and Short 1981, pp. 336–48; Short 1986) of the somewhat ironic or even sarcastic thoughts of some man who has just made love with a woman who appears to be rather naive and less experienced sexually than the man (hence her guilt as she runs home at the end of the poem). He could conceivably be talking to her (the free direct representation is potentially ambiguous as to whether speech or thought is represented, as there is no 'narratorial' indication to resolve the ambiguity), but as what he says is rather rude and unflattering, and generally inappropriate for a speech situation, a thought-presentation interpretation is much more likely. This knowledge, in conjunction with the structural facts already presented, helps us to come to an interpretation of lines 9–14 whereby it is not the policeman and the mother who come into the room (after all, we would expect the mother to be at home, and making love is not normally a criminal offence). An interpretation that fits all the constraints is that the sunlight and the sound of the birds come into the room, waking the girl up, reminding her of her mother, and thus making her feel guilty for her actions. This interpretation explains the semantic oddities, and also accounts for the parallelism, through the relation of 'parallel meaning'. Note that the mother appears in this context not to be the soft and supportive stereotype we have come to love, but an authority figure, an interpretation which is arrived at through the parallel with the policeman who, we should notice, comes first in the sequence.

You may, of course, have understood the lines I have explicated without any difficulty. In which case, if you had not already formulated explicitly for yourself what I have pointed out above, you may well have just thought to yourself, 'Yes, I knew that already, but didn't realise that I knew it.' But the general point I want to make is that, if you do get stuck for meaning, knowing about stylistic analysis gives you something useful to try. Otherwise, there is not much more you can do than re-read, in the hope that 'something will click'.

3.5.2 Beginning to teach about deviation, parallelism and linguistic choice

Almost as soon as our students begin our *Language and Style* course, we want them to begin to understand the role that linguistic choice plays in meaning, as a prelude to helping them to notice the meaningful effects of deviant and parallelistic choices. In lectures as well as seminars, we are keen to have the students be active, discovering things for themselves, and *feeling* the significance of what they are told as well as *understanding* it intellectually. So, lectures for us are not just activities where the students sit and listen. Students also have to do things themselves. For the last few years, in the middle of the first or second lecture of the course, after appropriate introductory material, we give them the task of choosing for themselves alternatives in a poem by Stephen Crane. You may recognise the text, and the alternatives, as ones used by van Peer (1988) when discussing the use of the cloze procedure for helping students to become aware of textual cohesion. We use his materials and his task, but for different purposes. The students, working alone or in groups, as they wish, have to try to decide which of the three alternatives Crane actually chose at each point. They are then invited to 'vote' for their choices, so that the patterns of choice can be displayed.

I stood	(on) (upon) (in)	a high	(place) (mountain) (hill)
And saw,	(terrified,) (laughing,) (below,)	many devils,	
(Running,) (Dancing,) (Singing,)	leaping,		
And	(living) (indulging) (carousing)	in sin.	
(I) (They) (One)	looked up	(sadly,) (grinning,) (to heaven,)	
And said:	('Comrade! Brother!') ('Join us!') ('Help me!')		

Some choices the students almost always get right. For example, 'upon' works best in the first set of alternatives, not just because it satisfies the above/below structure of the text, as van Peer notes, but also because it satisfies the overall iambic metrical scheme of the poem. But few students choose 'Comrade! Brother!' for the last choice (although they quickly see its ironic superiority – achieved through its presuppositional structure – once Crane's own choice is revealed). And they almost never guess 'carousing' in the fifth set of alternatives, because it is so unusual a word. This exercise thus helps them (a) to feel deviation palpably when it occurs in the poem, (b) to appreciate Crane's originality, and (c) to understand better the role of the deviation in interpretation. It also gets them to focus on linguistic choice as a vehicle for complex and interesting meanings and effects. In other words, we have made them begin to feel the relevance of doing elementary stylistic analysis through an activity which they find fun, thus 'softening them up' for the more analytical work which it is going to be necessary for them to do if they are to become proficient at doing stylistic analysis.

Another way of teaching about linguistic choice is through the comparison of different versions of the same text. For the seminar associated with the lecture which I have just referred to, we ask them to compare a poem with which they are probably already familiar – Blake's *The Tyger* – with an alternative version which I constructed from the various drafts which Blake made. This 'amalgam' of earlier versions was chosen to be as different as possible from the original, while still remaining a reasonably consistent text.

Seminar exercise

Working with two or three colleagues in your seminar group, read the *final version* of Blake's *The Tyger* through a few times and discuss it until you think you have a reasonable understanding of it. Then compare it carefully with the version Mick Short has 'composed' from Blake's earlier drafts for the poem. Note down each difference, and at what linguistic level the difference occurs. Then discuss why you think Blake changed the poem at each place. Each time, can you specify any difference in meaning and/or effect which occurs? How does this difference relate to Blake's overall meaning strategy in the poem? Bring your conclusions to the seminar.

The Tyger

Final version

Tyger! Tyger! burning bright
In the forests of the night,
What immortal hand or eye
Could frame thy fearful symmetry?

In what distant deeps or skies
Burnt the fire of thine eyes?
On what wings dare he aspire?
What the hand dare seize the fire?

And what shoulder & what art,
Could twist the sinews of thy heart?
And when thy heart began to beat,
What dread hand? & what dread feet?

What the hammer? what the chain?
In what furnace was thy brain?
What the anvil? what dread grasp
Dare its deadly terrors clasp?

When the stars threw down their spears,
And water'd heaven with their tears,
Did he smile his work to see?
Did he who made the Lamb make thee?

Tyger! Tyger! burning bright,
In the forests of the night,
What immortal hand or eye
Dare frame thy fearful symmetry?

'Drafts' version

Tyger, Tyger, burning bright
In the forests of the night,
What immortal hand & eye
Dare frame thy fearful symmetry?

Burnt in distant deeps or skies
The cruel fire of thine eyes?
Could heart descend or wings aspire?
What the hand dare seize the fire?

And what shoulder & what art
Could twist the sinews of thy heart?
And when thy heart began to beat,
What dread hand? & what dread feet?

Where the hammer? Where the chain?
In what furnace was thy brain?
What the anvil? What the grasp
Dare its deadly terrors clasp?

When the stars threw down their spears,
And water'd heaven with their tears,
Dare he laugh his work to see?
Dare he who made the lamb make thee?

Tyger, Tyger, burning bright,
In the forests of the night,
What immortal hand & eye
Dare frame thy fearful symmetry?

We do not have the space to discuss all the variants in these versions, but a couple of simple ones will help to demonstrate the usefulness of the activity in getting students to appreciate the effect of fine linguistic choices. In stanza one, there are two changes. The final version has 'could' in the last line, not 'dare'; thus producing one highly significant change between the otherwise identical first and last stanzas of the text, and, consequently, a highly significant internal deviation interpretatively. Comparing the versions helps students to see the change and begin to discuss the resultant meaning, via their intuitions associated with the two modal verbs. Thus it helps to lead to initial discussion of the semantics of modality if the tutor desires it, as well as to discussion of the meaning and organisation of the poem itself.

The other change in stanza one is from '&' to 'or': a change which helps students to see the more uncertain character of 'or', an effect which they can relate easily to the poem's overall meaning, and more specifically to choices seen later in the text through this comparative method. In stanza four, 'where the hammer?' and 'where the chain?' become 'what the hammer?' and 'what the chain?', so that the question at issue is not where the hammer and chain are located, but what their very nature is, another step towards uncertainty about the tyger, a fact which is related to its fearsome character.

3.5.3 Deviation, parallelism and foregrounding checksheet

The first thing I should own up to at this point is that we have never, at the time of writing, actually used the checksheet below on the

Language and Style course. The other two checksheets, presented in 3.6.3 and 3.7.2 below, have been used extensively, however.

Example 3.1   *Deviation, parallelism and foregrounding checksheet*

A. Note down each deviation and parallelism you can find in the text.

Deviation

(a) Is the deviation *internal* (deviates from some established pattern internal to the text) or *external* (deviates from some norm external to the text)?

(b) If the deviation is external, what external norm does it deviate from (e.g. the norms for English, the norms for the genre, the norms of the particular author)?

(c) At what linguistic level does the deviation occur?

Discoursal	Graphological
Lexical	Metrical
Morphological	Phonetic
Pragmatic	Syntactic
Other	

(d) Are there any other deviations occurring at the same place in the text? (If so, re-apply (a)–(c).) Note the extra foregrounding.

(e) Do(es) the deviation(s) lead to new, non-literal meanings for the text-parts concerned? If so, what are they in each case?

Parallelism

(f) Are there any parallelisms? If so, note at what linguistic levels they occur by using the list of levels in (c) above. (Note that parallelism may occur at more than one linguistic level at the same time.)

(g) Does the parallelism 'rule' (look for same or opposite meaning) apply? If so, what is the meaning-result?

B. Examine cohesion and function of foregrounding.

(h) How do the foregrounded portions of the text relate together and contribute to the interpretation of the poem as a whole? Does looking at the whole pattern help you in any way to interpret particular deviations or parallelisms that you could not satisfactorily explain before, or reinterpret others?

(i) Note down any other points which occur to you.

A checksheet like this helps to make sure that students do not forget to note down significant items which they might otherwise forget in analysis, and incomplete, sometimes inadequate support for the view of the text they want to expound. This 'partial' kind of analysis can lead to interpretations which are not fully worked out. The checksheet thus helps to improve their interpretative as well as their analytical abilities.

It is not necessarily the case that when students receive a checksheet they will have covered every aspect of its operation in detail. This fact tends to annoy them, of course, but it also, valuably, sets up a desire in them to know about the parts which have not yet been covered. For example, section A of the above checksheet lists a number of linguistic levels at which deviation might occur. But students may not yet have learnt about all of these levels, or may have learnt about some in only sketchy detail. They are now almost bound to ask their tutors about them in their next seminar. It is not just the case that this process keeps their interest up. It also means that they learn new terms and concepts in a rather more natural way than in the standard lecture, where a new term is introduced and immediately defined, the students often ending up with an imperfect understanding as a consequence of trying to write down the word and its definition at the moment that they are trying to understand it. I am not, of course, advocating a sloppy approach to teaching, where tutors can get away without explaining all that they should. I merely point out that knowingly withholding information can have strategic benefits, if it is done carefully.

3.6   Fictional prose

3.6.1   *The linguistic control of point of view*

The example of prose stylistics which I have chosen to use is designed to show stylistics at work in the understanding and explication of point of view. In the following example, we have a number of indications that the viewpoint which the omniscient narrator is taking on is that of Mr Verloc:

> Mr Verloc heard the creaky plank in the floor, and was content. He waited. Mrs Verloc was coming.
>
> (Joseph Conrad, *The Secret Agent*, ch. 11)

Mr Verloc is subject of a verb of perception and a verb of cognition. His state of mind is portrayed with 'was content', and the verb 'coming' in the last sentence clearly relates Mr Verloc as deictic centre. Mrs Verloc is coming towards Mr Verloc. This raises the issue of why it is that the narrator has restricted his description of the events to Mr Verloc's viewpoint. The answer is that Conrad is setting up a combined effect of irony and horror. Mr Verloc, who has had a bad day and is lying on the sofa, waiting for his wife to bring him his evening meal, has not yet perceived what the readers of the novel already know, that Mrs Verloc is coming towards him with a carving knife in her hand. She kills him by plunging the knife into his chest before he can move. She murders him because Mr Verloc has been the unwitting instrument of the death of her witless younger brother, Stevie. Mr Verloc is, unbeknown to his wife, a secret agent. He has set off to blow up the Greenwich observatory with a bomb, and Mrs Verloc, who wants her husband to like her brother and agree to look after him when her mother dies, has forced Mr Verloc to take Stevie with him. Moreover, she has badgered Stevie to be helpful to Mr Verloc. Stevie thus insists on carrying the case with the bomb in it, and accidentally blows himself to smithereens when he trips over the root of a tree in Greenwich Park.

Mr Verloc does not feel he is to blame. After all, he did not want Stevie to come with him, and certainly did not want him to carry the bomb. Arguably, Mrs Verloc is at least as responsible for his death as anyone else, but she does not see it that way, and her husband does not realise. *The Secret Agent* is clearly a novel about isolation and lack of communication, and understanding what is happening in terms of viewpoint control in the three sentences above is a small, but significant, element in Conrad's strategy to help us appreciate the way in which the characters, in this case man and wife, are isolated from one another.

Recognising viewpoint manipulation and understanding its strategic part in the novel is obvious enough in the above example, but it is unlikely that many students will be puzzled over the meaning of this extract. The following example may be rather more difficult, however. It is the very beginning of Ken Kesey's *One Flew Over the Cuckoo's Nest*:

> They're out there. Black boys in white suits up before me to commit
> sex acts in the hall and get it mopped up before I can catch them.

It is the very first sentence that I am interested in. In viewpoint terms, it is clearly related to the I-narrator who tells us the story, and it is a very dramatic and extreme version of what has been called the *in medias res* effect (see Leech and Short 1981, p. 179), where readers feel that they have started a story 'in the middle', with some important information apparently withheld. The subject pronoun is unanchored (though resolved in the next sentence), as is the deictic adverb 'there', a lack of specification which is only partly explained by 'the hall' in the next sentence. We still don't know where the hall is, or what kind of hall it is.

The issue for the reader is whether this particular *in medias res* beginning is just another, more extreme version of a technique we have become used to in the twentieth century, or whether it is more than that. Is it reasonable for the narrator to treat us so unreasonably? This issue signals the beginning of an important 'structural' aspect of the novel. The narrator, we discover later, is an inmate of a lunatic asylum. So, there is a problem about whether we can trust what he tells us, and how. Yet he is also an I-narrator, someone with whom we would expect to sympathise, and he describes the nursing staff as treating him and his friends in ways which are unreasonable and at times decidedly inhumane. This sympathy tension constitutes a major aspect of the book's interest, something which is being signalled to us in the interpretative puzzle set up in its opening sentence.

3.6.2 Beginning to teach about the linguistic control of point of view

The linguistic analysis of point of view is by now well established (see, for example, Leech and Short 1981, chapters 5, 8 and 10; Fowler 1986, chapters 9 and 10; Simpson 1993), and students who have already come across the concept repeatedly from their more traditional literary studies generally have no problem with feeling the relevance of what stylistics have to say in this area. But our students, straight from school, may well only have a hazy notion of viewpoint in literary terms. We thus begin by establishing what viewpoint is and how they already intuitively understand its workings. The example below is used for the first seminar on point of view, after they have attended an initial lecture session on the topic.

Example 3.2   Being the author!

(a) Below is a description of an event which we have invented. We have tried to tell it in as natural a way as possible. Please read it through.

> A woman is sitting in a room with the door closed. (1) She is stroking a cat which is sitting on her lap. (2) A man, who has a gun in his hand (he is a policeman looking for an escaped murderess), enters the room suddenly. (3) The woman jumps up in fright. (4) The cat runs past the man and out through the door. (5) The woman attacks the man with a knife. (6) In reaction he shoots the woman, who receives a wound in the arm. (7)

(b) We want you to rewrite the *last three sentences* of the story, paying close attention to steps of perception, *either* from the point of view of the woman *or* from the point of view of the man. In both cases, we would like you to avoid first-person narration, and use instead *third-person narration in the past tense* (i.e. the 'usual' form for narration).

(c) Avoid using words we have used in the '*neutral*' version above, as far as this is possible. This will help you to characterise better, and will assist you in giving one person's point of view. The only constraint is that you should not alter the basic story.

(d) *Important*: We would like you to do two things before you begin your seminar task this week.

　　1. *Working in pairs*, play out the roles of the man and the woman in the passage. Don't try to do this alone – you need someone to work with so that you can discuss the following points:

　　　(i) When playing the role of the man, what do you know that the woman doesn't know? What do you *see* that she doesn't see? What feelings or reactions do you have *that the woman can't know about*? What are your thoughts during the episode? *In what order* do the events impinge on your consciousness? And *vice versa*:

　　　(ii) When playing the role of the woman, what do you *know* that the man doesn't know, and what do you have that he doesn't? What feelings or reactions do you have *that the man can't know about*? What are your thoughts during the episode? *In what order* do the events impinge on your consciousness?

　　2. Discuss with your partner (in crime?) all these aspects, and decide how they will affect the language in your re-telling of the story. One of you should then choose to tell the story from one point of view, and the other from the other.

Remember
You know/see different things according to the point of view. The *sequence* in which things are perceived or appear to happen may change according to the point of view. The *descriptive focus* (*nearness* or *distance* from the fiction) can interact with point of view.

Bring your re-telling of the story, clearly written out, to the seminar. Our discussion will centre on such questions as:
  (i) What are the differences between all three versions? Is it possible to *specify them in detail* (i.e. in terms of the language features)?
  (ii) Which of these differences are a result of the change in viewpoint?

Others, particularly in relation to language and literature integration in the EFL context, have explored the use of students' own writing, and changing what others have written, in language learning and language understanding (e.g. Maley 1989; Carter and Long 1987, unit 7). This work builds on that kind of model, and on similar proposals concerning role-play in language-learning situations. When students come to the first point of view seminar, they feel involved with issues to do with viewpoint because they have written what is discussed in class. Some even rewrite the passage from the viewpoint of the cat! As a consequence, they are very prepared to learn about the detail of the linguistic mechanics of viewpoint, and discuss their different versions with considerable animation. This knowledge is then, of course, available for them to use in the more academic analytical discussion of interesting novel extracts.

An alternative approach, which we sometimes use, is one where students rewrite passages produced by well-known authors. For example, we have asked students to write alternative versions of extracts from Sue Townsend's *The Secret Diary of Adrian Mole* when it was in vogue with students. This example is very like that proposed in Montgomery *et al.* (1992, p. 190).

Example 3.3

Below are two extracts from *The Secret Diary of Adrian Mole*. Re-cast extract (a) from the point of view of Mr Lucas and (b) from the point of view of Adrian's father. What did you change and why? What does this tell you about how point of view is manifested linguistically?

(a) Monday February 9th

There was a removal lorry outside Mr Lucas's house this morning. Mrs Lucas and some other women were carrying furniture from the house and stacking it on the pavement. Mr Lucas was looking out from his bedroom window, he looked a bit frightened. Mrs Lucas was laughing and pointing up to Mr Lucas and all the other women started laughing and singing 'Why was he born so beautiful?'

(b) Sunday February 8th

FIFTH AFTER EPIPHANY

My father came into my bedroom this morning, he said he wanted a chat. He looked at my Kevin Keegan scrapbook, screwed the knob off my wardrobe door back on with his Swiss army knife, and asked me about school. Then he said he was sorry about yesterday and the shouting, he said my mother and him are 'going through a bad patch'. He asked me if I had anything to say. I said he owed me thirty-two pence for the Chinese chips and soy sauce. He gave me a pound. So I made a profit of sixty-eight pence.

3.6.3   A point of view checksheet

We give the checksheet below to students in the lecture following the 'softening up' week described in 3.6.2. It is accompanied by a sheet of short extracts from stories and novels which are interesting in terms of one or more of the categories in the checksheet. Some of the examples are worked through in the lecture. Students discuss others themselves, either after a category has been explained to them, or before a category is explained, as a way of getting them to feel the need for the information before it is given to them. The checksheet is not perfect (in fact we have changed it recently by incorporating point of view aspects of situational frames using the insights of schema theory), but it covers most of what is needed to account for the linguistic manipulation of point of view. Students then use the checksheet in examining a passage from a novel as their associated seminar task. I will not go through the checksheet in detail here, partly for space reasons, and partly because many readers will already know about this area in some detail. If you do not, reading the works referred to in 3.6.1 above would be a good beginning.

Example 3.4 Point of view in prose: Checksheet of linguistic indicators of point of view

1. Given *vs.* new information, e.g.
   - (a) definite/indefinite articles (*a/the*);
   - (b) textually referring (anaphoric) pronouns (*you, it, they*, etc.).
2. Deictic (shifting) expressions related to place, e.g.
   - (a) adverbials (*here/there*, etc., *to my left, in front of him*);
   - (b) demonstrative pronouns (*this/that*, etc.);
   - (c) verbs (*come/go*, etc.).
3. Deictic expressions related to time, e.g.
   - (a) adverbials (*now/then, today/that day, tomorrow, the following day,* etc.);
   - (b) past and present tenses.
4. 'Socially deictic' expressions, e.g.
   - (a) personal and possessive pronouns (*I, you, he*; *mine, yours*, etc.);
   - (b) variant socially relevant expressions for the same person, e.g.
     - (i) the naming system: *Mick, Mr Short, Dad*;
     - (ii) varying expressions in third-person reference (sometimes called 'elegant variation'): *Bunter, the hapless owl, the fat ornament of the Remove, the grub raider of the Remove.*
5. Indicators of the internal representation of a particular character's thoughts or perceptions, e.g.
   - (a) verbs of perception and cognition (*see, hear, imagine, think, believe*);
   - (b) verbs related to factivity (cf. *It was obvious that he was ill* vs. *It seems that he was ill* vs. *He pretended to be ill*);
   - (c) adverbs related to factivity (*actually, apparently*).
6. Value-laden and ideologically slanted expressions, e.g. *I saw Mick Short* vs. *I saw that awful Mick Short; He is a freedom fighter* vs. *He is a terrorist; the Far East* vs. *South-East Asia.*
7. Event coding within and across sentences, e.g. *The man burst the door open* vs. *The door burst open; Robin Hood ran past me* vs. *Someone ran past me. It was Robin Hood.*

3.7 Drama

3.7.1 Turn-taking and the understanding of character relations and dramatic meaning

In the extract below, from Shakespeare's *Richard III*,[3] Buckingham asks Richard for the reward Richard has promised for

Buckingham's support in his various machinations and wrong-doings:

> Buckingham: What says your Highness to my just demand?
> King Richard: I do remember me, Henry the Sixth
>   Did prophesy that Richmond should be King,
>   When Richmond was a little peevish boy.
>   A king . . . perhaps . . . perhaps –
> Buckingham: My lord!
> King Richard: How chance the prophet could not, at that time,
>   Have told me – I being by – that I should kill him?
> Buckingham: My lord, your promise for the earldom –
> King Richard: Richmond! When I was last at Exeter . . .
>   (William Shakespeare, *Richard III*, IV iii)

In spite of the fact that he does not openly say so, Richard is telling Buckingham that he will not reward him after all. He does this, of course, by his manipulation of the turn-taking rules (see, for example, Herman 1991 and Bennison 1993 for accounts of turn-taking patterns and the production of meaning in drama). Buckingham asks a question, which Richard pointedly ignores, talking instead of Richmond, and thus breaking Grice's maxim of relation (Grice 1975) and taking over control of the topic. Whenever Buckingham tries to bring Richard back to his original topic, Richard continues with his own, interrupting Buckingham as he goes along. Richard's interruption and ignoring of Buckingham's attempts to get his reward here are part of a larger, similar pattern seen in this scene. Indeed, when that wider context is taken into account, Richard's behaviour can be seen as even more rude: the conversation takes place in the presence of other powerful members of the Court. Richard is using the 'meaning' of established conversational behaviour to indicate that he is in absolute power and can ignore, at whim, the just demands of an important supporter. From this, we can, in turn, infer that Shakespeare is portraying him as a tyrannical king, who is continuing the unpleasant and unreasonable behaviour which he has already used in murdering his way to the top. The extract is thus a clear example of how we infer meaning from the observation of turn-taking and other discoursal patterns, a skill which it is important that students develop if they are to cope with the subtleties of dramatic conversation.

3.7.2 Combining the 'softening up' technique and the checksheet

Turn-taking is an extremely useful area for introductory work on stylistics, precisely because the technical terminology is very like the vocabulary that ordinary English speakers use to talk about the same sort of thing. Moreover, because most people are clued in to understanding everyday conversations (we get a lot of practice, after all), they catch on reasonably fast to the way in which we infer meaning from discoursal patterns. As a consequence, we have experimented in the past with beginning the *Language and Style* course with work on drama. We have now gone back to starting with poetry, because the most fundamental concepts of stylistic analysis, those of foregrounding theory, are most easily exemplified through the examination of poems. Although prose is the easiest genre to read with understanding, it is perhaps the hardest genre to analyse stylistically. So, we usually begin with poetry, move on to prose and then end with drama, so that students end the course (and enter the examination period) on an easier, and higher, note.

Partly because students are by this time used to our methods, and partly because of the 'intuitive' aspect of turn-taking terminology and analysis, we combine the 'softening up' process and the checksheet work, using a version of the checksheet as a way of establishing in a lecture what the students already know intuitively about conversation. We give them the Conversational structure and power checksheet below, and ask them to imagine a conversation among a group of people, where one person is clearly more powerful than the others. The turn-taking parameters are introduced in the form of a series of straightforward questions which the students have to answer, singly or in groups, 'voting' for their choices as they did in the exercises on the Stephen Crane poem reported in 3.5.2.

Clearly, the powerful participant tends almost exclusively to be the one who is ticked in the students' answers to the above questions. Once the stereotype is established, it is then possible to make the model more sophisticated by exploring the effect of particular contextual conditions (for example, the fact that in interviews the least powerful person, the interviewee, tends to speak longest, precisely because this divergence from the general pattern is in the interest of the powerful participants, the interviewers). This work in turn helps us to establish that, in order for an interpretative conclusion to be reached with respect to turn-taking (or other textual

Example 3.5   Conversational structure and power checksheet

CONVERSATIONAL BEHAVIOUR	POWERFUL PARTICIPANT	POWERLESS PARTICIPANT
Who has most turns?		
Who has longest turns?		
Who interrupts whom?		
Who allocates turns to whom?		
Who initiates?		
Who responds?		
Who controls/changes the topic of talk?		
What terms of address are used by one character/ person to another?		
Other significant features e.g. paralinguistic features, actions		

patterns for that matter), not every single factor has to point in the same direction, but that in order for one's interpretative conclusions to be well-founded, it is helpful to have a number of factors which all point in the same direction.

After the general turn-taking rules and the effect of typical patterns has been established in the lecture, we can use the seminar task to ask the students to use the checksheet in text analysis. The last section on the checksheet is there not for use in the lecture, but to help them notice other significant features when they analyse texts. Currently, we base the seminar task on a passage from *Richard III* which includes the short extract discussed in 3.7.1.

Example 3.6

The following passage is taken from Shakespeare's *Richard III*. Buckingham has been promised a title and wealth in return for his loyal support. He now seeks to claim them from Richard. (Passage from *Richard III*, IV iii, 85–123, not quoted here for space reasons.)

A. Read the passage carefully.
B. Using the 'Conversational structure and power checksheet', examine the following aspects:
    (i) turn-length and overall distribution of word-counts for each character;
    (ii) interruptions;
    (iii) topic control;
    (iv) terms of address;
    (v) any other features which strike you.
C. What does your analysis reveal to you about the interaction between the two characters, and how does this contribute to characterisation?

3.8 Concluding remarks

I have not commented in any detail on the seminar exercise in 3.7.2 as, given its straightforward nature and the context of the rest of this paper, its purpose should be easy to infer.

What I hope to have established in this paper is that 'stylistics upside down' is an invaluable tool for students when grappling with the understanding of texts, as well as when they have the task of stating interpretations and supporting them through textual evidence in the traditional manner of stylistic analysis and good practical criticism. But, for my students at least, persuading them to give sufficient attention to the *minutiae* of language in the texts they read, and their effect on textual understanding, is a task which has to be undertaken with considerable care and attention. I cannot assume an automatic interest in textual detail and, in any case, many of my students do not have a metalanguage for text description – a fact which probably explains their tendency to talk about their feelings after reading, to the exclusion of talk about the text itself. It is not surprising, then, that they do not properly understand how readers interact with texts to generate meaning, and have to be persuaded that it is interesting to explore this interaction in detail. It·is also not surprising that they need support in becoming more analytical. We cannot merely *tell* them to be more systematic, we have to help them; even when they accede in general terms to the usefulness of our strictures. The checksheet, I would suggest, is a useful tool in this enterprise.

Notes

1. A version of this paper was first given as a plenary paper to the Conference of the Poetics and Linguistics Association (PALA), 'Interdisciplinary Approaches to the Teaching of Language and Literature at All Levels', held at Abo Akademi University, Turku, Finland, August 1993, and first appeared as *PALA Working Papers* 4. It was subsequently republished in *Textus* **VI**: 3–30. Tilgher, Genova, Italy, 1993.
2. With particular relation to section 3.3, I would like to thank all those who have helped in the *Language and Style* course since its inception in its present form in 1986. The most important, by far, is Mike Breen, who co-designed the course in its new form with me. (It had been running in a different form for many years, and the general course structure and philosophy changes are described in Breen and Short 1988 and Short and Breen 1988.) Mike and I taught the course together in the first three years of its new design. Geoffrey Leech, Greg Myers and Elena Semino have also co-ordinated the course at various times. Others who have been involved in the course (and who, through our weekly team planning meetings, have contributed significantly in course planning and the design of materials as well as in teaching) are Tom Barney, Carol Bellard-Thomson, Hywel Coleman, Jonathan Culpeper, Hazel Medd, Judith Poole and Stef Slembrouck. Carol Bellard-Thomson used her experience of teaching on *Language and Style* as the starting point for Bellard-Thomson 1992.
3. The quotation from Shakespeare's *Richard III* was brought to our attention by Jonathan Culpeper.

4

Designing groupwork activities: a case study

ALAN DURANT

Whilst acknowledging the availability of good commercially produced materials, Alan Durant recommends that teachers themselves are the best source of tasks for use by their own students. Using the example of the opening of Elizabeth Smart's *By Grand Central Station I Sat Down and Wept,* he investigates questions concerning text choice and the design of groupwork, considering also teaching strategies and pedagogic pay-off.

Syllabuses will often dictate text choice, but in all cases the actual text is less important than what is done with it. However, difficulty and relevance of chosen passages are addressed. Problem-solving and 'working by doing' are considered as desirable workshop modes, and varieties of task type and instruction-giving are compared for effectiveness. Guidelines for handling feedback and evaluating learning are then discussed, both in theory and in relation to the author's example. Possible extensions of groupwork are dealt with in the concluding section.

4.1 A groupwork activity

One result of work in 'language through literature' or 'pedagogic stylistics' approaches to literature teaching over the last two decades has been the publication of an impressive range of materials for use in pairwork and groupwork (see, for exemplification of this range, McRae and Boardman 1984, Maley and Moulding 1985, Benton and Benton 1990, Durant and Fabb 1990). Many teachers now use such commercially produced materials. Over the same period, too, a considerable body of more theoretical and descriptive material has also built up, exploring general principles and priorities in such approaches (see, for example, Brumfit and Carter 1986, Short 1989, McRae 1991, Carter and Long 1991, Widdowson 1992); such commentaries and descriptions provide a helpful framework for discussing and evaluating practical initiatives in this area.

It is commonly agreed, however, that commercially produced materials do not travel well: they work best when designed with a particular group (or at least kind) of student in mind, and with a sensitivity to linguistic, cultural and other factors which characterise a given teaching situation. Teachers, many people would therefore advocate, *should as far as possible develop their own materials, simply using published resources as a starting point.* This emphasis on local production of materials is inspired partly by recognition of a risk inherent in the circulation of commercial materials: that some teachers may come to feel dependent on them for good classroom practice, and so may become actually disempowered or even de-skilled by them (see Apple 1982), despite the ethos of individual and group empowerment implicit in such work. Between the now well-established practical level of implementing workshop materials in the classroom and the theoretical level of educational discussion, therefore, a less explored middle ground exists, of general strategies for selecting suitable texts and designing tasks for classroom use. Not very much time is generally given in teacher development or during in-service training to reflecting on how workshop materials can be designed, however, rather than merely used. What sorts of texts should be chosen? How is the basic idea for a groupwork activity decided on? How are tasks best formulated? What sorts of unexpected problem arise? These are difficult questions, both theoretically and simply in terms of useful practical guidelines, as they probe elusive areas of teachers' creativity and improvisation.

In this chapter, I consider a number of issues which arise in the design of groupwork materials, dividing my comments between brief consideration of each of the following topics: choosing the passage; devising the tasks; implementing the activity in a class session; and evaluating the learning which takes place. To focus my discussion, I have organised it around discussion of an activity I recently formulated for use at a specific workshop; and towards the end I report briefly on participants' findings when I have used the activity on two experimental occasions. In presenting a particular activity in this way, I am not claiming that it is of special interest in itself; in many ways it is less sophisticated, and less original, than many activities to be found in published collections, or which teachers around the globe regularly devise. Nevertheless, using one activity as a case study does offer a concrete starting place for analysing issues which arise when the attempt is made to translate spontaneous skills of individual improvisation (which teachers regularly deploy) into more public forms of agreed strategy or pedagogic planning.

As a way into the issues of selection and design which form the main concern of the chapter, therefore, consider the following activity, presented here in roughly the form in which it was given to participants:

Example 4.1 Activity: investigating implied relationships in the opening of a novel

(*Time:* one hour, including final plenary session; pairs or groups)

The passage below (which is the opening of a novel) describes the novel's narrator waiting for two people arriving on a bus. In this activity, we explore *how much we can infer about the relationship between the narrator and those two people*; in doing so, we investigate the various linguistic clues offered about that relationship.

1. Please read the following passage [*allow 5 minutes for this*]:

I am standing on a corner in Monterey, waiting for the bus to come in, and all the muscles of my will are holding my terror to face the moment I most desire. Apprehension and the summer afternoon keep drying my lips, prepared at ten-minute intervals all through the five-hour wait.

But then it is her eyes that come forward out of the vulgar dis-embarkers to reassure me that the bus has not disgorged disaster: her madonna eyes, soft as the newlyborn, trusting as the untempted. And, for a moment, at that gaze, I am happy to forego my future, and postpone indefinitely the miracle hanging fire. Her eyes shower me with their innocence and surprise.

Was it for her, after all, for her whom I had never expected nor imagined, that there had been compounded such ruses of coin-cidence? Behind her he for whom I have waited so long, who has stalked so unbearably through my nightly dreams, fumbles with the tickets and the bags, and shuffles up to the event which too much anticipation has fingered to shreds.

For after all, it is all her. We sit in a cafe drinking coffee. He recounts their adventures and says, 'It was like this, wasn't it, darling?', 'I did well then, didn't I, dear heart?', and she smiles happily across the room with a confidence that appals.

2. Working in pairs or small groups, discuss the questions below, selecting responses from the alternatives provided [*allow 20 minutes for this*]. For each answer you choose, add a note of words or expressions in the passage which suggest that this is the most appropriate response. For each alternative you reject, make a brief note of evidence which in your view disqualifies it. (If you think more than one answer is appropriate, add a note indicating why you think so.)

   (i) Is the 'I' who narrates the passage
     (a) a man?
     (b) a woman?

  (ii) Which of the two people is the narrator waiting for more?
     (a) the man
     (b) the woman
     (c) neither; both are awaited equally

 (iii) Has the narrator met either or both of the two people before?
     (a) neither of them
     (b) one of them (indicate which)
     (c) both of them

 (iv) What relationship exists between the two people being waited for?
     (a) relatives
     (b) casual friends
     (c) professional colleagues
     (d) some other relationship (be as specific as possible)

  (v) What feeling(s) does the narrator have about the arrival of the two people?
     (a) excitement
     (b) anxiety
     (c) boredom
     (d) some other feeling(s) (be as specific as possible)

 (vi) What relationship exists between the narrator and the two people being waited for?
     (a) relatives
     (b) casual friends
     (c) professional colleagues
     (d) some other relationship(s) (be as specific as possible)

3. When you have completed your responses to these questions, and discussed them briefly with other pairs/groups [*allow 10 minutes for this*], consider the information provided in the passage on the second, separate sheet [*this second passage needs to be presented separately, so that participants can't simply consult it as they respond to the initial series of questions*]. This second passage is the first half of the

short biography of the author given at the beginning of the most recent paperback edition of the novel from which the passage is taken.

Elizabeth Smart was born in Ottawa, Canada, in 1913. She was educated at private schools in Canada and for a year at King's College, University of London. One day, while browsing in a London bookshop, she chanced upon a slim volume of poetry by George Barker – and fell passionately in love with him through the printed word. Eventually they communicated directly and, as a result of Barker's impecunious circumstances, Elizabeth Smart flew both him and his wife to the United States. Thus began one of the most extraordinary, intense and ultimately tragic love affairs of our time. They never married but Elizabeth bore George Barker four children and their relationship provided the impassioned inspiration for one of the most moving and immediate chronicles of a love affair ever written – *By Grand Central Station I Sat Down and Wept.*

4. Does this additional material affect your responses to the questions above? If so, how?
5. How much should an interpretation of this passage be based on information learnt separately from the author's biography? How far does such information serve to *justify* one particular interpretation of the passage?
6. Make a note of some headings under which you might present an argument assessing how far, as readers, we project our own concerns and lives onto a passage we are reading. Are readings which are not 'anchored' by reference to biographical or historical information:
   (a) equally valid?
   (b) incorrect?
   (c) more inventive and imaginative?
   (d) Add your own alternative description here if you wish.
7. Finally, during whatever time remains, discuss how important it is for any given reading to fit with details of the language of the passage. Circle a number below to summarise your response to this question:
   (not very important) 1 2 3 4 5 (very important)

Using the activity presented here as an example of a particular type of teaching approach, we can now formulate a number of questions which arise regarding how such activities are chosen and designed.

4.2 Which comes first, passage or tasks?

There is no firm answer to this, and for good reason. In some
syllabuses, the texts are in any case already prescribed. Such
courses are corpus-driven (and subscribe to some more general
logic of text selection which has already been decided). In these
cases, innovation lies in the originality and suitability of the tasks
devised – especially in situations where the particular texts seem to
the teacher inappropriate to the interests or current levels of linguistic competence of the students. In other cases, courses are
skills-driven, and units are organised around such topics as irony,
figurative language, or implied meanings; the course objectives
are conceptual or procedural, so many different texts could
almost equally be used (so long as they provide instances of the
topics in question). In such courses, selection of appropriate texts
or excerpts is a far more continuous activity; and what becomes
crucial is that the *tasks* are clearly focused in the particular concepts, terms or skills which constitute the syllabus (so that sessions
do not become open-ended discussions of response, rather than
work towards given – albeit narrower – learning objectives). Other
courses again (e.g. courses in 'commentary and analysis' or in
'extended reading') aim to offer general experience of reading;
in these cases, it is the range or generic breadth of texts selected
which arguably contributes most to the overall development of
reading experience; and what is important is broad comparison
and contrast. (Often, in fact, it can be effective to encourage
students to choose the passage themselves, in order to provide an
initial personal 'investment' or 'stake' in the materials being read
and discussed.)

What is common to all three types of course is that, for different
reasons, the initial choice of text is less important from the
teacher's point of view than what is done with the text once it has
been selected. The style of any text reflects choices which have
been made in its production; and choice involves an underlying
level of system which becomes amenable to analysis as soon as
alternative choices (and so the consequences of choice) are
assessed. By working outwards from a given passage, therefore,
into the ways it might have been different, it is possible to use
virtually any text as a resource in discourse analysis. The danger in
'language through literature' sessions is less that there will be
nothing interesting to investigate than that the session merely

opens the door on personal responses, which are difficult to channel back towards specified learning objectives without impeding
the participants' enthusiasm and talents.

4.3 What sort of passage or text?

Even if choice of passage is not crucial, passages *do* have to be
chosen; so it may be helpful to make explicit some of the general
principles on which texts are often deemed 'suitable'. The question of suitability is frequently formulated by teachers in terms of
two distinct parameters – difficulty and relevance – each of which
deserves consideration.

4.3.1 Difficulty

As in other areas of ELT, especially the grading of class readers,
difficulty in the language of literary passages is in principle
measurable (for an introduction to readability research, see
Alderson and Urquhart 1984). As regards literary passages in
particular, alongside questions of word identification and structural analysis (especially as regards idiomatic expressions), there
are likely to be special considerations of stylistic difficulty (e.g. use
of literary registers or archaism). And such specifically linguistic
difficulties need then to be linked to referential issues (e.g. problems posed by culturally remote allusions), as well as issues of
more specialised literary competence (e.g. awareness of specific
interpretative techniques appropriate in allegorical or symbolic
interpretation). Such issues posed in literature classes by specialised ways of reading are analysed in detail in Montgomery *et al.*
1992.

  With intermediate and more advanced learners, immediate difficulty with the language of the passage is less likely to be intractable
than other kinds of obstacle. It is possible to support work on local
language difficulties with established techniques, such as use of
contextual clues to infer meanings of words. Difficulties as regards
stylistic variety and implicature are more persistent, however, and
are exacerbated by the fact that second-language users rarely have
easy access to the social matrix within which to locate register variation, nuance, or bodies of cultural assumptions mobilised in
inferential interpretation. Use of specifically literary excerpts is

accordingly likely to be more effective where stylistic and inferential concerns form the main pedagogic interest, rather than specialised grammatical or lexical issues.

But in assessing the 'difficulty' of a passage it is necessary to consider not only the language but also what *tasks* are to be undertaken. It is possible, after all, to carry out very simple formal tasks (e.g. classifying texts as poetry, drama or prose) on passages which are scarcely understood at all. The fact that 'difficulty' is a function of the tasks we create as well as of the language of the text itself is only obscured by our tendency to think in terms of an unspecified task of 'reading and understanding', which disguises a complex of unanalysed ideas of what 'reading and understanding' means.

Because the nature of tasks affects considerations of difficulty so fundamentally, we need to distinguish our concept of 'difficulty' (a negative attribute, inhibiting productive work) from some notion of intellectual 'challenge' (the puzzle or unknown element which stimulates enquiry in problem-solving work). One person's challenge, of course, is another person's difficulty; so part of the skill in devising workshops involves ensuring that suitable support in tackling challenges is provided. In this context, it is usually more important that participants in a given session gain confidence from being able to achieve something they can value as a learning experience than that they have been presented with texts of a higher level of difficulty which only confirm their diffidence at being unable to carry out the prescribed tasks effectively.

4.3.2   *Relevance*

If literary texts are to serve the function in the language classroom of motivating and stimulating interest, then their relevance to student concerns is important. With this in mind, materials writers sometimes choose passages for the assumed relevance of their themes or topics. Passages grouped around topics such as war, love, nuclear power, green politics are often chosen, and are illustrated by pop songs, fashion magazine articles and adverts, in addition to well-known poems or prose passages. Such selections are justified by the idea that students will already feel interest in and have opinions in these areas, and will therefore be more motivated to work on and discuss them than if presented with more remote historical or literary materials.

Some topics will clearly engage participants' interests more than others. There is a risk, however, that the tendency to second-guess student tastes can become patronising, to the extent that it draws on images of young people's interests, held by teachers whose age and cultural experience and aspirations are often very different. And such selection of materials raises two additional problems. Firstly, some of the texts drawn from popular culture may be part of a deliberate anti-culture, which can be devalued by being appropriated into the classroom. The second problem is that one commonly-asserted aim of literary education is to broaden students' reading habits and horizons; selection of already-popular materials only contributes to this aim if it forms part of a strategy of gradually introducing new and possibly unexpected materials, providing fresh challenges and opportunities. When organised thematically, 'relevance' based work can become reductive, and often deeply ahistorical: even when selections are not exclusively of twentieth-century extracts, different cultures and previous ages tend to be read through present concerns; and, in travesty of many of the humanistic claims made by literature teachers, the densities of cultural and historical difference are turned into merely a sounding board for modern linguistic usage.

4.4 Selecting a particular passage

Questions of difficulty and relevance underlie much of our discussion of the suitability of particular passages. Within such general parameters, however, it is also important to note more specific pedagogic constraints. In the case of the passage chosen for the activity above, for instance, two specific features merit consideration.

The first is that the extract is the *beginning* of a work. One effect of this is that readers in the classroom are faced with a situation analogous to that of 'real' readers, inasmuch as there is no presupposed information from earlier in the work that would be available to general readers but which is denied to students carrying out the activity. In a useful chapter on selection of extracts, Guy Cook has shown how far passages chosen from later in works rely on preceding information; he concludes:

> As by far the greatest part of cohesive ties are *anaphoric* (referring to the preceding text) . . . the least destructive form of extraction is

that which takes either the beginning of a text or at least a part of a
text which represents a new introductory departure in the narrative.

(Cook 1986, p. 152)

Cook's analysis provides backing for what is in any case common
practice in many teachers' selection of extracts, including in
earlier 'practical criticism' approaches; and while it is easy to think
of famous beginnings of novels which have arguably been overused, using the opening passages of works does have distinct
pedagogic advantages. One is that it is possible to use the prescribed task to initiate a sequence of other workshops or lessons
which follow in a sequence loosely replicating the linear process
of first-time reading (or traditional classroom 'working through'
of a book). In the activity reproduced here, for instance, complex
and changing perceptions of the relationship between the three
characters are central; much of any later reading of the novel will
almost inevitably be concerned with the representation of contradictory feelings already intimated in this opening passage. Using
the opening passage as the basis for a hypothesis-forming activity
in this way draws on a general feature of texts: that opening passages encourage especially strongly inferential activity concerning
the possible significance of local textual details. In more general
terms, too, using opening passages of works can motivate students
to read further after the session, by offering a guided 'beginning'.
(Again, this draws on a general function of opening passages: that
of activating a narrative dialectic of enigma and closure which
Roland Barthes, in *S/Z*, describes as a work's 'hermeneutic code').

A second issue raised by the passage selected for this activity
concerns the *suitability of its content*. Are there, in fact, topics which
should not be talked about at all? In this extract, for example, the
beginning of an adulterous relationship is presented without
apparent moral judgement. The first-person narration represents
the point-of-view of one of the people involved in the relationship;
and the focus is on feelings rather than moral quandaries or
dilemmas (while the feelings may vividly convey moral questions,
those questions themselves are not explicitly formulated). As a
result of the passage's point-of-view and other literary techniques,
readers' sympathies are likely to become aligned with the narrator's view; and some teachers may feel that moral issues are in this
way being overlooked or misrepresented.

One practical way of dealing with such issues of moral sensitivity
is to ensure that a variety of texts is used: foregrounding textual

sensitivity by frequently using potentially problematic material creates a delicate classroom climate. On-the-spot judgements of suitability are essential, as there can be significant variation even between individual cohorts of the same category of class (which is partly why commercially distributed materials can bring unwanted problems). Alongside evident ethical issues, a more directly pedagogic question also arises: that distortions in the teacher/class dynamic can make subsequent activity-based work more difficult or even precipitate student hostility (which cannot always be discounted as merely formative resistance). When students become absorbed with the *choice* of text, they don't necessarily focus on the particular tasks or learning objectives associated with it; unless the shock value of a passage forms part of your instructional strategy, it may simply distract attention for your actual pedagogic goals and cloud responses in the activities you create.

4.5   Deciding on tasks

To design a groupwork activity, at its simplest you simply gather together materials you think may be appropriate; then, instead of giving instruction (e.g. by illustrating your points with reference to material you have selected), you 'translate' any ideas, skills or information you want to investigate into a participatory activity. Through carrying out the activity, students discover things for themselves, and are likely to become more motivated to learn than if you require them to respond in the more passive mode of listening, copying or taking notes. Working on problems and tasks leads to greater independence among students in their work, and can act as appropriate pre-activity to instruction or input, preparing students to engage with – but at the same time adopt a more critical and analytical attitude towards – material you yourself present. Work which students themselves do in an activity also creates an agenda for later class discussion aimed at investigating difficulties and issues which have actually arisen in their own activity.

These elements form part of most standard explanations of how workshops work ('learning by doing'). But are things in practice really this simple? Is it even clear what the goals of an activity are? (It is possible, after all, to have many enjoyable and apparently productive workshops in which it nevertheless remains slightly unclear how much or what kind of learning is actually going on.)

In general, what makes a workshop activity function as something more than directed discussion is its inclusion of a foreseen,
determinate end-point. This can either be completion of a set of
responses to given questions or, generally better, a decision made
regarding a central question around which cluster a set of subordinate, prior or related questions (as in the activity presented
earlier in this chapter). Problem-solving work is built on the idea
of an information gap, where something is left out in presenting
the passage (e.g. individual words are removed from a passage in
cloze procedure; the title is omitted and has to be guessed; part of
the passage is not by the original author but which part is not
indicated, etc.). Many different sorts of activity can be devised
using information-gap procedures, and vary from ones which are
highly directive and goal-oriented through to ones which are
extremely open-ended and act more like a checklist of seminar
elicitation questions. (For a list of different *types* of activity, formulated by making generalisations from a corpus of given instances,
see Durant and Fabb 1987.)

4.6   Formulating instructions

A list of activity types can be useful. But once you have decided on
the general principle of the activity, how do you actually formulate
the tasks?

A useful initial distinction can be drawn here between interrogatives and imperatives. While interrogatives can be short and
direct, they tend to make the activity resemble a traditional series
of comprehension questions, and imply a power relation at odds
with the collaborative ethos of groupwork learning. (There may
be a problem with the instructions in the activity above in this
respect.) Interrogatives also raise issues familiar from studies of
interview techniques (e.g. in human resources management):
questions of processing difficulties presented by double- and
multi-headed questions, or of the different value, as elicitation, of
open and closed questions. But there is also a more practical problem with interrogatives: that they do not specify the form in which
answers should be given; and this can result in participants merely
thinking of answers, but not keeping written notes on which to
base responses or feedback during the plenary stage. Usually,
therefore, it is better (where possible) to formulate instructions as

tasks – in imperative form – rather than as questions: the aim of a workshop is to enable students to learn through doing, not to present them with simulated exam questions or to conduct an oral elicitation by proxy. (In oral elicitation, you would in any case almost certainly mediate the abruptness of interrogatives with preambles, follow-up questions and supplementary remarks or instructions.)

Irrespective of whether tasks are formulated as questions or as instructions, however, procedures need to be made fully explicit. (Indicating precise procedure is perhaps especially crucial in literature classes, where analytic procedures are generally very informal and ill-defined.) In designing activities, it is easy to underestimate scope for misunderstanding, even where there is goodwill from participants. And where groupwork is being introduced for the first time, activities can be sunk altogether by difficulties with the wording of instructions: with classes used to sitting and listening, participants need to be invited to move chairs or form groups, informed how long has been assigned for each stage of the process, and instructed whether they should take notes of their discussion, etc.

Making aspects of the workshop process explicit creates difficulties of its own, nevertheless. The resulting length and complexity of instructions itself becomes a problem. A page of dense and detailed instructions can be daunting, and displaces attention from reading the passage itself – shifting what should be encouraging workshop guidelines towards the register of regulatory examination rubrics. In addition, the more time participants spend in a first reading, the longer the silence before they start talking or working together. And particular care needs to be taken regarding the relationship between the complexity of instructions and the complexity of the tasks themselves. Sometimes an over-sophisticated metalanguage is used in instructions, given the tasks being prescribed (especially where teachers are determined to keep strictly to English-medium teaching). A likely result is that anyone who could read the instructions would learn very little from carrying out the tasks, and would probably find the workshop process trivial.

By comparison with expressing personal response, formalistic and classificatory tasks are intellectually demanding. While students do undoubtedly face difficulties in expressing personal views in class – especially in a second or foreign language – they are likely to be relatively comfortable with the *concept* of personal interpretation and reaction. In workshop classes, difficulty typically lies in channelling such responses towards a given analytic or problem-solving goal, working through issues in a systematic way rather than simply juxtaposing personal reactions in an unresolved montage of individual points of view. In designing an activity, accordingly, it can be useful to build into the sequence of questions a gradience of difficulty, from concrete and specific to more open-ended tasks (as has been attempted in the activity above). As well as enabling work on later questions to build on operations carried out for earlier ones, such a design allows groups or individuals to find their own level or pace, and so facilitates mixed-ability or mixed-experience teaching.

4.7 Trying out the activity

Before even starting, it is important to ensure that there are adequate resources available for what you have in mind. How much photocopying do you anticipate, and is there time (and money) to do it before the session? If a photocopier is not readily available, it may be necessary to consider other ways of distributing the passage – perhaps by a separate, prior session of dictation, or by writing the passage on the blackboard for copying. The size of groups you propose may need to depend on room-space and furniture (e.g. where chairs are screwed to the floor, groups of two or three people are likely to work better than larger groups, simply because eye contact and conversation are easier in smaller groups in such circumstances). By visualising the activity as precisely as possible as a process or event in advance, you may well be able to pre-empt procedural difficulties which could otherwise undermine the seriousness or interrupt the flow of the session.

On the first occasion an activity is tried out, problems are especially likely to arise with timing, since it is difficult to anticipate how long any particular analytic procedure will take. (It is not even easy to guess how long participants will take to arrange themselves in groups – since this varies depending on prior experience – or how long they will take to read through the passage and instructions.) Problems of an activity going too quickly are potentially as serious as it taking too long: you can adapt a session if participants finish too soon by having contingency plans for further work; but if you are forced to postpone tasks integral to the workshop to a subsequent session, or ask participants to finish on their own later, there is a risk of failing to deliver the promised sense of a determinate end-point within the session itself. Be realistic about time: try only to create tasks that your participants – working in their actual given conditions – will be able to carry out in the time allocated. Think, too, of your own time: what will you do while students are carrying out the tasks? Will you leave them to work with each other, free from your own – potentially inhibiting – presence? Or will you attach yourself to each group in turn, creating opportunities for small-group interaction that students are often deprived of, in classes with adverse staff–student ratios?

Before or during the session, it is also necessary to anticipate how you will handle participants' findings in the feedback stage. Procedurally, this may mean deciding whether you will note key words on the board; or ask group secretaries to move to another group and relay findings; or invite participants themselves to write on the board (encouraging a sense of shared ownership of the event and room-space). At another level – where practical procedures and learning theory interact especially closely – handling participants' contributions means dealing with the issue of whether there are 'correct' and 'incorrect' responses (as well as whether there are 'relevant' and 'irrelevant' ones). Undoubtedly there *can* be local misunderstandings (e.g. about individual words, grammatical structures, or allusions); at the same time, you are likely to want to signal that you recognise many issues as being far more open to argument (e.g. does knowledge of a writer's biography help in interpreting a text?). As coordinator of the session, it falls largely on you to discourage participants from becoming fixated on the notion of correct answers, even as you seek to commit them, for the sake of the workshop, to at least interim decisions on the questions you ask. As in many other areas of teaching, exploring the *grounds* of different answers – in concrete observation, structures of argumentation, and in more general theoretical constructs – offers a way into comparison of different views. Celebrating all responses equally as helpful contributions, on the other hand – while it does build confidence and confers value on participants' experience – can, if carried too far, detract from the point of anyone taking their contribution seriously at all.

Finally, if you intend to use an activity again, it can be useful to take notes of what participants have said, as well as of directions –

including apparent tangents – in which debate has developed. Such notes provide ideas for follow-up tasks, as well as ways of re-sequencing the existing tasks (since sometimes the routes through an activity which you yourself think likely are not the most obvious or interesting ones). In cases where the assumed lines of continuity – which depend on the accessibility of bridging inferences that need to be made between tasks – are not particularly evident to participants, you may wish to modify instructions in order to provide the activity with more obvious coherence. It may also be worth noting down headings which seem appropriate to the discussion which might take place during the feedback session, or particularly apposite examples from the text or analogies with other texts; in this way, later uses of the activity can benefit from contributions (even, where appropriate, specific editorial suggestions) made by participants. One necessary restraint needs to be imposed on such preparation, nevertheless: that the activity shouldn't be allowed to become formulaic or mechanical as a result of what you take to be a predictability in the pattern of people's responses. As in other kinds of pedagogy, individual judgements need to be made regarding a conflict between the value of the teacher's detailed preparation and prior experience on the one hand, and the freshness of novelty and genuine interest on the other – even if this means rough edges in delivery.

4.8   Evaluating the learning which takes place

It is generally recognised that workshop activities can generate interest, lively conversation and the appearance of work. But how do we assess whether anything is actually learnt? Little detailed or convincing research has been done on individual sessions, partly because empirical study and evaluation in this area are so complicated to carry out. The tendency, instead, is to assume informally that as teachers we somehow know from experience whether a session has been effective or not, without establishing criteria or indicators against which learners' achievements might be monitored.

It does seem possible in general terms, however, to say that where an activity has functioned effectively in the minimal sense of generating discussion and responses to the questions asked, the following learning opportunities have been presented:

(i) a new passage has been introduced and read;

(ii) reading of the passage involves observation and 'close read-ing' skills to the extent that interpretative judgements offered in the feedback session are based on linguistic features;

(iii) almost irrespective of the answers and comments offered, efforts made in responding to the tasks involve cognitive effort and organisation, especially analytic reasoning;

(iv) some degree of discussion has taken place with a partner or partners, either in the target language or in the first lang-uage, but certainly *about* features of the target language (and some element of learning from peers may well have taken place during this dialogue);

(v) a pre-structured sequence of analytic procedures has been worked through, which presents one possible model or tem-plate of a process of investigation;

(vi) participants have been grouped together in ways which require them to use social skills to negotiate a task-related conversational register for at least the duration of the activity;

(vii) in preparing for and presenting class feedback, speak-ing/writing opportunities have been presented (including debate and practice with technical terminologies).

We should note, immediately, of course, that a 'learning oppor-tunity' is not necessarily a learning outcome. Some members of the group may have achieved a considerable amount under most or all of the above headings; but it is equally probable that other participants will have been passive and others again will have been actively resistant or cynical (taking the opportunity to talk about topics entirely unrelated to the session, or to satirise the process in which the class is engaged). Group dynamics are in these respects unpredictable and need sensitive handling. Despite criticisms that workshop-based pedagogies devalue teachers' creativity, much of whatever learning takes place will depend on the skill of the teacher in guiding discussion during the feedback session, especi-ally to coordinate comments and findings with other areas of the students' studies (and, in this sense, workshop tasks enrich rather than replace the interactional dynamics of teaching).

In order to avoid becoming naively idealistic about groupwork teaching, however, the contribution made by a particular work-shop session to a curriculum can be evaluated more concretely by making a direct comparison between the workshop and how the same resource of teacher, time, audio-visual aids and/or xerox could have been used differently. Where opportunities for learning are compared in this way with those provided by a lecture or open-agenda seminar, then, despite all the evident difficulties, results can begin to seem rather more favourable.

4.9   Discussion of sample activity

The activity presented in this paper, as I indicated above, has been tried out so far on two occasions. One involved a group of non-native-speaker teachers from a range of linguistic and cultural backgrounds; these participants had advanced language skills in English, were used to groupwork, and were interested in analysis of the activity as part of a teaching strategy, as well as direct participation in it. The second occasion involved a group of twelve first-year undergraduate students, all native speakers, on a first-year undergraduate course at a British university.

On both occasions, during feedback after the first stage of the activity, participants outlined hypothetical scenarios as a basis for their interpretation. In each case, the majority view expressed was that the passage describes an 'eternal triangle' or 'love triangle'. In response to Question 2 (i), most participants thought the narrator must be a woman (claiming support for this view from the third line, where the narrator's lips are repeatedly 'prepared' in anticipation of the two people arriving). A dissenting minority on each occasion thought the narrator a heterosexual man in love with the woman who arrives on the bus (basing this view on the observation that the woman remains quiet while the two men talk, linking this information to the more general social script of 'two men struggling over a woman who is herself excluded from the contest'). Another minority thought the narrator possibly a gay man involved with the man arriving (pointing out that it is not only women's lips which can be 'prepared' with lipstick). Interestingly, as regards later stages of the activity, no specific linguistic evidence was adduced for either of the minority views; indeed, in discussion, proponents of these two views offered no explanation of other, potentially significant details of the passage which seem to conflict with the view they were putting forward. Rather, discussion at this stage focused on the idea of *possibility in principle*: on an 'openness' in texts which could or should make them amenable to alternative, 'non-conformist' or 'dissenting' readings. One further variant on the 'eternal triangle' theme was also voiced: that the passage involves an Oedipal drama, in which the narrator is meeting his or her parents off the bus (though this view was challenged by other participants who thought it unlikely that the narrator would not have seen or even imagined his or her own mother ever before).

As regards Questions 2 (ii) and 2 (iii) – who the narrator is waiting for more, and whether the narrator has met either or both people previously – on each occasion there was consensus around the view that it is the man who is awaited more keenly. While it remains unclear from the passage whether the narrator has met the man before, there was agreement that it is the first time the narrator has met the woman. The paired phrases 'her whom I had never expected nor imagined . . .' and 'he for whom I have waited so long . . .' were taken to provide compelling evidence for these inferences. Attention was also drawn to the role of the connective 'but' in 'But then it is her eyes' at the beginning of the second paragraph. The adversative effect of this word, coupled with the way the pronoun 'her' is brought into focus by the cleft construction, was taken to signal contrast with what the narrator was expecting (i.e. that it would be the man who the narrator would see first after waiting so long). The sudden and unsettling effect caused by the narrator's seeing the woman's expression ('at that gaze, I am happy to forego my future') was also thought to suggest that the narrator hadn't seen the woman before.

Relatively clear evidence, of the sort used in conventional comprehension exercises, was accumulated in response to Question 2 (iv) concerning the relationship between the two people arriving. Participants concluded that the two are a couple, probably a long-standing married couple. The man, participants pointed out, is reported by the narrator as addressing the woman as 'darling' and 'dear heart'; and the fact that one person carries 'the tickets' and 'the bags' while travelling (the use of 'the' was considered significant), and narrates 'their adventures' on behalf of both of them, was taken to indicate a couple rather than two unconnected individuals. Evidence from the passage's cohesive devices was brought in again, too: the 'after all' in 'for after all, it is all her' was taken to imply that the narrator makes clear his or her *presumption* of a close connection, or bond of primary importance, between the man and the woman (as does the final phrase in this context, 'a confidence that appals').

Participants' responses to Question 2 (v), concerning the narrator's feelings about the arrival of the two people, explored several different kinds of evidence. Most obviously, participants took account of clear statements such as 'apprehension' being one cause of the repeatedly dry lips, and that the event is one which 'too much anticipation has fingered to shreds'. Alongside such statements, however, more contradictory feelings were identified in paradoxical, figurative wordings such as 'all the muscles of my will are holding my terror to face the moment I most desire'; desire for the man, detectable in the linking of phrases such as 'he for whom I have waited so long' with 'who has stalked unbearably through my nightly dreams', is coupled with a sense of guilt conveyed by the unusual semantic set employed in the description of the woman's eyes and expression – not colour, shape or size, but innocence, surprise and trust ('madonna eyes, soft as the newly-born, trusting as the untempted').

In the final question of the first section (Question 2 (vi)), participants are in effect invited to combine and sum up their responses to previous questions; in doing so, most concluded that the narrator is a woman with strong but as yet unconsummated desires for the man (cf. the 'miracle hanging fire'), who is suddenly troubled by conflicting feelings of guilt on seeing the woman with him.

When provided with the second sheet, of biographical information about the author, on both occasions the dominant interpretation of the passage constructed by the group was considered to have been reinforced by parallel reading of the two paired passages. Indeed, several participants who had previously argued for alternative views decided that their readings were now 'wrong'. Discussion during this section of the activity on each occasion centred on the way the biographical blurb sets out to make its connections as direct as possible with the opening passage (e.g. 'Monterey' in the passage, 'flew both him and his wife to the United States' in the blurb; the first-person narrator somehow desiring the man in the passage without having definitely met him, in the blurb knowing him from his poetry, etc.).

When participants came to consider Question 5 (roughly: 'how much does contextual information of the sort provided in the second half of the activity justify a particular interpretation?'), discussion became predictably more open-ended and wide-ranging. Along with statements of more formulaic positions drawn from critical theory, discussion focused on the fact that the passage is only a short extract from a much larger work; and argument turned on whether the contextually 'embedded' aspects of the book (such as its autobiographical relation to the life of the author) would take on a different significance if viewed in the light of the whole novel. Questions were also raised about how far a book can transform autobiographical concerns in the process of being written, and whether this should be perceived as fraudulent misrepresentation of a 'real' life or as valuable creativity.

Question 6 also elicited a wide range of different viewpoints. Views ranged from the opinion that the life and intentions of an author guarantee the meaning of the work to the view that we can make whatever we wish of a text, irrespective of local details (since it is creative reading which is important rather than more passive consumption of patterns written into the work). Each of these views – which of course reflect a spectrum of current critical positions – was presented in a precisely illustrated form, so creating opportunities for further work that might bring together various literary and cultural concerns of the curriculum.

Finally, Question 7 (which was added orally on the first occasion, then fully incorporated for the second) encourages participants to commit themselves to a judgement about the extent of the contribution made by stylistic features to the interaction of text with reader which makes up the reading process. Although the full 1–5 spectrum of numeric values was used in participants' responses, a clear majority opted for the higher end of the range (so suggesting that linguistic features *are* important). Debate in this brief closing section of the activity touched on quite a number of topics: the valuably catalytic, emotive force of reading (through which deep personal experiences and recollections are released, whatever the text itself actually says); ways of taking stylistic features coherently into account in a reading when there may be contradictions, ambiguities and indeterminacies in the text itself, or alternatively exploiting contradictions to open up the text for other, alternative readings; and I.A. Richards's disparaging notion of 'mnemonic irrelevances' or failure on the part of some readers to follow texts closely because contingent memories and associations get in the way.

4.10   Conclusions

In view of the large number of different concerns which surround
the planning and implementation of any one workshop activity, a
wide range of directions for further comment now open up.
(This, in itself, contributes to the problem of analytic work on
pedagogy: that there are so *many* variables in play.) In this paper, I
confine myself to two types of preliminary conclusion.

Firstly, it is possible, on the basis of comments I have made
above, to visualise a series of follow-up activities to the workshop
outlined here. Each could be designed along the lines I have
indicated, and the series as a whole might be interspersed with
presentations by the teacher and other kinds of study. One possibility based on the excerpt I have used above, for instance, would
be to delete all gender-specific words and ask participants to fill
them in, following this up with tasks based on point-of-view (again:
who is the narrator?) and the role of gender assumptions and
stereotypes in our reading. With later extracts it would be possible
to employ other sorts of cloze procedure, investigating individual
metaphors and patterns of metaphor which pervade the work.
And activities which explore allusions and stylistic imitation – possibly using additional hand-outs to present source texts and
literary. analogues – might help locate the language of the novel
(including, of course, its title) in relation to literary traditions;
such work would open up questions both of the meaning of the
term 'poetic fiction' in general, and the suitability of Biblical
imagery to adultery narratives in particular. As regards writing
work, it is easy to see how tasks might be created inviting participants to compose dialogue for the characters as they get off the
bus, or to extend the conversation in the cafe. At later points in
the novel, writing outwards from the text itself might involve simu-
lating the style of newspaper and police reports, or reworking a
passage in a contrasting idiom (e.g. in modern romance genre, in
the style of publications by Mills and Boon). Equally, it would be
possible – again by examining the fabric of metaphorical language
– to guide students' studies towards philosophical or moral issues
raised by the work, or (with training teachers) into arguments for
and against use of 'sensitive' texts in the classroom, or issues of the
formation of a twentieth-century literary canon. Each of these
kinds of study combines work on the novel itself with investiga-
tions involving other kinds of English discourse; and the value of

such work would lie in the extent to which it is successful in using that broadened range of texts and tasks to reflect back on the specific kinds of choice made in writing the prescribed passage or work.

Secondly, it seems reasonable to ask whether the comments I have made above about workshop design allow any general evaluation of the activity presented at the beginning of the chapter. I think they do, at least in a few simple respects. It is possible to say, for instance that, in view of the points I have made above, the activity remains problematic in terms of the number, length and style of instructions. This may be merely a question of local re-writing; or it may be that what is signalled by the complexity of instructions is a more serious design failure: that of trying to incorporate too many different topics or tasks within a single lesson plan. It also seems reasonable to query the level of verbal skills presumed of participants; while complex issues are often expressed most succinctly by reference to concrete examples, it is questionable how many students can conduct the sorts of discussion reported above – and in any case no indication of the precise sort of student ultimately aimed at is provided.

In view of plausible criticisms along these lines, the general issue of focus needs to be re-emphasised. While the activity described above stimulated discussion and a certain amount of problem-solving work on the pilot occasions (in arguably more interesting ways than would have been possible within a conventional comprehension-class format), the risk remains of work diffracting in too many different directions. Open-endedness in an activity may offer a valuable stimulus at the beginning of a course on a particular work, where each of the many different topics raised can be revisited in later sessions; or alternatively, it might be appropriate in a 'commentary and analysis' type class. Much of the interest of groupwork materials in 'language through literature' approaches lies, however, at least in my opinion, in the assumption that they can facilitate more specialised kinds of learning than merely general exposure to English discourse or enhancement of practical reading skills by group discussion linked to conversation and writing practice. If this is so, then it might be argued that an activity like the one presented in this chapter fails to focus sufficiently clearly on any one principal theme. Students are encouraged to investigate semantic sets, cleft constructions, discourse connectives, metaphors and other linguistic features, and to explore how these contribute to their interpretations of the passage; but arguably they do this in ways which do not allow conceptual development or targeted learner feedback as clearly as the more directed problem-solving work routinely presented in workbooks in linguistics or second-language acquisition. And whatever an activity's role in a course, it seems important to establish clearly a link between the focus of the individual activity and the focus of the overall course in which it takes place (something which is again not signalled in the version presented above).

Given such difficulties with focus in activity design, one appropriate task for research – as much in relation to workshops and open-learning materials as in the development of experimental multimedia learning packages – would be to investigate and define specific educational purposes and values served by directive workshop learning, as compared with more open-agenda, discussion-based activities. In order that such research should not merely fall back into assumed educational values or impressionistic judgement, one useful interim project would be empirical analysis of data from a series of sessions involving the same single activity. Such analysis could draw on recordings of dialogue during the sessions, to investigate cohesion and deveopment within group responses, as well as examining forms of learner–teacher interaction. Work along these lines (which has been tackled in a slightly different context in Benton *et al.* 1988) might finally enable us to link together, more concretely than current work permits, the existing richness of experience and case law in the field of 'language through literature' teaching with an equivalent richness of research in the fields of reading theory, pragmatics and conversation analysis.

5

Reconstructing and deconstructing: drama texts in the classroom

MICHAEL McCARTHY

Michael McCarthy begins by stating that his principal aim is to discuss 'drama-as-literature' rather than as a performance-based activity, although creative tasks will emerge in the course of the paper. Teachers as facilitators must approach dramatic texts as spoken language and not merely a vehicle for discourse analysis.

In his chosen text, Alan Ayckbourn's *Woman in Mind*, the main character is caught between reality and fantasy, and normal rules of discourse are repeatedly broken. Rewriting tasks are suggested, to bring out the incoherence, allowing students to experience this directly, before an analytical reading is undertaken. Open-endedness of interpretation is likely to result from reconstruction having preceded deconstruction, which the author argues is in keeping with modern drama discourse.

5.1 Introduction

Few language teachers need reminding that the typical experience learners have of the drama of the target language is as drama *texts*, rather than as plays in performance. This has been one of Short's main justifications for analysing drama text rather than plays in performance (Short 1981; 1989). Indeed, the EFL/ESL world in many cases has got itself into a situation where students either *do* drama as meaningful language-learning activity (that is to say, they create and improvise) or else they study the texts of plays as 'literature'. The robust tradition in language teaching of two or three decades ago, of getting students to perform famous plays as end-of-term productions, seems to have taken third place to the more 'meaningful' activities of self-expression, analysis and interpretation. This is not to criticise the excellent products of the drama-as-self-expression trend (e.g. Maley 1982; Hayes 1984; Dougill 1987), nor to suggest that the drama-as-literature approach (referred to in greater detail below) necessarily goes too far the other way. Both serve the ends of language learning and greater understanding and appreciation of the significance of drama in their different ways. Although the present paper will lean towards the drama-as-literature end of the scale, it will offer activities that attempt to engage the analytical abilities and the creativity of students and give them a chance to do a bit of performance, based on both their own and famous dramatists' scripts. As such I am attempting to get the best of all three worlds, and, as with all composite proposals, it may lose something from its three springs as they merge into the real-time flow of activity in the classroom.

5.2   Drama as spoken text

Getting students to engage with drama as a 'text of speech' is not an easy matter. It is all very well for discourse analysts to tease out the underlying mechanisms that make dramatic texts more, or less, comparable to modes of everyday speech, but the anodyne script that faces learners on the page can be very off-putting. We need ways of appreciating for ourselves (and here I mean teachers in their most admirable role as facilitators rather than as providers of knowledge) what is special about a dramatic text so that we can design activities that facilitate our learners' appreciation of the same text. Their goal may well be 'understanding' the text for some crudely instrumental motive such as passing an examination, but that does not mean that the path towards understanding need be sterile and abstract. Analysis can afford that luxury; teachers, in a way, have to consider both paths: some rather mechanical thinking and analysis of the target text, but also a good deal of creative thinking as to how to bring to life in the classroom the dead fish that the analytical net has trawled up.

This primary, analytical stage the teacher is faced with is not merely to get from the text the most high-sounding phrases or to sketch character and plot from the web of intrigue and event that resides in the text's content, but, as I have indicated, to get at the text as spoken language. If we cannot achieve this, we might as well read the drama text as a continuous piece of prose, stopping only to wonder at the clever turns of diction and rhetoric that the author indulges in. Some will have experienced this as the abiding memory of studying Shakespeare's or some other great playwright's texts in their own schooldays: unless one was lucky enough to see a performance, the play remained a written text punctuated only by change of speaker.

A growing literature now exists of studies of drama texts from a discourse-analytical point of view. Applied linguists have variously used models and principles of pragmatics, such as speech acts and conversational implicature (Short 1981; 1989; Gautam and Sharma 1986), models of interaction that focus on aspects such as face and politeness (Lakoff and Tannen 1984; Simpson 1989), the techniques of conversation analysis in relation to notions such as topic and turn-taking in speech (Gautam 1987; Herman 1991), and a well-established succession of books and papers using and adapting the exchange-structure models associated with British discourse analysis (Burton 1980; Korpimies 1983; Nash 1989). What they almost all have in common is the use of methods of analysis initially directed at non-dramatic spoken interaction to underscore the *defamiliarisation* of everyday language which the dramatist engages in. I say almost all, since Lakoff and Tannen's aim is more to show how a dramatic text reveals something about a fundamental communicative competence that speakers possess, in terms of their expectations of how conversation should normally progress, rather than to analyse drama *per se*. But what they all have in common is a sense that conversation is coherent and organised, does, in its day-to-day manifestations, orient towards certain norms and does reveal, in its manipulations of and deviations from such norms, the tensions, conflicts and power struggles that human beings are involved in when interacting.

Typical of these approaches are Herman's application of the principles of turn-taking (1991), as expounded in Sacks *et al.* (1974), to consider not only who speaks to whom in a dramatic text, but also 'who is *not* spoken to' (my italics); or Korpimies's inclusion (1983) in her model of analysis of the notion of *challenging exchanges*, originally categorised by Labov and Fanshel (1977, pp. 93–8) in their examination of therapeutic interviews, which Korpimies uses to illustrate conflict in a text by Harold Pinter.

The techniques of pragmatics and discourse analysis allow the analyst to specify the mechanisms that generate tension, conflict, irony, etc., but how can we help the student-reader to experience those qualities within the text and during their reading or activity with it? It is here that the notion of analysis leading to something more than observation is important. I shall argue and try to show that, from sound analysis, *performance* activities can be designed which mirror and highlight the key linguistic mechanisms of the drama text. I call these *reconstruction* activities: in some way or other they involve reconstructing a text. *Deconstruction*, understanding what the original drama text does with language, should ideally follow not precede reconstruction, hence the chosen sequence of the title of the present paper. In this way, the learner first experiences, and then analyses and understands (if that be the goal of the study of drama texts in class), the use and manipulation of language by the author.

5.3   Deconstructing Ayckbourn's *Woman in Mind*

I have chosen Alan Ayckbourn's play, *Woman in Mind*, which had its premiere in 1985, as an interesting text for the language-and-literature classroom and one which exemplifies much of the linguistic technique that is characteristic of modern British drama. Evans (1977, p. 208) points at the emphasis on language as 'confrontation' and at the treatment of relationships between individual characters that stresses 'less the uniqueness of the relationship than its typicality' as two principle features of modern drama, and Ayckbourn's play gives us both. It is a story of a woman who goes mad, ostensibly following a ridiculous accident in which she is struck by a rebounding garden rake. In her madness, the mundane world of her marriage to a boring husband is replaced by a romantic fantasy world where she, her husband and the family of her fantasies live on a beautiful country estate. Her real world and her fantasy world frequently collide, and the fantasy world ultimately takes over as her madness deepens. Despite the risible lunacy of Susan, the main female character, Billington (1990, p. 181) has described *Woman in Mind* as 'one of the most sympathetic, imaginative, compassionate accounts of womanhood written by any British dramatist since the war'. Susan's madness is primarily manifested in her inability to communicate with the world around her, whether her real or her fantasy world, and her increasing inability to do so as the play develops into a 'frantic oscillation between the reality of her life and the desperate hope of her dream world' (Carlson 1991).

The key to the play lies in the structuring of the interactions of the characters rather than any overt intrigue or dramatic series of events. Susan is someone for whom language, which ought to be the tool for shaping her environment, progressively *decreases* her power over her own situation. From the moment of her absurd accident, she enters a world where language separates her from the people around her. In the opening scene, she is being assisted immediately after her accident by the family doctor, Bill Windsor, and finds herself in a world where words no longer seem to make sense:

Bill: Squeezy, cow, squeezy . . .
Susan: I've no idea what you're saying. What are you saying?
Bill: Saul bite. Saul bite.
Susan: Who are you, anyway? Where am I?
Bill: Octer bin sir. Climb octer bin sir. Mrs sure pardon choose'un.

But nonsensical dialogue of this kind is restricted to the first thirty turns of speech in the play. Most of the time, Susan's disempowerment through language occurs because of a breakdown of discoursal norms. These include disturbance of turn-taking patterns, topical incoherence and defective exchange patterns. Susan's fantasy characters violate normal turn-taking by intruding into her 'real' conversations.

In this scene, her conversation with her real husband, Gerald, is interrupted by unsolicited contributions by her fantasy brother, Tony, and daughter, Lucy:

Gerald: Why didn't he tell us?
Susan: I should have thought that was fairly obvious.
Gerald: Yes. I suppose so. All the same, I don't think it's fair to lay all the blame at your door . . .
Tony: What?
Lucy: What?
Susan: What?
Gerald: There are probably two sides.
Lucy: Mother, don't stand for this . . .
Susan: My door? Did I hear you correctly?

Tony's and Lucy's contributions are coherent but violate turn-taking (they are neither 'selected' to speak by any of the participants nor do they have speakers' rights, since they are not participants but 'eavesdroppers'). Incoherence also frequently arises out of these clashes between Susan's two parallel worlds.

In this next extract, Bill Windsor pretends he too can see Lucy, Susan's fantasy daughter, and addresses her:

Bill: (*Quite avuncular*) Hallo, there. You're a big girl, aren't you? How old are you, then?
(*Lucy stares at him mystified*)
Bless my soul! Is that all? You look older than that. You must have been eating a lot of green vegetables.

Lucy: (*Getting up*) Mother?

Bill: They make you grow big and strong, did you know that? Did your Mummy ever tell you that? I bet she did.

Lucy: Mother, who is he? What does he want?

These are just some examples of the many scenes in the play where normal discourse is warped into mad dialogue. Held up as a mirror to Susan's real world, we are forced to conclude that the mad dialogue of fantasy is no more, or less, satisfying than the stifling and frustrating conversations of her real relationships. Neither type of dialogue empowers Susan; both types trap her in their own prison. Much of the play's dialogue is therefore of the type that lends itself to just the sorts of discourse analyses mentioned earlier in this paper, and the reader is referred to those sources for examples of the techniques their authors employ to quantify the modern dramatist's defamiliarisation of everyday talk. Employing the techniques of discourse analysis to bring out the significant features of the text as spoken interaction is a useful first step. Deciding how to exploit those features in class is the next.

5.4   Reconstructing the script

One of the ways of approaching this particular play is to begin with classroom activities that focus on the experience of incoherence from Susan's point of view. This can be done before any of the play itself is read. Working in pairs or groups, one half of the class can be given an extract from the play's opening scene (the conversation with Bill Windsor cited earlier, but with Bill's nonsensical dialogue restored to normality, such that 'Squeezy, cow, squeezy' becomes 'Easy, now, easy', etc.) and asked to 'Rewrite Susan's words in your own words, changing the meaning as little as possible'. This is a decoy exercise while the other half of the class have the same normalised script but with the instruction: 'Rewrite Bill Windsor's words with nonsense words that sound similar to his real words. An example is given to help you.' Those rewriting Susan's part do not know this, and think the other half are rewriting Bill's part in the same way as they are doing. The script both halves work on is given below.

Example 5.1 Activity A

Susan, a married woman, has just had an accident in her garden. She has been struck on the head by a garden rake and is semi-conscious. Her doctor, Bill Windsor, is helping to bring her around.

Bill: You're bound to feel somewhat groggy after that hit on the head.
Susan: Hit on the what?
Bill: Easy, now, easy.
Susan: I've no idea what you're saying.
Bill: It's all right.
Susan: Who are you? where am I?
Bill: Doctor Windsor, this is your garden, Susan.
Susan: Oh God, I've died. Nobody speaks English. What am I to do?
Bill: Susan, we speak English.
(plus more lines as deemed appropriate).

Those rewriting Bill's words can be given an example: Instead of 'Easy, now, easy', you could say, 'Breezy, how breezy' or anything else that sounds similar.

When both sides are ready, pairs can act out the Bill and Susan parts as rewritten. Those playing Susan can be asked how they experienced the surprise of hearing nonsense from Bill, and the rest of the class who watch the performance can also comment on the experience of absurdity.

An alternative, and one which is excellent for highlighting the kinds of topical incoherence which regularly occur in the inter-mingling of Susan's fantasy world and the real world, is to use a dialogue dove-tail. In the next activity example, which again can be done before any of the play is actually read, in order to sensit-ise the students to the problems of incoherence, students work in pairs, with each one initially *not* seeing his/her partner's script.

Example 5.2 Activity B

Student A: fill in A's part in this dialogue. *Scene:* a group of people are standing in the grounds of a big estate which belongs to B:
A: ... ...
B: Yes, it's all ours.

A: ... ...
B: Since 1386.
A: ... ...
B: Yes, we go right to the river that way.
A: ... ...
· B: Oh, that's Thailand.
A: ... ...
B; We held on to the shooting rights, but it's theirs officially.
A: ... ...

Student B: fill in B's part in this dialogue. *Scene:* a group of people are standing in the grounds of a big estate which belongs to B:
A: Glorious spot, this. Is it all yours?
B: ... ...
A: How long have you lived here?
B: ... ...
A: Oh, quite a time. Vast.
B: ... ...
A: Oh, yes. I see. What's the other side, then?
B: ... ...
A: Oh, is it? Is it?
B: ... ...
A: Lucky little chaps.

When each partner has his or her version ready, the original typed version is ignored and the two handwritten scripts are performed as a continuous dialogue. The actors naturally find the experience increasingly incoherent and confusing, rather as Susan herself finds the language around her. Once again, discussion can follow, in which ideas concerning the experience of incoherence can be raised. It must be stressed again that the purpose of these activities is to experience the disjointed dialogue in performance. This is done prior to reading and conventional analysis, not as a follow-up. In this way, concepts such as 'incoherent' and 'disjointed' can be related to immediate experiences and are not just dealt with abstractly.

Many other types of pre-reading activities which lend themselves to performance and discussion can be created. Students can be encouraged to write 'intrusive' lines of their own by imaginary characters into ordinary dramatic text and to judge the effects such violations have on judgements of the characters. (Do perfectly sane characters suddenly become lunatics by this process? What sort of communication is going on between characters?)

Real lines from the text can be jumbled and used as a text re-assembling exercise just as is often done with prose texts.

This becomes a far more memorable exercise if the original script itself displays features of incoherence (how easily can one re-assemble a jumbled version of Bill Windsor's conversation with the imaginary Lucy, above?). Another activity could be to remove all the contributions by the fantasy characters from zany conversational sequences. If such defective passages are 'tidied up' and normalised, does Susan still appear to be mad? This last question underlines the basic assertion that Susan's madness lies in her inability to separate the discourse of the real world from that of her fantasy world, not in the fact that she says daft things.

Such activities as are described here not only engage students in creating dialogue and performing their own scripts, but can also lay the necessary foundations for post-reading analytical work in a non-threatening way. I have found them particularly useful for presenting *Woman in Mind* to my students of discourse analysis, but they can be equally effectively used with students of literature and for many different modern drama texts. It is when the features of discourse, manipulated by the dramatist, have been experienced and discussed in lay terms by the students, in some sort of meaningful activity, that the terminology and techniques associated with rigorous analysis can be most effectively introduced and absorbed. The purpose of the activities suggested is not just self-expression or to have fun, invaluable as both those things are in any classroom. It is to bring the text to life so that analysis can be seen to be anchored in some tangible concepts and goals based on an already shared language.

5.5   Conclusion

Throughout his book on dramatic language, Birch (1991, p. 11) argues for 'variation and multiple meanings and the need to make variability and multiplicity the centre of critical practice, rather than the idea of a single, writer-oriented meaning.' So often, traditional reading-plus-commentary on dramatic texts simply delivers the orthodox interpretation, which is accepted passively, since to seek alternative interpretations would involve too much effort directed at the fossilised text. Pre-reading reconstruction activities by their nature encourage the personal response of the participants, and ask questions of the text rather than merely expect it to deliver up its one 'correct' meaning. But another advantage accrues from concentrating on the language of the text as discourse rather than just as vocabulary or 'diction', or merely addressing content, which is that the concept of open-endedness in meaning and interpretation can be linked to the open-endedness that deviant, 'unclosed' discourse structures necessarily create. Furthermore, with a writer like Ayckbourn, one can focus on the playwright's own input in creating such open-endedness. The text, rather than the play in performance, may actually contain more cues to open-ended interpretation than we think, and these can be exploited from a language-in-literature point of view. In the case of *Woman in Mind*, simple language activities based on the *stage directions* can yield much insight. For example, students can be asked to highlight any words that make the directions less precise and more vague in some way, for it does seem that Ayckbourn's stage directions for *Woman in Mind* deliberately ask for a blurred interpretation of what is happening, as in this example, which is one of many where the directions emphasise the imprecise qualities of the scene before us:

> *Susan:* Gerald, just go away. Go on, get away! Get away!
> (*She is ignored. In fact, from this point on, people appear to be less and less aware of Susan. As if she herself were slowly slipping from the dream whilst it carries on without her.*)

The number of times Ayckbourn's directions include words such as *seem, appear,* and modal words that lessen the assertion of any one particular reality on the stage, is notable, and can be brought out by straightforward language activities. The directions are part of the experience of blurred reality, madness, incoherence and powerlessness that Susan herself is the victim of. The directions are no less a part of the *text* than the dialogue itself.

I have argued that the text can be exploited in a number of ways in class, to get away from traditional, unmotivating modes of analysis, by combining guided writing activities with mini-performances, by looking at the text as samples of spoken language and by concentrating on the open-endedness of interpretation that a text-as-discourse approach allows. There is no reason why rigorous analysis should be excluded from the total process of confrontation with the text, but it does seem, that when analysis becomes an end in itself, the open-ended world of modern drama discourse so often becomes closed off by product-oriented activity that plods relentlessly towards the 'right' answers. Birch (1991) and, one suspects, Ayckbourn, would argue that there are no 'right' answers, just as there are rarely right answers to the day-to-day interpretation of our own and others' spoken interactions off the stage. The drama text is merely an imperfect template for possible discourses, and, if approached as such, can be just as effective a vehicle for interpretation as the play in production.

6

That's for your poetry book!

ALAN MALEY

The author begins by discussing the nature of poetry, pointing out its equal relevance as a subject of literary study and a resource for the development of language skills.

The first part of the paper mentions several faults and misconceptions about the poetic medium, including the role of 'inspiration' and so-called 'poetic' language in the early twentieth century. Then the focus shifts to a consideration of what constitutes good poetry; the five linguistic criteria of Accuracy, Appropriacy, Economy, Clarity, and Elegance are suggested, with examples drawn from the efforts of student writers.

The second part moves to an examination of teaching approaches to pairs of poems on similar themes, with rubrics directed to the hypothetical student, of either language or literature, concluding that the two disciplines interpenetrate to a greater or lesser degree according to the students' purposes. Readers may like to consider Chapter 9 by Guy Cook as a natural theoretical complement to this highly practical chapter.

This article will be in two parts. In section 6.1 I shall examine some common misconceptions about the nature of poetry. In section 6.2 I shall suggest a number of classroom activities which can be used with pairs of poems to enhance language learning as well as literary awareness.

At long last the traditional hostility between Literature as a subject of study and Language as the acquisition of a set of practical skills seems to be waning. It is now increasingly recognised that Language and Literature can and should be mutually reinforcing. Also that learners have different goals, needs and expectations, depending on where they are positioned along the cline from Literary Studies at one end to down-to-earth, no-nonsense

Language for Communication at the other. The first part of this article will be angled towards the literary end of the scale, and will, I hope, be of relevance to classes where the literary artefact is the main focus of study. The second part will be of more relevance to teachers wishing to draw upon poetry as one resource, among others, for developing language skills.

6.1 This is a great poem!

In this section I shall examine some common misconceptions about what poetry is. These misconceptions have cropped up repeatedly in discussions with teachers and students of English literature in many different parts of the world. In my view, they tend to get in the way of an informed reading of poetry. Their effects are also all too evident in the texts which many aspiring writers produce under the banner of 'poetry'.

6.1.1 What poetry is not

1. It is not the uncontrolled, spontaneous outpouring of the writer's emotions on to the page. It is rare for us to be able to write well when in the grip of powerful emotions. It may be therapeutic for the writer, but all too often it is embarrassingly turgid for the reader.

2. Neither is poetry 'inspiration' – in ninety-nine percent of the cases. The image of the poet seated with a wet towel about his head, burning the midnight oil as he waits for inspiration to strike through his pen into immortal lines on the page is a fantasy. Quite often, what is written under the influence of 'inspiration' turns out to be junk. The white goddess of the night before proves a deceiving doxy in the cold light of the morning after.

   This is not to deny that inspiration has a role to play. But it rarely does more than get the writer started. It may be a chance good idea, a near-perfect couplet which 'just comes' to us and will not stop resonating in our ears, or a striking image. However, to turn these into a successful poem involves long and hard work.

3. Many people continue to believe that, in order to qualify as poetry, a text must be written in special 'poetic' language. In other words, there is an assumption that there are two separate registers of language; one for poetry and another for everyday matters.

This poetic register is thought to be made up, among other things, of archaisms, (e.g. thou, ye, doth, dieth, oft, a-blowing, etc.), of 'poetic' equivalents of everyday words, (e.g. sylvan / wooded, bliss / happiness, billows / waves, damsels / girls, raiment / clothing, tarry / stay, verdure / greenery, etc.), and of syntactic oddities, chief among which is inversion of various kinds, e.g.

> But knowledge to their eyes her ample page,
> Rich with the spoils of time, did ne'er unfold.
>
> Thomas Gray

Inversion is, of course, a device often used to shift a rhyme conveniently to the end of a line.

It is understandable that people should think of poetic language in this way. Until the cataclysm of the First World War (1914–18), most English poetry had indeed been couched in a special 'poetic' idiom. So, for those raised on a diet of predominantly pre-1920 poetry (which included, until recently at least, most overseas students of English literature), it was quite natural to think of poetry in this way.

It is also possible that some students/teachers are influenced by their experience of poetic conventions in their own literatures, where poetry may still be written in a special register. This would be the case, I believe, for Arabic and Tamil, among others.

In contemporary English poetry however, such conventions long since ceased to be observed. Anyone who continues to write in this way would be judged anachronistic and quaint. If a contemporary poet were to write in this idiom, we would have to suppose that he was doing it for some special, possibly comic or satirical, effect.

4. Allied with this misconception is the notion that only certain topics or themes form the proper subject matter of poetry: Love, Beauty, Death, Nature, etc. Though this may once have been the case (though in English poetry, even this is doubtful), it certainly is the case no longer. Poems can be about anything at all: bad breath, babies' nappies, space travel, battery hens, etc. As we shall see below, however, it is the gift of the good poet to transmute the particular, however seemingly trivial, into something of universal significance.

5. Poetry, contrary to much popular belief, does not have to rhyme. Unhappily, many students, who attempt to write it, behave as if it did. All too often, the result is a kind of rhyming prose of

the William McGonagall variety.[1] On the whole, rhyme in contemporary poetry, where it occurs, tends to be somewhat more subtle.

6. Poetry is not a literary crossword puzzle. Indeed there is something self-defeating about poems which resemble a thorn hedge of obscure references, offering no chink for the reader to peer through.

Much of what passes for 'modern' poetry, and a good deal of what does not, is simply obscurantist. It may refer to phenomena, emotions, ideas or events which are so personal that they are inaccessible to others. Or it may simply be mesmerised by the cleverness of its own technique.

There is always a danger when 'teaching' poetry of this kind, for the teacher to explicate the poem, in the manner of an exegesis, rather than to help students to respond to it in a personal way. The way in which T.S. Eliot, (who came perilously close to constructing perversely impenetrable poetry at times), is 'taught' is a case in point. The teacher passes on the secrets of *The Waste Land* to the uninitiated acolytes.

7. The misconceptions listed above (1–6) tend to place both readers and writers of poetry in a position of deference towards poetic texts. If such texts are the product of high emotion, of inspiration and so on, then they take on a sacrosanct quality. It is no longer possible to question such texts; it is sufficient to admire them. This relieves teachers and students alike of the tiresome necessity of trying to evolve an independent response to them. They can fall back instead on received wisdom. Such an attitude of excessive respect for the rest also precludes dismembering it in pedagogically fruitful ways.

6.1.2   What poetry is

Having spent some time on enumerating what poetry (for me at least) is not, it is not unreasonable for the reader to inquire of me what it is. I will confine myself to four key aspects.

1. It is discipline and control. The control is exercised in two main ways: over form and over content. The writer has to decide on a form which will best carry his content. Once chosen, he has to submit to the discipline of it. The form may be highly constraining, as for example in the sonnet, the villanelle or the haiku. But, even when working in so-called 'free verse', there are constraints

of choice in the patterning of rhythm, metre, internal rhyme, alliteration and assonance. The poem has to 'sound right' to the inward ear. It is a three-dimensional web which, if touched at any one point, will vibrate all over.

Likewise with content. We may have a whole host of ideas, images, metaphors we would like to cram down the throat of the poem. But only what is relevant to, and what resonates with the form in the most economical and elegant way will do.

Discipline then is exercised through the difficult choices the poet has to make at all levels. He is constantly having to choose, to reject even some of his choicest gems if they do not fit this particular crown. The discipline of throwing away, of revising, re-drafting, of starting again from scratch if need be, is an essential quality for the poet. Indeed one of the most productive ways of approaching a poem is by looking at the choices the poet made and comparing them with the choices he might have made.

Donald Davie once referred to poetry as 'articulate energy' – energy rendered articulate through control and discipline.

2. Poetry is seeing unfamiliar things in unfamiliar ways, and making unexpected connections. Perhaps the most characteristic way in which 'inspiration' works is by throwing together previously unconnected elements in the mind, and making new sense from the connection. To do this the poet has to develop a keen sense of observation, and to remain open to the unpredictable. In fact a kind of Zen state.

This process is difficult to reconstruct retrospectively for established poems. An example may be helpful however. The writer is on the way to the airport in a foreign country early in the morning. He *sees* many things on the way, but what he *notices* is a goat calmly stripping off a political poster from a wall and eating it. This suggests to him the key word 'digestion', and his imagination goes to work on the metaphorical possibilities this raises. Eventually, after several abortive attempts, he comes up with a more or less satisfactory version, which incorporates his observation and the unusual connection he has made.

> *Airport Road*
> An early morning goat,
> Rampant against a wall,
> Calmly chews strips
> Of the Chief Minister's face.

Like the electorate,
Goats can digest anything –
But he at least
Is getting
Some nourishment.

Alan Maley

3. Poetry is also about using ordinary language in extraordinary ways. I made the point earlier (see 6.1.1(3) above) that the language poets use is not necessarily part of a special register. But this is not to say that they use words in exactly the same way as they might in everyday contexts. They are constantly experimenting with language, stretching it to test the limits of the meanings it can be made to take on. They do this:

– by creating striking new metaphors:

His legs were blistered sticks on which the black sap
Bubbled and burst . . .

Anthony Hecht

– by transforming the syntax in unconventional ways:

he sang his didn't he danced his did

e e cummings

– by dramatically extending the semantic range of common words:

Hands have no tears to flow

Dylan Thomas

– by creating new collocations:

as radiant as wine

Student

and so on.

Poets are linguistic risk-takers and stunt-men. They are constantly pulling the language out of its well-worn ruts. Yet, to change the metaphor, they are still using the old warp and weft to weave the new cloth.

4. Poetry is also about making universal meanings from precisely-observed particulars. These examples may demonstrate this best:

The feather from the raven's breast
Falls on the stubble lea;

> The acorns near the old crow's nest
> Fall pattering down the tree;
> The grunting pigs, that wait for all,
> Scramble and hurry where they fall.
>
> John Clare

> . . . the dark waves,
> The sea-birds bathing, spreading their wings,
> Rime and snow falling, mingled with hail.
>
> Thomas Hardy

> Or the swan stirs the reeds, his neck and bill
> Wetting, that drip upon the water still.
>
> William Wordsworth

In these poems there is very closely observed detail which acts as a symbol of a universal truth.

In other words, poems should work at more than one level of interpretation. Each reader will find different meanings in them. And, in the very best poetry, the same reader can return repeatedly to the same text and continue to find new meanings which had not surfaced before.

6.1.3   *Implications for teaching*

It is not my intention in this first part of the article to propose a set of detailed procedures for the teaching of poetry. I would suggest however, that the points raised under 'What poetry is not' could form the basis for the critical examination of any given text – a sort of 'beware' list. Likewise, the points made under 'What poetry is' could help in raising students' sensitivity to key factors in the reading of poems – a sort of 'be aware' list. I would further suggest that students be trained to look at poems (or indeed any kind of written text) in terms of five criteria:

Accuracy, Appropriacy, Economy, Clarity, Elegance.

These acid tests could be applied both to poems written by themselves and to published poems. (The quotations in this section are all taken from students' work.)

Accuracy

Are the words being used in their normally accepted meanings? If not, can an accurate interpretation be derived?

Is the syntax correct? If not, is it an acceptable distortion? (Even the syntactic violations of e e cummings and Dylan Thomas conform to a higher-order set of rules in English. By contrast, 'the achieve of man' does not.)

Are the images accurate? Do they correspond with the idea the writer was trying to convey? 'The slinky thread of a deluded aeon' is somewhat resistant to interpretation, for example.

Appropriacy

Is the language chosen appropriate for the writer's purpose? Does it contain archaisms or anachronistic turns of phrase?

Is the tone appropriate to the intended reader? Does it shout too loud? Is it too low key?

Is the form appropriate to the content? (For example, it would not generally be thought appropriate to select the limerick form to convey a sense of awe.)

Are the images used appropriate to the message? There is something odd about this, for example:

> The freezing blood
> brought us back to our coops.

Economy

Is it too long? Too short? Pointlessly repetitive? Is there anything which could be removed without seriously affecting the impact? (Some of Wordsworth's poetry is a suitable case for treatment in this context.) Are the images too densely spaced? For example:

> You seem a perspective
> intagliated on
> the palm-clustered vertical myth.

Clarity

Has the writer made his meaning clear? Are any passages obscure or ambiguous (in what seem to be unintentional ways)? Are there too many 'private' meanings? Does the writer seem to be clear in his own mind about what he intended to say? Does he show off at the expense of clarity? For example, it is difficult to assign a clear meaning to the following:

> In determined antwilding over
> saccharine pots
> Anticipation finds lip salve.

Elegance

Do the elements which make it up – the sound patterns, the metrical form, the ideas, the images, the tone – come together to make a complex whole which is in perfect balance; which resonates to an internal harmony? Does it have just the right measure of tension, like a tiger before the spring, the arrow before release? Does it have wit, in the sense of intelligence – 'the ability to relate seemingly disparate things so as to illuminate or amuse'? Does it make us say, 'I wish I'd said that'? Is it seemingly effortless? Does it sound as good as it means? Does it mean as good as it sounds?

6.1.4　Conclusion

I would suggest that discussion based on such criteria would yield useful insights for students whose primary goal is a literary understanding of poems. There is one further activity to be recommended however; namely, writing poetry. Experience with groups of teachers and students in many parts of the world has convinced me that there is no better way of understanding other peoples' writing than by engaging in the writing process oneself.

6.2　'Where you get that nose from Lily? / Got it from my father, silly.'

In this section I shall take a pair of poems and suggest some ways in which they could form the input for language-focused work. (I would not wish to play down the incidental spin-off the activities might have for literary insights however.)

I have suggested elsewhere (Maley 1994) that it is helpful to develop a set of generalisable tasks which can be applied to virtually any text. What follows is based on a modified version of this scheme. I have grouped the activities:

Responding; Analysing/Using Critical Judgement; Writing.

I have chosen to take two poems rather than one because I believe that we notice a great deal more about a text when it is contrasted with another text on the same theme than we do when it stands alone.

> *Well Caught*
> These days I'm in love with my face.
> It has grown round and genial as I've become older.
> In it I see my grandfather's face and that
> Of my mother. Yes – like a ball it has been thrown
> From one generation to the next.
>
> Gerda Mayer

> *Heredity*
> I am the family face;
> Flesh perishes, I live on,
> Projecting trait and trace
> Through time to times anon,
> And leaping from place to place
> Over oblivion.
>
> The years-heired feature that can
> In curve and voice & eye
> Despise the human span
> Of durance – that is I;
> The eternal thing in man,
> That heeds no call to die.
>
> Thomas Hardy

6.2.1   *Responding*

(The rubrics are all directed to the hypothetical student.)

Interpretation

1. Do you look like anyone in your family? In what ways? (colour of eyes? shape of nose? type of hair? etc.) Talk to your partner about this, then report back in the whole class discussion.
2. Do you have any photographs of your parents or grandparents when they were your age? What do you notice? Compare your observations with a partner.
3. Read the two poems. Which one do you find more difficult to understand? Why? Compare your ideas with others in the class.
4. Write out your answers to these questions in relation to each poem.
   – Who is speaking in each case? Who are they speaking to?
   – What are they talking about? What are they saying about it?

– When are they talking? When were the poems written?
– Why are they telling us this?
– How would you describe their different ways of telling us?
Use your answers to take part in the class discussion.

5. Imagine you are going to interview the authors of these two poems. Work with a partner to prepare some questions to ask them. These can be about themselves (e.g. How old are you?), about some aspect of their writing, (e.g. Why did you call your poem *Well Caught?*) or about the subject matter of their poem, (e.g. What made you choose this subject?), etc.

   Share your questions in a full class discussion. Can any of the questions be answered by members of the class?

Extension

1. Try to find other types of text on the same subject (e.g. extracts from popular science magazines, newspaper articles on genetic engineering, extracts from biology textbooks, etc.).
2. Develop a classroom display project based on photographs and other documents relating to family resemblances of the class members.
3. Prepare a debate on the pros and cons of genetic engineering for future generations.
4. Try to find other pairs of poems on some different themes (e.g. mirrors).

6.2.2   Analysing / Exercising Critical Judgement

Comparison/contrast

1. Make a list, with a partner, of all the ways in which the two poems are different from each other (e.g. length, rhyme, type of vocabulary, tone, images, etc.).
2. Then list all the ways in which they are similar. Compare notes with another pair. Then report back in full class discussion.

Selection/matching

1. Choose the paraphrase which fits the sense of the poem *Heredity* most accurately:
   – The family face is what survives when people die. It can jump over several generations. This helps to make us eternal.

- There is no need to worry about dying because our faces will live on in other people. We are immortal.
- Physical features are passed on genetically from one generation to the next. Even if we die, our characteristics live on in our descendants.

Discuss your answers in groups of four.

2. Here are four short poems. Which one do you think comes closest to the ideas expressed in the original poems? And which of the four do you like best? Discuss your answers with your teacher in the class discussion session.

   (a) Even when I die
   I will live on in others –
   See – there's my grandson.

   (b) Though death's cold breath is sharp and keen,
   It is no match for the subtle gene;
   For though I'll pass from off the earth,
   My features will enjoy re-birth,
   And generations later will surprise
   Death with my voice, my nose, my eyes.

   (c) From this photograph
   My father, aged twelve, looks out –
   Through my own son's eyes.

   (d) Death cannot harm me
   For I leap from birth to birth;
   And, seed within seed, I spread through time
   To the ends of the earth.

   Alan Maley

Analysis

1. Look at the vocabulary in *Heredity*. How many unusual words/ phrases (or ordinary words used in unusual ways) can you find? Make a list with your partner. Then try to find more common equivalent words or phrases for each of them. Finally, compare your answers with another pair.

2. Practice reading the two poems aloud in small groups. (You may find it helpful to mark the sense groups.) What do you notice about the rhythm? Can you speak each of the poems at the same speed? Discuss this with your teacher.

3. Write a question to test the comprehension of some aspect of the two poems (e.g. What does 'anon' mean? What is the

connection between the title *Well Caught* and the poem which follows it?) Then exchange your questions and try to answer the one you have been given.

6.2.3   *Writing*

1. Read the poem *Heredity* again. Then choose ten words from it which you think are especially important for the meaning. Write them down on a separate piece of paper and put the poem away out of sight. Now use the ten words you have chosen to write a new text on the same theme as the poem. Your text could either be a new poem or a piece of prose. Of course you will need to add other words to make a complete text.
2. Choose a content word from either poem. Write it in the middle of a blank sheet of paper. Then write down all the words which come to your mind in connection with the word. Write them in the form of a word-star. Here is an example:

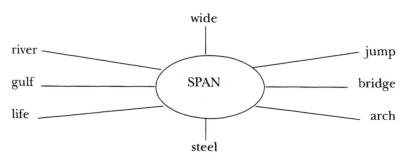

Now use the words you have written to write a new poem. Show it to your partner.
3. Write a refrain (a chorus) which could be spoken at the beginning, in the middle and at the end of the Hardy poem. You may use fragments of the poem itself if you wish. Here is an example:

> I am the family face;
> The eternal thing in man.
> I win the mortal race –
> Despise the human span.

Compare your refrain with others in the class.
4. Add a third verse to the Hardy poem which continues with the same theme. Here is an example:

I chart my passage through the gloom
Of centuries of tears.
Avoiding treacherous reefs of doom,
I navigate the years,
Until from the ancestral womb,
This face once more appears.

Check your versions with your teacher.
5. Write a parody of the Mayer poem. Remember that a parody is a comic or mocking imitation of the original. For example, the famous first line of Shakespeare's sonnet 'Shall I compare thee to a summer's day?' could be parodied: 'Shall I compare thee to a plastic bag?'

Here is an example.

These days I really love my face –
Before I thought it a disgrace –
I've got my grandfather's pink eyes,
And Mum's ears (twice the normal size).
My family's there in every feature;
I'm really glad I am their creature.
They've thrown my face round like a ball –
It seems it's theirs not mine at all.
But though I don't mind being thrown,
It's not much fun to be a clone.

6.2.4   Experiment further

The activities suggested above by no means exhaust the possibilities of these two poems. You may wish to experiment with other pairs of poems in the same way. Maley and Moulding (1985) has fifteen sets of paired poems. Here is another pair:

Haiku
quietly dozing
under a clock without hands;
the museum keeper.

                                    Eric Amann

Still Life
On a chair by the door
between Still Life with Flowers
and Portrait of a Lady (artist unknown)
she sits, shading the seconds into minutes,

'. . . and here in the corner (if we could *all*
keep together), Portrait of a Lady –

possibly from Flanders.
Note in particular how, wherever you stand,
you seem to be followed by the eyes,
and how the hint of disillusionment
at the corners of the mouth
is echoed in the folded hands.
Notice too (before we move on)
how well the whole figure
blends with the background . . .'

Eyes weary of galleries
scan the canvas of her face
searching for the frame
and, finding none, move on
noting in passing
how well the whole figure
blends with the background.

On a chair by the door
between Portrait of a Lady (artist unknown)
and Still Life with Flowers
she sits, shading the minutes into hours.

                                                    Alan Duff

6.3 Conclusion

In this article I have tried to show how poetry might be approached
at the two ends of the continuum extending from Literary studies
to Language teaching. I would however re-state my view that
Literature and Language interpenetrate in varying degrees
depending on the student's purposes. The activities suggested in
section 6.2 could equally well be used with some groups of
Literature students, and the kinds of questions addressed in section
6.1 could also be of relevance for advanced students of Language.

Note

1. William McGonagall (1830–1902) was one of the worst poets ever to
   be published. Here are some of the deathless lines from his poem on
   the construction of the Tay bridge:

   Beautiful Railway bridge of the silvery Tay,
   And prosperity to Messrs. Bouche & Grothe,
   The famous engineers of the present day.

7

Picking holes: cloze procedures in prose

ANITA WESTON

The author states that the well-known ELT practice of gap-filling is often seen, in literature study, as building on post-structuralist theory, where the reader constructs the meaning of the text by recreating it; although many theoretical and practical drawbacks are raised, initially with reference to aural cloze procedures.

Moving to literary prose, it is acknowledged that an approach essentially geared to language teaching must be undertaken differently in the language/literature classroom, as texts will go beyond the purely informational. Mischief may be found in the denotational meaning of words – 'goblins' – in a representational context. Replacing their omission in a literary text therefore represents much more than simply making grammatical or linguistic sense in a cloze passage.

Practical examples are given: from George Eliot and Virginia Woolf (with an example of her own rewritings) to Paul Theroux and Anthony Burgess. Stylistic points arising, such as omniscient narration and the register of characters' discourse, are brought out, as are the differing benefits to be gained from single-word and whole-sentence deletions.

7.1   State-of-play

L'endroit le plus érotique d'un corps n'est-il pas là où le vêtement bâille?

Roland Barthes

Cloze procedure has come to the respectable age of thirty, and some variation of it – pure, 'objective' cloze, when every nth word is removed, or 'controlled', more properly gap-filling, when selected items are chosen for deletion – still seems to be a popular exercise for a variety of teaching or testing purposes, both of language and, increasingly, literature. The gaps can be one word only, several words, or whole sentences; they can be filled (a) at the student's choice, (b) from a multiple-choice selection per gap, or (c) from a word-bank for the whole passage, either with one solution per gap, or, more perversely, more solutions than gaps, so that some words are 'blanks'. In this last case, and particularly where the cloze is targeted for vocabulary work, it is sensible to ensure that the blanks are extensions of semantic chains existing in the passage – antonyms, synonyms, hyponyms, or superordinates, morphological variants, etc.; this makes for a more meaningful discussion of choices and rejections, and, from work done on field-theory and the importance of context-relevance (cf. Carter and McCarthy, and Nation and Coady, in Carter and McCarthy eds. 1988, pp. 18–38, 101–109), would seem to increase their chances of being retained.

Cloze is, then, or seems to be a extraordinarily versatile tool, the philosopher's stone of ELT. It requires a combination of comprehension and production skills; it provides, for vocabulary work, a closely-woven syntagmatic and paradigmatic mesh in which the 'right' word has more contextual chance of being caught, taught/learnt, retrieved or consolidated, and it allows a guided and 'real language' context for the testing or underlining of specific points of grammar or vocabulary.

It is praised for its 'overall usefulness' in 'aim[ing] at a multitude of abilities [as regards] the lexical, semantic and syntactic inter-relationships which characterise the unique structure of a language' (Soudek and Soudek 1983), and, even more important for hard-pressed examiners in vast universities, state examining bodies, etc., as being, like multiple choice tests, attractively objective and 'fair': 'a reliable, valid, highly efficient instrument for measuring readability and reading comprehension and for estimating the level of proficiency of learners of a second or foreign language' (*ibid.*): the best thing since sliced bread.

When applied to literature it has apparently proved the butter and jam as well, offering, its supporters claim, direct experience of the literary-specific, an interactive form of practical criticism, and a creative encounter with the 'open' text. As an explicit concretisation of the implicit gaps in both text-external reference and text-internal relations, cloze is 'simply' an extension of the hermeneutic gap-filling which the post-structuralist reader automatically performs in actively constructing the meaning of a text (see van Peer in Short ed. 1989, p. 281 ff.). This is also, however, an altogether more contentious area. The language appraising cloze has thickened: on the plus side, it is a readily-wielded teacherly tool with which students experience 'the pleasure of the text', and learn some necessary facts of critical life about norm and deviancy; on the minus, it is accused of being a Jack-the-Ripper, destroying, in an act of violent lexicide, all the text's instantial charms once it has pleasured it, and the enemy of literature and civilisation as we know it: a McCarthy-like witch hunt of what seemed an innocent activity between consenting adults provided they were equipped with the necessary language-protection, namely competency.

There are indeed (to review the above points in a more user-friendly register) considerable advantages to cloze in both language and literature teaching. It seems to be extremely efficient for the active processing of a grammatical structure or item of vocabulary (although arguably no more than other guided production exercises), and a sensitive, 'hands-on' approach to a literary text (cf. Carter and Long 1987, 1991). Not least, it is also enjoyable. There are equally, in the 'pure' cloze procedure generally used in the language classroom, a number of doubts and grey areas, although as the present article is concerned with literary prose, these will simply be touched on.

7.2 Clozed, open and black holes

Mais si le language exprime autant par ce qui est entré les mots que par les mots? Par ce qu'il ne 'dit' pas que par ce qu'il 'dit'?
Merleau-Ponty, quoted in Culler 1975, p. 75

It has frequently been my experience that the hole in a clozed text is much deeper for students than the temporary gaps in their lexical knowledge when they are required to produce a sentence in any other way, and that the elusive word is perfectly familiar to them once it has been proffered. Nor does it seem to be a problem of collocation or context, of knowing the word but not *there*, in that particular hole, although studies like those by Aborn, Rubenstein and Sterling (1959) would seem to prove that immediate context has a significant role (obviously) for native speakers' prediction of missing words, and therefore for non-native speakers too. These studies demonstrate, among other things, that 'increasing the context beyond ten words does not increase predictability' and that a 'polo-mint', as it were, of text around a hole is more helpful for retrieval than a sizeable chunk on one side or the other.

Since, however, set phrases and 'top-down' processing of language will inevitably be more prevalent in native or bilingual speakers (who have acquired language in a native context, in a world built of language blocks which were gradually broken down as competence was acquired) than in EFL students (who, for all our efforts, have had to do a lot more 'bottom-up' processing, brick on lexical brick), it is arguably that these results do not necessarily carry over to EFL teaching in their entirety, since there is no 'automaticity of context', no shared 'language-set' to match the shared mind-set of a native-language community, other than the temporarily cohesive/coherent one provided by the text. This does not mean that guessing strategies for unknown words such as those suggested by Nation and Coady (Carter and McCarthy eds. 1988) – making use of relative clauses, breaking down into simpler sentences, etc. – are any the less useful, but they may well have to be more frequently deployed.

In the same way, strategies for guessing included, unknown words will have only a limited application to non-included but possibly known words. It is not simply that morphological or syntactic clues – syntagmatic interrelations generally – are far more transparent in a given but unknown world, but that the 'silence within margins', to misquote Genette, i.e. a gap, is considerably more eloquent than we as teachers intend, and often has the effect of silencing a gap-filler who would be perfectly able to produce the same word in any other form of language production, as I suggested above.

Surprisingly, the 'aural cloze' I want to look at briefly here often proves simpler, after initial panic. I have used this only with 'referential' texts, on the language side of the interface, and generally on 'seen' rather than 'unseen' passages (as a follow-up activity to dictation, for example). Unseen passages make it a hopelessly demotivating affair. In my experience, students start by hating it and end up finding it great fun (even when the passage is not a joke, as in my example).

7.2.1   Aural cloze procedure

A number of items from a particular word-category are deleted from a short passage, one category after the other, for a total of three (after which boredom sets in). I suggest first verbs, then nouns, then a mixed bag of adjectives, adverbs, prepositions, conjunctions, etc. The passage is first read out in its entirety.

> Breznev had recently been made head of state, and was showing his elderly mother around the Kremlin. The old woman, of peasant stock, was open-mouthed at the wealth and luxury on display. As they entered the state guest-rooms, Breznev asked her: 'Why are you so silent? Don't you like it?', but the old lady didn't say a word. And so on, through the bathrooms, the ballroom, the bedrooms and his office. Finally, in the kitchens, where cupboards and fridges held foods which she had never seen before, he was simply bursting, and had to ask, 'But mother, aren't you pleased your son has been so successful?' 'Oh, of course,' she replied. 'But – what if the Communists take over?'

The students are then told that the passage will now be read with a particular word-category omitted and replaced either by a 'joker' word such as 'dash', or silence, or something between the two. (Personally I have found a sort of significant 'hmm' the most useful, since it provides an empty container for the natural intonation pattern of the sentence without being a distraction which would make the students momentarily ponder over the meaning of 'his dash mother', or quite simply make them laugh. The teacher will feel foolish anyway for the first few times.) As in all cloze procedure, the first sentence should be left intact. Gaps should be pre-marked before the first reading with 'holes' begins, using a different code for each, and the number of gaps should be more limited than in written cloze, given memory-span and the difficulty of the processing involved. There can be slightly more in the third category omitted: by this reading, the students have the passage almost off by heart, which is a significant advantage of aural cloze. The subsequent readings might go as follows:

> Breznev had recently been made head of state, and was showing his elderly mother around the Kremlin. The old woman, of peasant stock, was open-mouthed at the wealth and luxury on display. As they entered the state guest-rooms, Breznev asked her . . . etc.

The subsequent readings might 'sound' as follows:

> (*nouns*) Breznev had recently been made head of state, and was showing his elderly mother around the Kremlin. The old . . ., of peasant stock, was open-mouthed at the . . . and luxury on display. As they entered the state . . ., Breznev asked her . . . etc.

(*verbs*) Breznev had recently been made head of state, and was showing his elderly mother around the Kremlin. The old woman, of
peasant stock, . . . open-mouthed at the wealth and luxury on display. As they . . . the state guest-rooms, Breznev asked her . . . etc.

(*adjectives, adverbs, conjunctions, and prepositions*) Breznev had recently
been made head of state, and was showing his elderly mother
around the Kremlin. The old woman, . . . peasant stock, was . . . at
the wealth and luxury on display. . . . they entered the state guest-
rooms, Breznev asked her . . . etc.

This aural procedure clearly has the advantage over the average
written cloze passage of not being unseen (although there is many
a slip between the cup of passive processing for comprehension or
dictation, and the lip of active cloze retrieval), but it remains a
sophisticated activity requiring a number of skills. That it should
prove easier than a cloze encounter of the standard kind causes
me unease. The debate is opened up by Carter (in Carter and
McCarthy eds. 1988, pp. 178–179): 'How useful is it to delete
items such as *however, for example, and so* [. . .] which serve to propel arguments forward [. . .]? Is the deletion of such items,
especially as they tend to be in clause or sentence initial position,
more or less important than deletions from lexical chains which
constitute thematic and propositional development?' In cloze
texts I have consistently found gaps along the syntagmatic axis to
pose more problems than those on the paradigmatic, precisely
because they *do* 'propel the arguments forward', and require a
control over anaphoric and cataphoric data. In an aural cloze
there is considerably less difference in student production
between the two axes, presumably because of clues provided by
intonation – the students 'hear' the missing conjunction, and
'hear' the causal/cohesive link.

As teachers of literature, we are well aware of the influence of
the typographic sign on expectation and interpretation; if rear-
ranging the layout of a piece of banal journalism can, as Genette
argues, totally alter its effect and make us read it as a lyric poem,
is it not perhaps possible that something analogous occurs in
cloze?[1] The formal nature of a gap on the page seems to provoke
a visual and neurological block, a sort of black hole which sucks
the reader in where an unknown word would simply be, for the
sake of metaphor, an unknown but negotiable planet capable
of sustaining normal lexical life: an unscientific observation,

certainly, but one which I have systematically verified by eliciting the same word from the same student by other means. This should perhaps give us pause – particularly when using cloze for testing purposes.

7.3 Gap-fill in literary prose

There has indeed recently been 'an explosion of interest in the use of literature in ELT and a corresponding [. . .] use of ELT techniques in literature teaching' (Mackay 1992, p. 199), but, however enthusiastically the symbiosis has been accepted, it is as well to remember that there will always be a difference in objective between the use of literature in E L(anguage) T and in E L(iterature) T. Techniques which are central to language teaching may well be marginal (although often invaluable) for literature: cloze, prediction, conversion, etc. are all excellent approaches to the literary micro-text, but in my opinion they remain essentially *language* activities: more traditional approaches to the macro-text and context continue to be necessary (and in no way at variance). Many of the supposed defects in cloze procedure, such as those discussed below, arise from mistaken targeting and the implicit assumption of so many writers and teachers that the common denominator of language is sufficient to make 'the language/literature classroom' the same place. More than a slash separates the two disciplines; in other words, 'Do not forget that a poem' (or any literary text), 'even though it is written in the language of information, is not used in the language-game of giving information' (Wittgenstein, quoted in Culler 1975, p. 162).

At a more general level, the widespread reappraisal of stylistics over the past few years may be a useful theoretical position from which to review some of its practical applications, including cloze. Jean-Jacques Lecercle's article 'The Current State of Stylistics' in the *European English Messenger* (Lecercle 1993, p. 17), while in no way demonising the discipline (the article ends '*La stylistique est morte, vive la stylistique*'), criticises 'the idiosyncratic pole of stylistics' and reviews carefully some of the more extreme claims which have produced 'analyses of style in terms of either the construction of individual grammars [or of] the dead end of norm and deviancy', and 'the extension [in stylistics] of the field of *langue* to the detriment of *parole*'.

7.4   Virtues and vices of cloze in literature teaching

What, then, are these marginal but invaluable advantages of cloze in the teaching of literature, and what are the possible pitfalls? Before looking at some practical examples, it is as well to clear the decks of theoretical clutter such as van Peer's justification of explicit gap-filling as a concrete, bottom-up extension of the implicit, top-down inferencing and integrating which all readers, L1 or L2, perform to supply the missing information of writerly world-views which is our readerly contribution to textual meaning. This, he states, is 'to bridge the incompleteness' with regard to 'the reality the text purports to depict'; he goes on to claim that cloze techniques will 'therefore' develop students' interactive reading skills (Van Peer 1988, p. 289). They most definitely do, but the ability to arrive at cohesion in a passage may, firstly, be a wholly inadequate integration/reproduction of that particular text's literary specific coherence (for a discussion of cohesion without coherence, see Carter, in Carter and McCarthy eds. 1988, p. 162 ff.); secondly, by extension, the ability to 'process' a text is in no way an ability to 'process' the 'reality the text purports to depict'.

7.4.1   Literary cloze

'To be or not to be, that is the . . . . .' may lead us usefully into Hamlet's syllogistic logic and question-and-answer clauses, but the 'inferencing', as we read, from our previous knowledge of his father's death and mother's remarriage, and from our knowledge of the Elizabethan theory of melancholy, is of a different nature altogether. The correct gap-fill of 'shallow' in the *Middlemarch* passage below may well proleptically point to other textual clues – Casaubon's hours in the library, Dorothea's tears before bedtime on their honeymoon – to reveal the actual state of Casaubon's 'gap', his impotence and Dorothea's consequent frustration ('consequent' for George Eliot, although see Jennings in this volume for contemporary expectations of female behaviour). Is, though, the localised integration of metaphoric cohesion required here really useful in developing skills by which students will be able, from their world-knowledge, to fill in the *implicit* gap in the text: the Victorian view of female sexuality, and the physiological consequences of geriatric impotence, however rigorously 'bottom-up' they work? Word-knowledge is not world-knowledge.

7.4.2   'As kill a king' . . .

Another problem sometimes adduced when considering cloze procedures in literature is that many teachers, of language or of literature, are unqualified to deal with literary cloze. Mackay thoughtfully but over-scrupulously argues (Mackay 1992, p. 204) that since we ourselves, as teachers, are often ourselves unable to guess an author's choice of word unless we ourselves have doctored the text, it is unfair to expect our students to do so. He then asks what seems to me the right question: 'Does it matter [as long as] what you produced was "acceptable" or "appropriate"?' but in answering allows himself to be browbeaten by Ted Hughes into believing that there are fairies at the bottom of the literary garden which are killed by our cloze scrutiny.

'Words which live [. . .] belong to several of the senses at once, as if each one had eyes, ears and tongue, or ears and fingers and a body to move with. It is this little goblin in a word which is its life and its poetry.' Connotations of one word collide with those of another, Hughes explains, and 'In bad poetry the words kill each other' (Mackay 1992, p. 205).

By allowing students to substitute one word for another, as long as its denotation is acceptable, with no respect for the 'goblin in a word', Mackay insists 'we are aiding and abetting the possibility of lexicide and increasing the probability of bad poetry. It is this aspect of literature that *users* of literature are often unaware of, simply because they are not *producers* of literature. By using literary texts in this way [. . .] we are, in our ignorance, effectively destroying the very quality that made us choose literature in the first place' – making the words play 'the language-game of giving information', i.e. denotation, referential prose. Coleridge makes the same point: 'Whatever lines can be translated into other words of the same language without diminution of their significance, either in sense of association or in any worthy feeling, are so far vicious in their diction' (Samuel Taylor Coleridge, *Biographia Literaria*).

This, however, is precisely the point. While the acceptance of literature as just another variety of discourse rightly causes unease among teachers of literature, literary cloze as close reading for critical analysis is an exciting interactivity which allows the student/reader to recognise and respect a goblin when s/he sees one, and sometimes create some of her/his own. It is for analysing the effect rather than guessing the meaning, and all the better if this comes sometimes from an unpredictable choice. (Too many surprises, however, can put the gap-filler in a 'heads the author wins, tails I lose' position, which soon discourages any real interaction or feeling of complicity; Mackay's chosen poem, Hughes's 'Slump Sundays', reaches a degree of abstraction which makes it an unlikely cloze contender anyway).

The following example is Carter and Long's much-quoted cloze of Wilfred Owen's 'Futility' (in Carter and Long 1987), with its now famous 'f. word':

> O what made f. sunbeams toil
> To break earth's sleep at all.

Now, the meteorological conditions obtain nowhere in the world which would make 'fatuous sunbeams' a normative, referential collocation, and no right-minded teacher would cloze the word for language-based vocabulary activities, unless 'fatuous' were being used by default, to evoke more predictable choices (a perverse, goblin-killing exercise). Nevertheless, as a final step (these are the last two lines of the poem) in the development of students' awareness of assonantal emphasis, alliterative patterning, general lexical gist, or content schemata, the goblin leaps out alive and kicking, accepted as 'the surprising word that is inevitable' by those who did not guess it, and with the gratification of its being co-created by those who did. From being users of literature we become *quasi* producers.

7.5   Practical examples

The practical examples which follow have all been used both on teacher-training courses, and with advanced students. The degree of difficulty was gauged specifically for teacher-training, to provide scaled-up examples of the comprehension difficulties involved in cloze for students. It is notoriously easy to underestimate cloze difficulty: how many teachers have not had the experience of leaving a prepared text to marinate for a day or so – here Mackay is quite right – only to find that they are then quite unable to retrieve the general sense, let alone the missing word?

All of my examples have at least one whole clause or sentence deleted. No statistics are available condoning or condemning this practice (tentatively advanced by Carter, in Carter and McCarthy eds. 1988, p. 178), but in the use of cloze for analysis of a literary text, whole-unit/sentence gapping allows a range of applications – guided composition, prediction, register-recreation, and a limited form of creative writing which glances at parody – which I have found no other circumscribed, controlled means of producing. The larger the chunk to be reproduced, the more sophisticated the activity involved and the wider the range of targetable points (whole similes, for example). Supplying one whole Jamesian sentence is felt on the pulse (and, indeed, the wrist) significantly more in qualitative terms than supplying the single word. The teacher is freer in this way, but so are the students: they see the next wave of text some way off without being immediately deluged by the next word, and, obviously, cohesion can be negotiated in a more relaxed way without the constraints of connectors, tense components, number, etc. Within the same sentence: freed of someone else's grammar, they can concentrate on style, register, and content.

7.5.1 Example 1

The first passage given below is taken from *Middlemarch* and comes early in the novel, when the young, lovely and idealistic Dorothea is engaged to the old, wart-nosed, egotistical scholar Casaubon. Its particular selling-point as a cloze exercise is in underpinning point-of-view and register shifts, and has been effectively used both as an unseen passage in a theoretical introduction to narratorial voice, and as part of a course on *Middlemarch*. (Cf. the cloze analysis of gender in *Middlemarch*, Carter and Long 1991, p. 194.) 'The Grange' is Dorothea's home, and 'the key to all mythologies' is Casaubon's life's work. As the first sentence is so long, I decided it was legitimate to cloze it. In this and all the following passages . .( ) . . denotes a one-word gap; where a clause or sentence is missing the dotted line is correspondingly longer, for visual and psychological effect.

> Mr. Casaubon, as might be expected, spent a great deal of time at the Grange in these weeks, and the . .(1). . which courtship occasioned in the progress of his great work – the key to all mythologies – . .(2). . made him look forward the more eagerly to the . .(3). . termination of courtship. But he had deliberately incurred the hindrance, having made up his mind that it was now time to adorn

his life with the graces of female companionship, to ..(4).. the gloom which fatigue was apt to hang over the intervals of studious labour with ..(5).., and to secure in this, his culminating age, the solace of female .. (6).. for his declining years. ..(7).. he decided to abandon himself to the stream of feeling, and perhaps was surprised to ..(8).. what an exceedingly ..(9).. rill it was. As in droughty regions baptism by immersion could only be performed symbolically, so Mr. Casaubon found that a sprinkling was the utmost approach to a plunge which his ..(10).. would afford him; and he concluded that ..(11)...

  (1) delay / hindrance / postponement / retarding
  (2) soon / gradually / naturally / quickly
  (3) ?
  (4) lighten / illuminate / gladden / irradiate
  (5) the play of female fancy / the pleasure of female company / the assistance of an intelligent woman / rest and pleasant company
  (6) company / companionship / tendance / assistance
  (7) ?
  (8) ?
  (9) inadequate / dangerous / deep / shallow
(10) stream / feelings / age / marriage
(11) ?

Answers

[(1) hindrance (2) naturally (3) happy (4) irradiate (5) the play of female fancy (6) tendance (7) Hence (8) find (9) shallow (10) stream (11) the poets have much exaggerated the force of masculine passion.]

Gap ploy

The free choices, given the complexity of the passage, should be kept as simple as possible. The job of the gaps is to draw attention to the shifts from omniscient narration ('Mr. Casaubon, as might be expected . . .'), which moves to omniscience with proleptic borrowings from Casaubon's register and content schemata (who but Casaubon would consider an engagement to a luscious young girl 'a hindrance', and be looking forward eagerly to his wedding night so that he could get on with the job in hand, his research?), then on to almost free indirect speech ('the solace of female tendance . . .' is straight from Casaubon's mouth and mentality). We watch Casaubon wading ever deeper into the Latinate pomposities of his own prose until he has confessed to us (a) that he wants, not a wife, but a nurse (which the choice of 'companionship' at (6) would completely destroy); (b) that, eager as he is to be back at his books, he has something of the voyeur's fascination with pretty young girls (few students have failed to comment on the strange 'play of female fancy' phrase), and (c) that he will fail to deliver the goods 'Hence he determined to abandon himself ...' Is surely his register, with its clichéd 'stream of feeling'; the narrator then promptly caps it, ushered in by 'and perhaps', taking his stream metaphor and, as it were, drowning him in it, superimposing vehicle and tenor with extraordinarily graphic and unvictorian force. Casaubon stands condemned by his own words: a male chauvinist pig, and impotent to boot.

Gaps (4), (5) and (6) require specific register-choices; (9) and (10) an understanding of the water metaphor and point-of-view. This metaphor is the major image associated with Casaubon throughout the novel, as students studying it should be encouraged to discuss as spin-off: cf. 'the cloudy, damp despondency of uneasy egoism' (Chapter 21); '[his soul] went on fluttering in the swampy ground where it was hatched' (Chapter 29), etc.. By the final whole-sentence gap some students are able to convey something of his register with either a token Latinism or syntactic complexity, and most produce something which tallies with his content schemata, female students generally wreaking some form of feminist revenge on him. If the students' level of production is considered inadequate, choices such as the following might be provided (the alternatives should, as far as possible, reinforce the points of style under view, or extend lexical chains: mere 'blanks' to be read through and discarded are a waste of time): (a) Dorothea was clearly unable to draw out his finer feelings; (b) the poets have much exaggerated the force of masculine passion; (c) the physical labours of a protracted courtship were proving too much for his fragile scholar's frame; (d) Mr. Casaubon's inadequacy clearly necessitated his seeking medical advice.

The 'right' answer is unimportant – the choice between (b) and (c) often proves difficult, the only 'clue' to the original being the word 'masculine' counterposed to the repetition of 'female' in the passage, although it has sometimes been observed that 'his scholar's ... etc.' indicates a detachment from the speaker which is more than free indirect speech (arguable). 'Mr. Casaubon', in (d), however, most definitely reintroduces an omniscient narrator at unproductive odds with 'and he concluded', making this a 'wrong' answer.

7.5.2   Example 2

The next passage is from the middle section, 'Time Passes', of Virginia Woolf's *To the Lighthouse*, the 'corridor' joining 'two blocks', Sections One and Three, as her notes describe it, or the darkness between two flashes of the lighthouse beam, as critics have more fancifully analysed it. Students should be reminded (or told) that the whole section describes the ravages of time on the Ramsays' holiday home and its former inhabitants, whose deaths – in war (relevance to 'poppies' could be elicited), childbirth (possibly relevant to the negative mating of the carnation and cabbage) and from illness – are all flashed telegraphically on the page in between square brackets, almost as interpolations. Mrs McNab is the only human presence; otherwise the animal, the abstract, and the absent become the protagonists. A brief discussion of the stages of decay in abandoned houses, and some related vocabulary, may be considered useful.

The second passage is the manuscript version,[2] which I find it less distracting to present once the cloze has been completed, although presenting it simultaneously gives a leg-up to less linguistically competent students without invalidating the gap-filling. Fascinating in its own right, like almost all manuscript versions of creative writing, it shows the writer's mind in action, the various stages in capturing meaning, or deciding which to capture from the 'open text' which is still being written – a sort of cloze procedure itself. Students always find manuscript choices immensely exciting and almost illicit (particularly when the author can't spell 'chintzes'), like spying on an actor before s/he's ready for the stage. This readily converts into complicity, and to have a hand in the writing of *To the Lighthouse* mostly proves very gratifying.

> What power could now prevent the fertility, the insensibility of nature? Mrs McNab's dream of a lady, of a child, of a . . (1) . . of milk soup? It had . . (2) . . over the walls like a spot of sunlight and vanished. She had . . (3) . . the door; she had gone. It was beyond the strength of one woman, she . . (4) . . . They never sent. They never wrote. There were things up there . . (5) . . in the drawers – it was a shame to leave them so, she said. The place was gone to rack and

ruin. Only the Lighthouse beam entered the rooms for a moment, sent its sudden . .(6). . over bed and wall in the darkness of winter, looked with equanimity at the thistle and the swallow, the rat and the . .(7). .. Nothing now withstood them; nothing said . .(8). . to them. Let the wind blow; let the poppy seed itself and the carnation mate with the . .(9). . . Let the swallow build in the . .(10). ., and the thistle thrust aside the tiles, and the butterfly . .(11). . Let the broken . .(12). . and the china lie out on the . .(13). . and be tangled over with grass and wild berries.

   (1) ?
   (2) wavered / wandered / flickered / danced
   (3) ?
   (4) ?
   (5) rotting / spoiling / lying / forgotten
   (6) scrutiny / stare / ray / glance
   (7) dust / mouse / straw / cat
   (8) ?
   (9) rose / dandelions / weeds / cabbage
 (10) eaves / drawing-room / trees / kitchen
 (11) ?
 (12) bottles / glass / mirrors / furniture
 (13) grass / lawn / patio / path

Answers

[(1) plate (2) wavered (3) locked (4) sand (5) rotting (6) stare (7) straw (8) no (9) cabbage (10) drawing-room (11) sun itself on the faded chintz of the arm-chairs (12) glass (13) lawn]

Manuscript version

         could prevail   the
What power against ~~all this~~ fertility & insensibility
of nature? Old Maggie's dream, her dim telescope vision of a
lady in a ~~grey cloak~~ stooping over her flowers? ~~had~~
flickering about the bedroom for a moment, but vanished.
~~watchers & preachers~~, Though the lighthouse came & went again,
the sudden scrutiny – its long look & then, sharply following,
its two quick glances, ~~met nothing in that~~
seemed perfectly satisfied with what they saw.
As for the watchers, the preachers, ~~the souls who who~~
had those spirits who, in sleep, had left their bodies, & dreamed
of some communion, of grasping the hand of a sharer, &
completing, down on the beach, ~~the~~ from the sky or sea

the cliff, ~~or the~~ the ~~fu~~ fullness that was incomplete, the
vision that asked for ratification, either they had been
woken from their dreams by that prodigious cannonading which
had made the wine glasses tinkle in the cupboard, or
that intrusion – that black snout – that purple foaming stain –
had so gravely ~~interfered~~ damaged the composition of the picture
that ~~w~~ they had fled. They had gone in despair. They had
. dashed the mirror to the ground. They saw nothing more.
They stumbled & strove now, blindly, pulling their feet out of the
mud & stamping them further in. Let the wind blow, let the
poppy seed itself, & the carnation mate with the cabbage.
Let the swallow build ~~on the works of Shakespeare; & the~~
~~butterfly flaunt~~ in the drawing room, & the thistle thrust up the
   up
tiles, & the butterfly sun itself on the faded chinzy~~es~~ arm chairs.
~~Let the ch broken china be~~ & all ~~beaut~~ civilisation lie
~~like~~ broken china to be tangled over with ~~the~~
blackberries & grass.

Gap ploy

The first and third gaps are motivating 'stocking-fillers' – something concrete and guessable, although in (1) the (flat) plate and
(concave) dish or bowl expectations are inverted. (Virtually
unguessable, however, is the composition of 'milk soup', although
it contrasts with the family's rather more aristocratic fare of *Boeuf
en Daube* served at the Last Supper which ends Section One.)
Once 'wavered' (2) has been indicated as the author's choice (but
cf. the manuscript version), most students will come up with the
water-association, and some with the alliteration, part of the passage's patterning of alliterative pairings of words. 'Flickering' has
the same idea of hesitation, and sometimes students will prefer it,
with its 'flames' and consequent association with 'sunlight', at the
micro-level, and may prefer to retain it even when reminded that
water imagery is an important text-cohesive feature at macro-level.
'Danced' is clearly too energetic. (It is worth varying word-length
in such self-consciously literary prose as Woolf's – she most certainly has not been speaking prose all her life without knowing it –
to elicit comments about rhythm.)

The speech verb (4) is sometimes not guessed by non-native
speakers, although it recurs three sentences on, because the shift
in point-of-view from the narrator's 'literary' prose to Mrs

McNab's homely register ('beyond the strength . . .. They never sent . . . rack and ruin', this last a more demotic alliterative pairing) is subtle and only momentary, but as it is indicative of Woolf's predominant use of free-indirect-speech/stream-of-consciousness generally, it is worth foregrounding.

Three of the choices for (6) are Woolf's own manuscript doubts, and all three personify the Lighthouse (lower key in the manuscript). Personification is generally deduced from 'looked' (attention to the verb giving the slightly forced pretence for underlining the parataxis of this sentence) and elicited through the 'wrong' choice of 'ray'; however, I have seldom found consensus over 'stare', the triple 's' sometimes causing offence and being rejected, with the manuscript's blessing, in favour of 'glance' (alliteracide?). (7) is a more neutral gap, and although rats and straw have vaguely literary associations of abandon and emptiness, no serious lexicide can be perpetrated here. Paying the words 'the compliment of unusual scrutiny' however, as Leech puts it (Leech 1969, p. 4), underlines the animate/inanimate coupling, the thistle/straw similarities, and the fact that the thistle and swallow are introduced more actively in the next sentence. As harbingers of spring and thus the return to life after the death of winter, the swallow is also a prolepsis of the house's return to vitality in Section Three, although its role in the passage seems purely destructive; this can emerge in discussion spin-off. (9), (10), (11) and (13) are all more concrete and content-geared, and can be given without solutions: (9), an example of the 'brute confusion and wanton lust' in the vegetable kingdom mentioned some paragraphs earlier, generally proves too shocking for students to condone, for all the alliterative nudging and horticultural recognition that carnations and cabbages are at different ends of the same visual continuum, as it were. (This might involve a drawing.) (10), sandwiched between the swallow observed by the lighthouse beam (6) which had 'entered the rooms' and the thistle wreaking havoc with the tiles, should elicit the idea of a civilised *interior* (preferably drawing-room, with its marked social register, rather than the unmarked 'kitchen') violated by the natural world, underscoring the passage's close semantic cohesion and pointing towards possible solutions for the open sentence at (11). (13) again alliterates, and is important in representing domesticated nature, in opposition to 'insensib[le] nature' which will tangle it over. Choices at (12) divide equally among bottles, glass and

- mirrors (furniture is generally felt to be too big to be 'tangled over with grass'). The 'wrong' choices here are often for the right reasons: those familiar with the novel's imagery plump for 'mirror', others go for the alliteration of 'bottles'. Some appreciate the half-rhyme of 'glass' with 'grass', and comments can be elicited on the close identity of the two words as signifiers, a lexical re-enacting of the 'tangl[ing]' of civilisation and nature which the manuscript states specifically by demoting the china to simile.

7.5.3   Example 3

The last two passages are offered as representative raw material, and will be dealt with in less detail. The first, from Paul Theroux's *The Kingdom by the Sea* (1983) offers engaging subject-matter for prediction and discussion, and enjoyable follow-up activities. Extremely culture-specific, unless very adequate pre-reading information is given, its use is obviously limited to students with a knowledge of Britain, who are able to take part in the English-bashing. British students themselves are confronted by a fascinatingly defamiliarised world, and reactions are strong (reviews were famously furious). Information can be pooled by working in pairs. It exemplifies the content-biased 'list passage' which generally provides good cloze material, although more concerned with language competence than with critical.

> Once, from behind a closed door, I heard an English woman exclaim with real pleasure, 'They are *funny*, the Yanks!' And I crept away and laughed to think that an English person was saying such a thing. And I thought: 'They . .(1). . their ceilings! They put iittle knitted bobble-hats on their . .(2). . to keep them warm! They don't give you bags in supermarkets! . .(3). .! Their government makes them get a hundred dollar licence every year for watching television! They issue driving licences that are valid for thirty or forty years – mine expires in the year 2011! They charge you for matches when you buy cigarettes! They smoke on . .(4). .! They drive on the left! They spy for the . .(5). .! They say ". .(6). ." and "Jewboy" without flinching! They call their houses "Holmleigh" and "Sparrow View"! They sunbathe in their . .(7). .! They don't say "You're welcome"! They still have milk bottles and milkmen, and . .(8). .! They love candy and Lucozade and leftovers called bubble-and-squeak! They live in Barking and Dorking and . .(9). .! They have amazing names like Mr Eatwell and Lady Inkpen, and Major . .(10). . and Miss . .(11). .! And they think *we're* funny?'

Answers

[(1) wallpaper (2) soft-boiled eggs (3) They say sorry when you step on their toes! (4) buses (5) Russians (6) nigger (7) underwear (8) junk-dealers with horse-drawn waggons! (9) Shellow Bowels (10) Twaddle (11) Tosh]

Gapploy

Perhaps one gap-fill choice could be provided, e.g.:

(8)   kings and queens / policemen who tell you the time / junk-dealers with horse-drawn waggons / houses with no central heating in them

since anachronisms are difficult to invent and may not have been experienced, and inserting a positive referent like the 'policemen' measures students' reading of the degree of negativity in the passage, which can later be discussed under a choice of pointers: affectionate humour? humorous but serious criticism? ethnic satire? xenophobia? the inevitable incomprehension of those 'divided by a common language'? etc.

Answers are always an interesting reflection of students' ethnic expectations (embarrassment at (6) is sometimes avoided by a generically offensive 'rat' or 'pig'), and always provoke hilarity. Few suspect that the British sunbathe in their underwear, and opt for 'parks' or 'gardens'. Past answers I have been offered for (3) include:

they eat with their cats on the table;
they don't rinse dishes after washing up;
they never shower;
they don't have bidets;
they call babies 'it' and animals 's/he';
they sleep with their dogs.

Follow-up activities

1. Discuss the writer's points one by one. Discuss their oddness and explain the relevant practice in your own country. Which do you find most odd?
2. Decide which of the author's observations most surprises you, and which is most typical of his expectations as an American visitor.

3. Discuss with a partner your own national characteristics which foreign visitors may find odd, and write a paragraph beginning 'They are funny, the . . .!'

7.5.4   *Example 4*

Finally, here is the beginning of Anthony Burgess's *Earthly Powers* (1980), one of fiction's most arresting openings as the narrator metatextually informs us. Clearly it makes demands on the reader's knowledge of lexis and the world, and has to be targeted accordingly. Its semantic cohesion is as tightly organised as a crossword puzzle, and demands some analeptic and proleptic zapping. Exceptionally, I have gapped the first sentence: its content is highly enjoyable for advanced students to reconstruct, and all the information needed is repeated in the passage.

> It was the afternoon of my eighty-first birthday, and I . .(1). ..
> 'Very good, Ali', I quavered in Spanish through the closed door of the master bedroom. 'Take him into the bar. Give him a . .(2). .'
> '*Hay dos. Su capellán también.*'
> 'Very good, Ali. Give his chaplain a drink also.'
> I retired twelve years ago from the profession of . .(3). . . Nevertheless you will be constrained to consider, if you know my world at all and take the trouble now to reread that first sentence, that I have lost none of my old cunning in the contrivance of what is known as an arresting opening. But there is really nothing of contrivance about it. Actuality sometimes plays into the hands of art. That I was eighty-one I could hardly doubt: . .(4). . cables had been rubbing it in all through the forenoon. Geoffrey, who was already pulling . .(5). . his over-tight summer slacks, was, I supposed, my Ganymede or . .(6). . lover as well as my secretary. The Spanish word *arzobispo* certainly means archbishop. The time was something after four o'clock on a Maltese June day, the . .(7). ., to be exact and to spare the truly interested the trouble of consulting *Who's Who.*
> Geoffrey sweated too much and was . .(8). . to fat (why does one say . .(9). .? Geoffrey never ran.) The living, I supposed, was too easy for a boy of . .(10). . . Well, the time for our separation could not, in the nature of things, be much longer delayed. Geoffrey would not be pleased when he attended the reading of my . .(11). . . 'The old . .(12). ., my dear, and after all I did for him.'

Answers

[(1) was in bed with my catamite when Ali announced that the arch-
bishop had come to see me. (2) drink (3) novelist (4)
congratulatory (5) on (6) male (7) twenty-third (8) running (9)
running (10) thirty-five (11) will (12) bitch]

Gapploy

Impossible as it seems for the gap-filler at (1) to catch anything
like the various deviancies of the original, the fact that this is the
novel's opening sentence means that no anaphoric reference can
exist in the ensuing passage which is not stated in this gap, so that
all surprising facts need only be sifted and transferred back into
this opening statement. The reader has 'simply' to reconstruct the
'actuality' from the writer-narrator's deconstruction of the 'art'
with which he constructed his first sentence. Then reading is not,
as Jonathan Culler has remarked, 'an innocent activity' (Culler
1975, p. 119): the word 'Ganymede', unusual enough to fore-
ground itself even without the clozed definition which follows
('my Ganymede or . . . lover'), and Geoffrey's antics with his over-
tight trousers in the 'master bedroom', whether they're to be
pulled 'up' or 'on', soon confirm for most readers the actual state
of affairs: few have our hero innocently sitting sipping tea.
'*Arzobispo*' is similarly foregrounded as a foreign signifier, and
clearly has to play its part in the 'arresting opening'; he is sometimes inserted into the bed in Geoffrey's place, but the presence
of 'his chaplain' generally discourages this ecclesiastical hanky-
panky. Ali presents no problem, being clearly his interlocutor;
even the word 'catamite' has sometimes been guessed, as the
degree of language awareness in the passage sends readers to their
dictionaries of synonyms to match like register with like.
Ganymede's age is a tease, and many readers decide on 'young'
lover (6), given mythological precedent and the description of
him as a 'boy'; the revelation that he is thirty-five (early middle
age actually being deducible from his 'running to fat') gives a
touch of humour, and makes the protagonist seem both older and
more malicious: Geoffrey is no spring chicken, and to be left with
nothing may be serious for him. Thus the novel's main protagonist begins his fictive life with his moral credibility undermined,
and the reader's interest is projected forwards for confirmation.
Any stirrings of readerly indignation can be vented at the deleted

expletive of (12). (The sexism of the original is generally a surprise.)

(7) may seem an odd choice of gap – the time more usefully reveals text cohesion, and can be inferred from the opening words of the passage. There is the possibility that the date will prove retrospectively important (is Geoffrey going to murder 'the old bitch', and be obliged to provide a strict alibi for the twenty-third? Is the fact that the twenty-third is the first day of summer in England, though not Malta, in any perverse way relevant?), but for the moment it seems totally arbitrary, not a goblin in sight. It is precisely this, though, which is found attractive: the chance of meddling with the *fabula*, the raw facts. Nothing is gained at the level of linguistic or literary insight, but there is a very hands-on sense of co-authorship.

7.6   Conclusions

Whatever doubts surround cloze in language testing, and literary cloze in language teaching, those using cloze in literature teaching can probably rest assured that they are doing something towards developing critical competence in their students while involving them in creative language production. Lexicide is instrumental in this, creating dead matter – standard, referential language – off which the goblins feed. Few of us are Ted Hugheses or George Eliots; most of us can provide a subject-adequate core language to fill their gaps, and virtually all of us (and our students on literature courses) are able to recognise where they succeed and we have failed to recreate a dynamic equivalence.

Whole-sentence cloze, by requiring the active production of a complete unit of the original's syntax, sense and register without the crossword-puzzle type restrictions of single-word gaps, increases the possibility of both inadequacy and, occasionally, adequacy. Competent students enjoy trying their hand at passable imitations after careful appraisal of word- and clause-length, and the less competent are able to see the contrast in their own simpler versions often at even a purely visual, typographic level, the sudden thinning out of the words on the page. For many of us, George-Eliot-by-numbers is the nearest we will ever get to creative writing, and for this reason alone is worth considering. The points made by a cloze reading could all be elicited by questions and straight input, but cloze is also writing. Embodying the author's choice by default is an exercise of considerably greater complexity, and very involving; it is also the students' own 'experience which is being [. . .] articulated, and they are not merely passive recipients of an account of someone else's encounter with the text,' as Rossiter puts it (Rossiter 1991). The simultaneity of someone else's meaning evolving before our eyes, under our pen, is exciting, and the greater the gap between our expectations and the text's fulfilment of them – the larger the goblin we kill – the greater is our surprised appreciation of the original, and our realisation that a piece of literature 'contains in itself the reason it is so and not otherwise' (Coleridge, *Biographia Literaria*). Our gap-fillers' 'otherwise' is an object-lesson in the specificity of literary language and how it manages to 'make things unfamiliar, [. . .] to make the stone stony', as Shklovsky famously puts it (Shklovsky, in Lodge 1977, p. 13), or 'unlocks the world' (Lecercle 1993). If the stone is sometimes destoned again, if Virginia Woolf's beam flickers instead of wavering, and Burgess's hero has to do without his catamite and settle for something linguistically less, our appreciation of the text will be none the worse for it.

Notes

1. I would like to draw attention to the following words by Gérard Genette (quoted in Culler 1975, p. 161): 'If one takes a piece of banal journalistic prose and sets it down on a page, surrounded by intimidating margins of silence, the words remain the same but their effects for readers are substantially altered.'

2. The manuscript version of the passage from Virginia Woolf's *To the Lighthouse* is taken from Susan Dick (ed.) 1982 *To the Lighthouse: the original holograph draft*, University of Toronto Press.

8

Learner autonomy and literature teaching

BARBARA SINCLAIR

This paper[1] explores the notion of learner autonomy and attempts to explain its relevance for literature teaching. It then provides a broad overview of techniques that may be used to promote learner autonomy with regard to reading literature. This overview is by no means intended to be exhaustive, but rather a guide for teachers wishing to take this aspect of teaching more systematically into consideration.

Barbara Sinclair begins by pointing out that learner autonomy is unpredictable and may be seen as disruptive to learning in the classroom. However, she argues, the use of representational materials such as literary texts demands individual responses, with some guidance from the teacher in the development of learners' capacities to discover strategies for their own learning.

Varieties of preparation and training are discussed, through which teachers can instil independence and confidence into their literature students, in a kind of two-way process, where the small 'l' approach fosters autonomy which itself leads to the development of personal responses to and enjoyment of literature.

8.1   Introduction

This article has, perhaps, a different focus from the others in this volume in that it looks at the teaching of literature (with a small 'l', McRae 1991) from the point of view of the promotion of learner autonomy. It will explore the notion of learner autonomy and then consider its relevance for literature teaching. It will then provide a broad overview of techniques that may be used to promote learner autonomy with regard to reading literature. This overview is by no means intended to be exhaustive, but rather a guide for teachers wishing to take this aspect of teaching more systematically into consideration.

I would like to start by presenting a sad but true anecdote: a student at university in Britain in the early 70s learning the Russian language (*ab initio*) attended Russian literature classes. She had chosen to study Russian because she loved the sound of the language, was entranced by popular images of the then Soviet Union, as portrayed by the film *Dr. Zhivago* and romantic Soviet films seen on TV, and wanted the challenge of a 'difficult' language. One term the class was obliged to study a novella by the Soviet writer, Sholokov. They were required to 'prepare' three to four pages of the story each week for the class. During the session, the lecturer would nominate one of them to read a paragraph or two aloud and then to translate it into English. After this, he might ask a question on the content of the story. They never knew, of course, who would have to read next, and so were obliged to prepare all the four pages in great thoroughness. The problem was, the text was rather too advanced in terms of its language level for novice Russian learners such as this group. The weekly preparation took the student hours of work with a Russian/English dictionary, checking almost every other word and then writing the translation, very faintly in pencil, above the text in the book. It was arduous. She did not dare leave any word unchecked, even if she thought she knew it, just in case she got it wrong in class. After two weeks of this, a strange thing happened; the student became so interested in the story, which was of a soldier and his tragic life, that she wanted to read the novella right through to the end as quickly as possible. She worked for hours through the night until she had read the last page, at which point she dissolved in tears, as much from the effort as from emotional response to the story. She thought it was wonderful! She was moved. She wanted to read more of this author. Unfortunately, her enthusiasm and impatience to read the story meant that she was less thorough than usual in pencilling in the translation. When she was called upon to read and translate in class the following week, there were some words whose meanings she could not recall and she was castigated thoroughly. The student explained that she had worked more hastily than usual because she had been eager to read *all* of the story, but the lecturer was not impressed. Worse still, when he noticed her pencillings in the book, she was held up to her classmates as the very model of a bad student.

Here was a lecturer whose objectives in getting his students to read this story were focused on consolidating and expanding their limited knowledge of Russian vocabulary and grammar, and on improving their pronunciation, stress and rhythm by reading aloud. Not only were this student's personal strategies for dealing with the text disapproved of, but also her autonomous decision to read the story to the end and to appreciate it in her own way.

8.1.1   Learner autonomy

Sadly, learner autonomy is disapproved of by many teachers. Such teachers often equate autonomy with lack of control and, possibly, chaos in the classroom. They may fear that allowing students autonomy will demand resources or knowledge from them that they do not have. While these fears may be real enough, they may also be founded on an inadequate understanding of the term 'learner autonomy' which proposes that, to be autonomous, a learner must decide for him/herself *what* to learn, and also *why, when, how, with whom* and *for how long* he/she should do it. This definition provides an absolute view which focuses on actual learner behaviour. Holec (1981) provides us with the more useful view that 'learner autonomy' is about *potential* learner behaviour, i.e. the *capacity* or *ability* to learn independently. Indeed, complete autonomy is an unlikely ideal; we live in a society in which what we do affects others and in which we are constrained by others. At different times in our lives and learning careers we operate at different levels of autonomy for different reasons, depending on a variety of factors, including how we feel at the time. We may, indeed, choose to be dependent. One language learner may well operate generally at a high level of autonomy when choosing texts to read outside the class in his/her own language, for example, but tend to be completely dependent on the teacher for direction while inside the class. Another learner may show great initiative in class on one day and none at all the next. It is important to recognise that learners' levels of autonomy are variable and that each learner is different from the next.

8.1.2   Learner autonomy and literature teaching

How is the above view of learner autonomy relevant to literature teaching? For one thing, the very nature of reading representational materials implies a focus on the individual reader by demanding that reader's response and personal interaction with the text. 'Representational material opens up, calls upon, stimulates and uses areas of the mind, from imagination to emotion, from pleasure to pain' (McRae 1991, p. 3). Using such materials in the classroom can promote the development of the individual as a whole person, providing access to new and different experiences, feelings, desires and creative impulses. This focus on the whole person means that teachers must recognise and accept their learners' individual differences with respect to their personal interpretations, responses, preferences, needs, wants and goals. Rather than ignore these, teachers need to help learners develop, be aware of, understand and articulate them.

To recognise that any group of students contains a wide range of individual differences implies two things: firstly, that such differences result in differing paths of development and, secondly, that one teacher cannot be expected to direct all such differing paths in his/her teaching. It follows then, that teachers have to be aware of the need for a balance in their teaching between helping individuals develop, on one hand, their personal and intellectual potential and, on the other, the capacity to be more responsible for their own development, i.e. to become more self-directed. Literature teaching offers an ideal context for such educational goals.

The issue of whether and how to promote learner autonomy has been the subject of debate for centuries. Educationalists have long argued against an education system which fosters passivity and dependency, rather than independence and motivation to learn. As Bruner (1966, p. 58) says, 'Instruction is a provisional state that has as its object to make the learner or problem-solver self-sufficient. Otherwise, the result of instruction is to create a form of mastery that is contingent upon the perpetual presence of a teacher.' Confucius (551–479 BC) puts the issue most succinctly in his famous saying, 'If you give a man a fish, you feed him for a day. If you teach a man to fish, you feed him for a lifetime.'

When teaching literature, whether with a small or large 'l', the teacher's ultimate aim is, presumably, to develop in the students the ability to read and understand the meanings embedded in the language and contexts of a wide number of text types, and to encourage in them an interest in reading English which will motivate them to choose and read texts independently, with understanding and enjoyment. Further, the teacher may be concerned with developing a faculty for critical reading (see Wallace 1992). Whether concerned with text-based techniques or fostering a 'lifelong love of English literature', the implication is clear; the teacher's role is not to impose total autonomy on the learners, which they may not expect, desire or be ready to accept, but to help them gradually develop the *capacity* for selecting English texts according to their own preferences and interests, as well as dealing with and understanding the language, discourse, style, form and contexts of these texts. In other words, it is part of the teacher's role to enable learners to be in a better position to take on more responsibility for their own learning. As Holec (1981) has suggested, 'For the time being, therefore, there is no question of wishing to force the learner to assume responsibility for his learning at all costs, and there probably never will be; what must be developed is the learner's ability to assume this responsibility.'

8.2   Learner training

It may be argued that literature teachers are, in fact, doing all of the above and, therefore, promoting learner autonomy without necessarily being aware of doing so. However, just 'doing' is probably not enough. Holec (*ibid.*) suggests that the capacity to be autonomous is not innate, but needs to be trained. The techniques and procedures for training learners to develop the capacity to be more autonomous in language learning have recently become known as 'learner training', which Ellis and Sinclair (1989a) define as follows: 'Learner training aims to help learners consider the factors which affect their learning and to discover personally suitable learning strategies so that they may become more effective learners and take on more responsibility for their own learning.'

Certainly, Ellis and Sinclair and others working in the field of learner training, such as Wenden and Rubin (1987), Wenden (1991), Oxford (1989), Willing (1989), Dickinson and Carver (1980), Dickinson (1987) have found that learners can benefit greatly from an explicit focus on 'learning to learn'. Dickinson and Carver (1980) suggest that learners need psychological and methodological preparation, as well as opportunities for self-direction in order to develop the capacity for autonomous learning.

8.2.1 Psychological preparation

Psychological preparation involves helping learners to make the leap from dependence to independence and to understand why it is useful. It also involves helping the learners to increase their self-confidence with regard to doing this. Such preparation is gradual and can take a long time. Initially, it might, for example, include discussion sessions in class where the learners consider the extent to which they act independently in different areas of their lives and how they feel about this. With school pupils the topic of parental control might be explored. There might then be sessions which focus more specifically on reading, such as discussing favourite topics for reading, favourite texts, etc. in the learners' own language and in English. Learners could discuss problems and phobias concerned with reading in English. The role of the teacher might be considered, and so on. These topics are all very general in nature, for autonomy is not only concerned with literature teaching. Nevertheless, such discussions can be a useful basis for developing autonomy in reading, as well. Indeed, they could involve a good deal of text-based work.

8.2.2 Methodological preparation and explicit training

Methodological preparation would include making sure that learners were familiar not only with the metalanguage used in reading literature which is appropriate to their level, e.g. 'headline', 'metaphor', 'genre', but also with the methodology used in the classroom for dealing with the texts. Learners need to understand *what* they are doing and *why*, and how this can be transferred to other texts. In other words, it is vital that the learner training should be *explicit*. Other writers in this volume have suggested many interesting and useful activities for dealing with texts. However, it is important that such activities are not carried out 'blindly' (Wenden 1986) so that learners are left in the dark as to why they are doing them. Once learners are aware of the importance of certain techniques and strategies, they can develop the capacity to apply them to different contexts and, thus, take more responsibility for their learning.

The notion of *explicit training* is crucial in the promotion of learner autonomy. Unfortunately, it is also the aspect most neglected by teachers. It can, however, be a relatively simple matter to include in one's teaching an explanation as to why the learners are doing a certain activity, to explain why it is useful and how what they learn from it can be applied to different texts or when they read alone. Many learners are so accustomed to following their teacher's directions that it does not occur to them to ask why. (In some cultures, of course, such questioning of the teacher would be positively discouraged and considered impolite. In cultures where the learners expect the teacher to be the fount of all wisdom, adding such explicit explanations to the teaching would not run counter to the learners' expectations, yet still be a useful way of empowering them to learn more independently.) Learners can be encouraged to ask questions if the teacher him/herself uses a questioning approach, e.g. 'Why do you think I asked you to do that?' 'How useful is this? Why?' Learners can also be encouraged to use new techniques on their own with different texts and to report back to the class on their usefulness.

8.2.3   Practice in self-direction

It follows that, if we are attempting to develop in our learners the capacity to learn independently, it is necessary to provide them with opportunities for self-direction. Such opportunities can be quite minimal at first, such as allowing students to choose who they work with, which text-related activity they do, or providing two or three texts for them to read and allowing them to choose which one they work on. Gradually, learners could be encouraged to bring in texts they have selected, choose books for the class library and decide on how they wish to respond to reading them.

A very common task imposed on learners by teachers concerned with developing 'extensive reading' is the 'report' they have to write after reading a book or reader. Obviously, the teacher requires some tangible evidence that the text has been read, but a more demotivating and unnatural post-reading task is hard to find. School students reluctantly write these because they know they will be graded, not because they enjoy doing them. It might be more useful to explore with the learners as many different ways of responding to a text as possible and encourage them to choose one particular way to experiment with and report back on. Some learners might prefer informal group discussions in which they talk about what they have read. Others might like to perform a scene from the story, hold a role-played interview with a character or the author, design a new cover, draw an illustration, keep a chart of gold star ratings, keep a 'response graph' to plot their reactions to different characters, chapters, part of the story, etc. (see Sevier 1991), hold a competition or debate to decide the best book and so on.

Teachers and learners need to discuss, too, the language to be used for such response activities. Is it really feasible or necessary for the students to do these in the target language? What advantages or disadvantages are there if they do not? Learners with a low level of English need to know how to select a text with a manageable level of language. The class could experiment with texts at different levels and draw up their own rule of thumb, such as, 'If there are more than six words on the first page you don't know, put the book back.' They need to know that it is not a matter of shame if they find a particular text too difficult for them. It is important, too, that learners should feel able to reject texts, and to say why.

8.2.4   Systematic training

Another important issue in learner training is that of systematicity. A survey of 65 teachers of English to German adults and French secondary school pupils conducted by Ellis and Sinclair (1989b) showed that, although these teachers were using certain learner-training techniques in their language classrooms, they did so in a generally unprincipled and unsystematic manner. Practitioners and researchers in the field of strategy training and learner training seem now to agree that the promotion of learner autonomy and learning to learn needs to be carried out in a systematic way in order for it to be of benefit to the learner. Before considering what might be meant by systematic learner training, however, we need to review what is meant by learning strategies.

8.3   Learning strategies

Researchers cannot seem to agree on the exact meaning of the term 'strategy'. However, a useful definition for our purposes is that of Rubin (1975, p. 43), who proposes that strategies are simply 'techniques or devices which a learner may use to acquire knowledge'. They are almost always purposeful and goal-oriented, but not always carried out at a conscious or deliberate level. Neither is there a consensus about the number and type of different strategies available to learners. (See O'Malley *et al.* 1985, Oxford 1989, Ellis and Sinclair 1989a, Wenden 1991, for suggested typologies of learner strategies.) Nevertheless, a useful distinction has been drawn between two major categories of learning strategies, which have been found to be significant for learner training in the language classroom.

Metacognitive strategies (also called 'Self-Management strategies' by Wenden) are those which involve thinking about learning, planning, evaluating and monitoring. Such strategies are general in that they may be applied to all kinds of learning, no matter what subject. Cognitive strategies are described by O'Malley *et al.* (1985) as those which involve actually manipulating the subject matter. These are different for different subject matters and tasks. For example, the cognitive strategies used by a learner learning to tap dance, such as feeling the rhythm, watching and copying the demonstrator, moving the feet in a certain way, etc. are different from those used by a learner involved in a language task, such as guessing the meaning of a new word by using clues from the context, practising spelling by writing down difficult words ten times each, etc. However, the metacognitive strategies of *planning* when to practise the new tap dance step or write down the words and then *evaluating* how well the task was performed are the same for both subjects.

Systematic learner training consists of activities and procedures which combine metacognitive with cognitive strategy training. As O'Malley *et al.* (*ibid.*) have noted, 'Students without metacognitive approaches are essentially learners without direction and ability to review their progress, accomplishments and future directions.' On the other hand, training learners in metacognitive strategies only is of limited use as it denies them the opportunity for active experimentation with their learning.

The model for systematic learner training proposed by Ellis and Sinclair (1989a) suggests an approach based on questions designed to stimulate reflection and experimentation by the learner. These questions may also be applied to the topic of literature teaching and may thus form the basis for learner training tasks and activities. (It is not suggested here that such questions are in any way new to literature teaching, but rather that they can be viewed as a sequenced and systematic learner training programme.)

Example 8.1   Learner training for literature

GENERAL QUESTIONS TO DEVELOP METACOGNITIVE LEARNING STRATEGIES

- – to promote introspection and self-awareness
- – to encourage exploitation of reading resources
- – to promote greater language awareness
- – to promote planning for individual reading

1   *Attitudes: how do you feel?*
How do you feel about reading in your own language? Why?
How do you feel about reading in English? Why?
What do you like to read in your own language?
What do you like to read in English?

2.   *Knowledge: what do you know?*
What do you know about reading in English?
What do you know about your English/literature syllabus?
What do you know about your set texts and writers?
What do you know about what is expected of you?

3.   *Self-assessment: how well are you doing?*
What have you read in English this week?
How much have you read in English?
How many different kinds of texts have you read in English this week?
How satisfied are you with your reading performance/understanding of what you have been reading? Why?

4.   *Goals: what do you want/need to do?*
What do you want/need to do to improve your reading in English?
What do you want to do to enjoy your reading in English more?
What do you need/want to do to have more opportunity to read English?
What is your reading plan for next week?

5.   *Strategies: how do you prefer to read?*
What do you like to read?
When do you like to read?
How long do you like to read for?
What conditions do you look for so you can read happily?

6.   *Organisation: how do you organise your reading?*
Where do you find things to read?
How do you organise your reading resources?
How do you keep record of what you have read?
Who do you talk to about what you've read?

Example 8.1 lists a number of questions which focus on developing metacognitive awareness. The sequence of these questions follows that of Ellis and Sinclair's model, and it is suggested that it is useful and appropriate to focus first on the learners' own feelings and attitudes. It is not envisaged that learners should be presented with all of these questions at the same time, but rather that different areas be tackled at different, appropriate stages during the learning period. Indeed, some of the questions, as they stand, imply a series of activities or further questions, e.g. Question 2, 'What do you know about reading in English?' might focus on reading strategies, such as skimming, scanning, etc., on recognising different genres, reading speed, the reading process, and so on.

Question 3: 'How well are you doing?' is vitally important. Self-assessment forms the crux of learner training, and learners should be encouraged to consider these questions on a regular basis. Teachers may wish to design questionnaires or feedback activities to encourage self-assessment, or, indeed, encourage the learners to formulate their own. Self-assessment, to be worthwhile, has to be followed by an appraisal of what needs to be done next, so question 4, 'What do you want/need to do?' encourages learners to plan short-term goals for themselves, based on the results of their self-assessment.

Question 5, 'How do you prefer to read?' encourages learners to consider their personal preferences, while Question 6, 'How do you organise your reading?' focuses on the exploitation of reading resources available to learners and encourages them to take on a more proactive role. All questions listed may lead to fruitful classroom discussion and further, related activities.

Figure 8.1 provides suggestions for tasks based on a specific text. These tasks together provide development in metacognitive and cognitive strategies. Again, each list may be extended into a number of activities for the classroom, but it is suggested that all of the major questions can be tackled during a learner training programme. It is, as already mentioned, vital that the learner training provided by such tasks be explicit, so that the learners are able to transfer the strategies they are practising to other texts and build up a repertoire of techniques and approaches which will help them when reading independently. For example, a text-based task under 'What do you know now?' might require the learner to guess or interpret the meanings of unfamiliar words or expressions. Here,

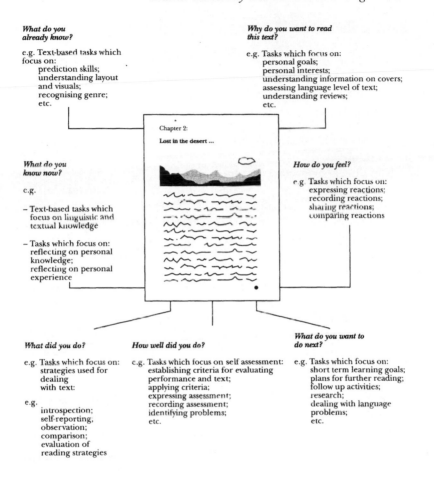

Figure 8.1 Questions to base tasks on, to develop metacognitive and cognitive strategies

the focus would be on using cognitive strategies to identify and make use of clues in the text, as well as learners' knowledge of the world, text genre, etc. A follow-up task under 'What did you do?' might ask the students to recall how they guessed these words and to discuss these strategies and compare them with those of fellow students. Here, the focus would be on developing meta-cognitive awareness. After considering these strategies in an explicit way in the classroom, learners should then be better placed to use them independently and confidently in their own reading.

8.4   Conclusion

To conclude, it is clear that many of the issues raised in this article are not new to literature teachers. The aim of this article, however, has been to explore the ways in which greater learner autonomy can be fostered through the teaching and learning of literature with a small 'l', and how, reciprocally, greater self-direction can help learners develop their personal responses to and enjoyment of literature.

It has been suggested that literature teaching provides an ideal context in which to develop not only the individual learner's intellectual potential, but also his/her capacity to take on more responsibility for his/her personal development. Further, it has suggested that a systematic programme of learner training can be provided through literature teaching which employs many of the techniques commonly used in such teaching, but which emphasises explicit training by the teacher and a self-questioning approach by the learner.

It is, of course, not possible in this article to describe in great detail the wide range of options available to the literature teacher concerned to promote learner autonomy. Nevertheless, it is hoped that some guidance has been provided which will stimulate such teachers to devise appropriate, explicit and systematic learner-training activities for their own students. Most of all, it is hoped that learners' acts of independence do not result in their being labelled 'bad students', as I once was.

Note

1. This paper first appeared in *GRETA: Revista para profesores de Inglés* **2**(2): 17–24, Granada 1994.

9

Making the subtle difference: literature and non-literature in the classroom

GUY COOK

Guy Cook engages in the debate as to where literature teaching might be going, and offers compelling reasons for the subject and for the values it might inculcate. He opens up discussion of the canon (which will be expanded in practical ways in the concluding article by Malachi Edwin Vethamani). Cook goes on to present some non-literary and some literary texts, bearing out the ideas already expressed by Carter and McRae, and leading to a closer examination of how artistic/literary merit may be judged. In particular he explores the varieties of language in modern media which are contrasted with the traditional approach to the study of English through the reading of books alone.

The second part of the paper moves to the practical level, with a selection of activities which confirm the earlier premises. Cook's selection of materials includes Blake and D.H. Lawrence with advertisements and popular fiction alongside them. The paper thus points forward to Mao Sihui's examination of 'culture' in the next contribution.

9.1 Language and influence

There is in Britain a continuing undercurrent of disagreement about the teaching of literature, which surfaces from time to time in bitter and strongly-worded debate. The debate is between those who defend, as the only source of texts for literary study, that set of classics referred to as *the canon*, and those who argue that many of the texts in this canon are irrelevant to contemporary students, who should rather busy themselves with learning to cope with the vast array of genres in the modern world: including such *non-literary* discourse as information leaflets, news bulletins, newspapers and casual conversations, as well as *sub-literary* genres such as 'pulp' romantic fiction, television soap operas and situation comedies, films, pop songs, graffiti and advertisements. The two sides in this debate are often quite wrongly associated with two political tendencies: advocates of the canon are associated with the right and its opponents with the left. Such a dichotomy is typical of the simplistic and unintelligent nature of party-political debate in contemporary Britain. In this paper I should like to argue for a more complex relationship between literature teaching which focuses upon the canon and literature teaching which looks outside it, and in conclusion to explore some classroom activities which might reconcile the two.

The banalities and posturing of political debate have infected pedagogic practice: extreme positions have been adopted and extreme practices indulged. As a secondary-school English teacher at the end of the 1970s, I was disturbed to meet a class of sixteen-year-old native-speaking English students who had completed their entire schooling in the subject 'English' without ever having read a poem; I was equally disturbed, when teaching a rowdy class of low-achieving fifth formers, to be visited by a school inspector who asked why my pupils could not distinguish anapests from iambs. Literature teaching, I believe, requires a subtler negotiation between tradition, the contemporary context, and the needs of students than either of these encounters suggests.

I shall assume for my purposes here that the majority of literature teachers are positioned somewhere between such extremes, and recognise that a discourse as subtle and complex as literature is unlikely to submit to the simplicities of a political 'either/or' resolution. I shall also assume that literature teachers (though they may disagree about the definition and nature of literature or about which particular texts are its best examples) share three premises. Firstly, they believe that there is such a thing as literature (fuzzy and indefinable as it may be); secondly, that it is something worthwhile; thirdly, that it is worth inculcating a knowledge and appreciation of it into others.

I have used the word 'inculcate' as more neutral than the word 'indoctrinate' which expresses disapproval of the methods used and of the values being passed on. Yet disapproval, when expressed by teachers, must surely be of *particular* values and *particular* methods, not of the act of passing on values itself, as this is integral to the very activity of education. For education (indeed all communication) is an attempt to change others – to interfere with them. The only alternative to this is silence, a *de facto* abandoning of the field to others. Inaction promotes the action of others and is thus a kind of action in itself. Someone will influence the young. There is therefore no way in which it is possible to be neutral in the literature-teaching debate. The issue is not one of *whether* teachers should inculcate value judgements into their pupils, but of *which* values those should be.

In the context of this opinion, the position I should like to argue in this paper is to some degree paradoxical. It is one which will allow the teacher to make a clear statement of his or her own values, making them available if the student wants them, while not trying to impose them by force (a tactic which, when applied to the young by teachers or to whole populations by governments, is thankfully likely to lead to the opposite outcome from that intended). It is an optimistic point of view, for it has faith in the assertion of value by each rising generation (even if the texts which they value are different from those valued by their elders) and recognises that each generation of teachers must relinquish to their students the task of selection and evaluation. A canon can be preserved only by popular acclaim. The sole alternative to this is the establishment of an elite whose judgements of such matters – what is valuable and what is not – are seen as intrinsically superior, an elite who promote (through the award of examination successes and jobs) only those who share their judgements. Thankfully, there is no need to preserve literary taste through the exercise of such power. Though the notion of 'literature' in its modern sense may be comparatively recent (see Williams 1983, p. 183), human beings from all times and places value some texts[1] above others for reasons other than their immediate usefulness. The reasons for this positive evaluation are perhaps not so dissimilar as cultural relativists would lead us to believe: dexterity with language, expressions of value and belief, insights into the human condition.

The argument I wish to develop, asserting the validity of a canon but allowing students to form their own judgements of what it should include, has an analogy in international politics. The closing of the borders around a country by its government leads usually to that government's downfall; the closing of the canon by the academic literary establishment may have a similar effect. Survival of both canon and state need immigration and emigration, free travel, the conversion of currency, the creation of alliances and trade communities. The longer-lasting regimes are open ones whose values, though allowed to change, are repeatedly chosen and re-chosen by their populations, as the literary canon can be chosen and re-chosen by its readers. And, if the analogy holds, one might add that people are frequently fondest of their native country when they are away from it.[2] Pursuing this analogy, what I am advocating is allowing the citizens of literature classes a trip abroad in the belief (perhaps mistaken) that most will return. What this means in practice is a syllabus which is a mixture: a mixture of canonised literary works with the non-literary or the sub-literary. There will inevitably be some intermarriages and off-spring of mixed parenthood, some change of citizenship too – with some of which the teacher will inevitably disagree. But the overall situation is a good one: active, and stimulating the kind of atmosphere in which literature and literary appreciation can thrive.

The strategy of mixing the literary, the non-literary and the sub-literary has the advantage of deterring the idea implicit in many literature courses that literature is a use of language somehow unaffected by the staggering technological changes in the uses of language which have taken place this century. (The details and timing vary from place to place, but the technological revolution has affected almost all societies to a greater or lesser extent.) Just as the nature of language was fundamentally altered by the advent of writing and print, so over the last century or so our relationship to language has also changed under the impact of a series of new technologies (photograph, telephone, tape recorder, radio, film, television, video, computer) which, while not usurping (so far) the dominant use and status of print, have nevertheless altered the nature of our relationship to it. As literature is a discourse whose mode is writing or print (the very word derives from the Latin *littera*, a letter of the alphabet), this change cannot but affect our relationship to literature too. This has happened, I believe, in one of two ways.

Firstly (most obviously but ultimately least significantly) there are ways in which these technologies have usurped some of the uses of print. For a reason about which no satisfactory theory has ever been advanced, people seem universally to take delight in, or even need, the narration of fictional events (Beaugrande 1987). This need, fulfilled so often in print, has in many people's lives been taken over (in whole or part) by radio, television, video and film, in all of which media an extraordinary high proportion of time is given over to the depiction of fictional events. On one weekday evening selected at random, for example, I estimate 42% of all television broadcasting on the four British terrestrial channels between 5.30 pm and 1.00 am to be taken up by fiction.[3]

Secondly, since the widespread availability of the computer, the nature of our experience of the written word is altered, not so much because new technologies replace the use of print but because they make its dissemination both easier and faster. (In this sense their effect on a literate culture is more comparable to the replacement of hand-writing by print than to the addition of writing to speech.) It is often forgotten, in the discussion of a 'computer culture', and the expression of fears for its detrimental effect on literacy, that the most widespread uses of computers involve writing. Computers bring us more written language rather than less; but their effect on our experiences of those written words may nevertheless be large. Word processing a manuscript is a very different linguistic activity from writing it by hand or typing. The ease of correction and redrafting adduces quite different creative processes (not always with better results); electronic mail and computer networking, though written, encourage an on-line interactivity quite unlike that in a time-consuming exchange of letters; desk-top publishing, by making print runs both cheaper and faster, leads to an increase in numbers of publications (not necessarily a desirable outcome, as works of quality may become lost in an increase in quantity). These are changes in the *production* of writing. On the side of *reception*, the existence of the book as a physical object, so integral to many people's experience of literature, may be continuously eroded. Texts may be handled more and more on screen; the libraries of the future will allow the retrieval of reading matter on a screen as friendly to the eyes as a page of print.

What effect should this new environment have upon the teaching of literature? Clearly it should have some effect. The worst response possible would be to continue as though nothing had happened, as though books were a unique means of disseminating linguistic art. The increased quantity of print made possible by new technology entails a greater need for selectivity by the individual. One of the most important skills for the contemporary language and literature student is to know what *not* to read. In a chirographic culture only the most valued texts are copied; in a print culture the range widens (hence the novel, which in its early

days was criticised as a frivolous genre unworthy of publication
(Watt 1963, pp. 36–61)); but a society with today's technology
inevitably prints material of ephemeral interest or of no interest at
all. Direct mail advertising is the most obvious example: an estim-
ated one and a half billion items are delivered annually in Britain,
and around 5 billion in the USA (Cook 1992, p. 199). In such a
society, an individual who cannot rapidly decide what is *not* worth
reading will be paralysed, unable to get beyond the front door
or down the street. Helping students to develop techniques of
eliminative evaluation is essential.[4]

The changes in our communicative environment, however, are
not only quantitative. They are also qualitative. The new media of
the twentieth century have not only added to the quantity of
written text, but also usurped some of its functions. Let us suppose
that – in a print culture without television, sound recording or
film – a literary text had the following qualities: it was highly-
valued; it had no ostensible utilitarian function; it was a text to
which people resorted in their leisure time; it was a text which
readers often re-processed with consequent knowledge of detail
enabling reference, quotation and even recitation. Such values
and well-known texts (like myths and prayers) become a point of
reference: 'this person is like Mr Micawber'; 'this behaviour is like
that in a Jane Austen novel'; 'this language is Miltonic' and so on.
I have said only 'let us suppose' that these were the characteristics
of the literary text in the past, for the picture I am painting has an
important flaw. It characterises the relationship of the reading
public to texts which, though they are *now* regarded as literary,
were not necessarily so regarded in their own time. This may be,
in the case of older texts, because they predate the modern con-
ception of 'literature' altogether or because, though dating from a
later time when there was a literary canon of vernacular prose,
drama and poetry, they were, although popular – indeed *because*
they were popular – excluded from it. Even such literary monu-
ments as Chaucer's *Canterbury Tales*, Shakespeare's plays and the
eighteenth-century English novel, were conceivably closer in
status for their contemporaries to the television soap opera and
the latest box-office movie than to literary classics. For literary
innovation is always one step ahead of the canon and the literature syllabus (which are often virtually identical). New classics
appear through a process referred to by the Russian formalists as
'the canonisation of the junior branch': the elevation by one

generation of particular works or entire genres which for an earlier generation were considered lowly (Eikhenbaum [1927] 1978, p. 32). The texts and genres of the junior branch – being outcasts with no responsibilities – are free from the constraints of noble lineage and can borrow and steal and abuse and mix; it is this which gives them vitality and creativity. Chaucer's vernacular verse, Shakespeare's theatre, the novel, the lyric poem were all once regarded as junior branches, as, closer to our own time, was the cinema film, once despised, but now indisputably recognised as an art form (Cook 1994, p. 134). The active critic and student should surely be on the constant look-out for the next bastard in line for promotion. Not every junior branch is worth later canonisation, but it may be instructive to wonder what today's candidates might be: the soap opera, the pop song, the advertisement? And if so, which particular ones. For if such genres may provide works of artistic merit this is not to say that any more than a handful of instances will be regarded in this way. In the same way, the majority of poems are hardly worth attention. The activity of assessing the artistic merit of examples of the junior branches has a particular pedagogic merit. As there are no established judgements of works outside the canon, students are left on their own, unprotected by the judgements of others.

The delayed nature of literary canonisation produces a double standard among many students and teachers. For many people, television has usurped the role of the book as the primary source of fiction and relaxation. When they become literature students, they are forced back into the earlier pre-television culture, which has never ceased to exist, but continues almost as a 'residual culture' (Williams 1977, p. 17) alongside the new one. In such a situation it is inevitable that many students and teachers will lead a double life *vis-à-vis* the standards of these two co-existing cultures. When it comes to a body of texts used for relaxation, for language play, for immersion in a fictional world, for pleasure, even for social and psychological insight, many literature students and teachers turn (at least some of the time) to the soap opera, the television comedy, the video film, the pop song, the magazine story. Though we profess greater allegiance to the texts of the literary canon, these can easily become part of the world of hard work and serious study: something *from* which rather than *with* which we relax. This leads to a paradox with which many teachers are familiar: the modern literature student, while professing honestly the greater worth of poetry, novel and drama, has a more thorough knowledge, a more accurate remembrance of the song and jingle, the romance and the soap opera. A further contradiction is that these newer, 'lower' genres are often recalled with more pleasure and accuracy than the supposedly 'higher' genres of the literary canon, while the attachment which this pleasure and knowledge would seem to indicate is simultaneously denied. The junior branches are viewed as lesser, trivial genres, something for the end of a hard day.

I am not suggesting that there is anything wrong with such double standards. On the contrary, single standards are perhaps both unusual and uninteresting. The conflict which arises when the two value systems are brought into contact is fertile and dynamic. Both Dr Jekyll and Mr Hyde as individuals are uninteresting – it is their irreconcilable but simultaneous presence within one body which intrigues. Students and teachers seem to alternate between one world of artistic values and another. Perhaps there is something to be gained from precipitating a clash. One way of doing this is to study works from the canon alongside texts from the technological profusion to which I have referred above.

9.2 Activities

The following are some suggestions for implementing the comparative study of literary and sub-literary or non-literary works. They all exploit a superficial similarity of form or content.

9.2.1 Activity 1

Choose an advertisement, a witty piece of graffiti, or a tabloid headline which compresses several meanings into a very few words. Consider it alongside a short poem on the students' syllabus which also generates more than one meaning. Ask them first to explain how the multiple meanings are achieved in both cases, and then ask why the literary example is generally considered more worthwhile.

One could take, for example, the two-page advertisement for Cinzano (Figure 9.1) which shows a sea urchin on the right-hand page, and a glass of Cinzano on the left-hand page, with the words over the sea urchin:

FOR A TASTE WITH
SPIKE YOU'LL PREFER
THE ONE ON THE LEFT
TO THE RIGHT ONE

with in smaller letters under the glass of Cinzano

OUR HERBS AND SPICES MAKE THE SUBTLE DIFFERENCE

For a taste with spike you'll prefer the one on the left to the right one.

Our herbs and spices make the subtle difference

Figure 9.1

and consider how many meanings and how many different read-ings are packed into these twenty-four words. 'Spike' refers both to the spikes on the sea urchin and to the herbs and spices which sharpen the drink. 'The one on the left' refers to the glass of Cinzano but sets up the expectation that the phrase will be con-trasted with the syntactically parallel phrase 'the one on the right'. The phrase actually used – 'the right one' – is thus foregrounded, a fact which helps draw attention to its double meaning. For 'the right one' (unlike 'the one on the right') can also mean 'the best one' or 'the correct one', and is indeed so used in the slogan describing Cinzano's main competitor Martini, which by analogy becomes equivalent to the sea urchin (an animal which, though painful to step on, is also positively associated with warm climates and holiday beaches). With all these multiple meanings set up, 'difference' in the smaller caption means all or any of the following: the difference between the sea urchin and Cinzano, the difference between Martini and Cinzano, the difference between the phrasing of 'the right one' and 'the one on the right', the difference between the right-hand and left-hand pages, the difference between a drink without herbs and spices, and one with them.

There are prosodic and phonological features of interest too. 'Spike' and 'spices' which are in this context both opposites and co-referential, are also very similar in spelling and sound, with only a 'subtle difference' between them. There is a fairly (though not exactly) regular rhythm, with most prosodic units being either iambs (an unstressed syllable followed by a stressed one) or anapests (two unstressed syllables followed by a stressed one). In the phrase 'the right one' two adjacent stresses bring emphasis at the end of the main slogan.

> for a TASTE / with SPIKE /
> you'll pre FER /
> the ONE / on the LEFT /
> to the RIGHT ONE /

If one reads the last line rhythmically as

> our HERBS and SPIces
> make the SUBtle DIFFerence

then both lines have so-called 'feminine' endings (i.e. unstressed syllables) in contrast with the 'masculine' endings (stressed syllables) of the larger slogan. This perhaps, together with the smaller print size on the left, iconically suggests the subtlety and delicacy of the Cinzano. The lay-out also plays a trick on our processing. The central position and larger size of the main slogan makes us read it first. We process the right page before the left page, reversing the usual order of reading. In advertising, right-hand pages are more expensive than left-hand pages as they are more likely to catch the eye of someone flicking through a magazine. What happens here, unusually, is that the product is pictured on the left page, presumably on the assumption that the words on the right-hand page, perceived first, will direct our attention towards it.

Students can be asked first to explain the word-play and the ways in which it exploits the linguistic system to create relevant multiple meanings. Secondly, they can be asked to evaluate the advertisement, to consider why it is not deemed 'equal' to poetry in its skill. Students may also wish to consider the interaction of pictures and words, the use and connotation of different typefaces and lay-outs. Though these are significant in many genres – such as advertisements – they are generally unimportant in literature.

The advertisement could then be contrasted with a short poem such as Blake's *The Sick Rose*, a favourite in poetry anthologies, and only ten words longer than the Cinzano ad.

> *The Sick Rose*
> O Rose thou art sick.
> The invisible worm
> That flies in the night
> In the howling storm,
>
> Has found out thy bed
> Of crimson joy:
> And his dark secret love
> Does thy life destroy.

Here multiple meanings are generated not by technical word-play as in the ad, but by the potential for the description of the rose and the worm to be interpreted metaphorically. Indeed, unless one reads this (somewhat absurdly) as a poem which is literally about a flower and a bug, it *must* be interpreted metaphorically. 'Bed', 'crimson joy' and 'dark secret love' may suggest analogies concerning (in)fidelity and sexuality, but it is the lack of precision as to what the infected rose symbolises which gives this image its power and potential to yield a vast variety of personal interpretations.

On a more technical level, it might be noted that this poem, like the Cinzano ad, mixes anapests and iambs.

> o ROSE / thou art SICK. /
> The inVIS / ible WORM /
> That FLIES / in the NIGHT /
> In the HOWL / ing STORM, /
> Has FOUND / out thy BED /
> of CRIM / son JOY: /
> And his DARK / secret LOVE /
> Does thy LIFE / des TROY. /

In both cases the use of words is skilful and meaning is com-
pressed. What is it that makes the second seem to most people
more serious, more moving, more profound?

Many teachers who have tried such an exercise encounter initial
incomprehension or derision, but once (and if) the activity can be
taken seriously, it will lead either to statements asserting the value
and difference of literature (perhaps that literary texts demonstrate skill with language in the service of some larger or more
serious goal), or to doubts about the judgements which the syllabus is handing down. In either case it will help students towards
more independent and thoughtful judgement. If students feel this
activity does not help them in their examinations, this may be
true, but that is also an indictment of the examinations.

9.2.2 *Activity 2*

Identify a soap opera or film which is popular with a substantial proportion of the class. Choose a scene (and show it on video) in which
the content is comparable with a scene from a play on their syllabus:
an argument between mother and son for those studying *Hamlet*; a
conspiracy to commit a crime for those studying *Macbeth*; accusation
of adultery for those studying *Othello*. If there is time, transcribe the
words from the soap opera and compare the language with a section of text from the play. Again, discuss why one is considered
literary and the other is not. Discuss the degree to which they are
dependent on images and acting, or can 'stand up' as written text.

There are some disadvantages of course. The search can be
time-consuming for teachers (though it can also be an excuse to
relax a little longer in front of the television) and the activity takes
time away from the acquisition of the detailed knowledge of a set
text demanded by examination syllabuses. 'Better' students may
feel peeved that an advantage is being given to those with greater
knowledge of popular culture. Yet again the activity may either
highlight the virtues of the literary example, or stimulate a fundamental re-evaluation.

9.2.3 *Activity 3*

Contrast videos of a poetry reading with a stand-up comedy act or
the performance of a solo singer-songwriter. They have a great
deal in common (see Cook 1995). In both cases an individual

stands on stage and delivers words which have been prepared in advance. In both cases, if the performance is successful, the audience approves of the soloist's skill with words and insights into life.

9.2.4 Activity 4

Take a passage from a 'lowbrow' successful novel and a 'highbrow' novel on the syllabus. Choose two passages which deal with comparable subject matters: a death, a wedding, a declaration of love, a funeral, a homecoming. Discuss why one work is elevated to the status of literature and the other – though perhaps 'gripping' and enjoyable – is not.

Consider for example these two passages, the first from Julie Burchill's best-selling novel *Ambition* (1990), the second from D.H. Lawrence's novel *The Rainbow* (1915).

There were two people in the Regency four-poster that swamped the suite overlooking the Brighton seafront but only one of them was breathing; deeply and evenly, as she sipped flat Bollinger Brut and decided what to do next.

Her name was Susan Street, and she was almost twenty-seven and almost beautiful with long dark hair, long pale legs and a short temper. Beside her lay a man who would never see fifty again and who now would never see sixty, either. He had been, until half an hour ago, the editor of the *Sunday Best*, a tabloid with teeth whose circulation was three million and rising. Unfortunately he would never see it reach four million, because his deputy editor Susan Street had just dispatched him to that big boardroom in the sky with a sexual performance of such singular virtuosity that his heart couldn't stand it.

His heart, like everything else about him, was weak, she thought as she kissed his still-warm lips.

When Anna Brangwen heard the news, she pressed back her head and rolled her eyes, as if something were reaching forward to bite at her throat. She pressed back her head, her mind was driven back to sleep. Since she had married and become a mother, the girl she had been was forgotten. Now, the shock threatened to break in upon her and sweep away all her intervening life, make her as a girl of eighteen again, loving her father. So she pressed back, away from the shock, she clung to her present life.

It was when they brought him to her house dead and in his wet clothes, his wet, sodden clothes, fully dressed as he came from market, yet all sodden and inert, that the shock really broke into her and she was terrified. A big, soaked, inert heap, he was, who had been to her the image of power and strong life.

> Almost in horror, she began to take the wet things from him, to pull off him the incongruous market-clothes of a well-to-do farmer. The children were sent away to the Vicarage, the dead body lay on the parlour floor, Anna quickly began to undress him, laid his fob and seals in a wet heap on the table. Her husband and the woman helped her. They cleared and washed the body, and laid it on the bed.

Both passages concern the reaction of a young woman to the sudden death of an older man. Both use comparable linguistic strategies, manipulating syntax to create rhetorical effect:

> A big, soaked, inert heap, he was, who had been to her the image of power and strong life.

> Beside her lay a man who would never see fifty again, and who now would never see sixty, either.

Yet one is instantly perceived as light-hearted and without pretensions to literariness, the other as (at least attempting to be) profound. Is this only because the dead man in one is the woman's adoptive father, and in the other a casual lover, or is it signalled stylistically by choice of language or semantically by choice of detail? Is levity necessarily non-literary? How exactly does Burchill signal that the death is to be taken lightly, while Lawrence identifies it as a matter for reflection and grief?

9.3   Conclusion

It is questions and activities like these which, I believe, help students to appreciate that literature (if not specific literary works) *is* something special, subtly different from the clever manipulation of language for non-literary purposes. Going outside the canon may lead students actively to confirm and create their own judgements of excellence in the present, rather than passively receiving the judgements of others from the past. It is a cause for optimism when these judgements confirm our own, and the power of literature to transcend generational difference.

Notes

1. I use the term 'text' here loosely to include oral performance as well as writing.

2. No analogy is perfect. If it were, the two halves would be identical rather than merely comparable. In this analogy the political state is compared to a set of texts, but the comparison does not imply other equivalences beyond those made explicit. No state is superior among others, in the way that (I believe) literature is a superior discourse; and whereas the erosion of the nation state would be a desirable development, the erosion of literature would not be.

3. Even allowing for differences of opinion about the definition of fiction, which might increase or decrease this figure, the general point (that there is a lot of fiction on television) remains true.

4. This point applies in both mother-tongue and foreign language teaching.

10

'Interfacing' language and literature: with special reference to the teaching of British cultural studies

MAO SIHUI

Mao Sihui talks initially about the widening of cross-cultural awareness, and the challenge this presents for the English language/literature classroom, with reference in particular to text-based approaches to literature and the importance of creativity on the part of the teacher.

The traditional 'canonical' approach is queried, as the author advocates a small 'l' approach to literature, and the discipline of British Cultural Studies – not as a replacement curriculum but as a complement to Literature, Linguistics, Language Skills, etc. especially for non-native-speaking students of English.

Consideration is given to the inter-relation of topics-teaching plans-texts, as well as the differing text types of novel-play-film. The inseparability of a third trichotomy – linguistic-literary-cultural – is illustrated with examples for classroom use based on Ted Hughes's poem *Hawk Roosting* and the script of Neil Jordan's film *The Crying Game*, with reference also to John Osborne's play *Look Back in Anger*.

> A linguist deaf to the poetic function of language and a literary scholar indifferent to linguistic problems and unconversant with linguistic methods, are equally flagrant anachronisms.
>
> *Roman Jakobson*

10.1   Introduction[1]

It is both fascinating and disconcerting to notice that when 'our' world is undergoing an unprecedented process of *globalisation* (of the economy, of images, of discourses, and of risks and problems), there arises a truly urgent need to cross geographical, national, political, cultural and even psychological boundaries and barriers, although one must also be alert to the unequal international flow of news, knowledge and information, the problematic geopolitical distribution of power and wealth between highly industrialised nations and the developing Third World countries. The rapid emergence of regional studies in the last decade or so does seem, at long last, to suggest a possibility of re-reading, re-thinking or even deconstructing the greatest cultural construct in human history – the East–West Divide. And here I am talking about the teaching of British Cultural Studies as a *dynamic, enabling,* and *inter-disciplinary* subject (drawing on methods developed in cultural studies, in literary studies, in 'a range of disciplines in the social sciences and English language teaching', 'a hybrid' in the process of 'acquiring its own distinct identity' (Bassnett 1994, pp. 63–4) which, I firmly believe, can help open our mind, widen our cultural horizons and promote our cross-cultural awareness. Aiming at the development of an active curiosity and sincere wish in both the teacher and the taught to find out and understand the peoples and cultures of the British Isles, this new subject will undoubtedly present new challenges to our English language/ literature classroom.

In this paper, I shall discuss a number of issues confronting us when we attempt to approach British Cultural Studies through literature in an EFL (English as a Foreign Language) classroom. First, we have to deal with our well-grounded anxieties about the present increasingly shrinking status of English Literature in our university curriculum and then explore the possibility of creating a space for negotiation and compromise over redefinitions of literature. Building on the integrated British Studies teaching models proposed by Carlin Dick (1992), I shall, no doubt very summarily, use three texts – John Osborne's *Look Back in Anger,* Neil Jordan's *The Crying Game,* and Ted Hughes's poem *Hawk Roosting* – to show how we can design teaching plans with units on specific topics while adopting a three-level comparative approach to the teaching of British Cultural Studies through literature.

While using some of the ideas from discourse analysis (Carter and Simpson 1989) and also suggestions for activities from the brilliant book *Literary Studies in Action* (Durant and Fabb 1990), the final part of this essay will be devoted to a discussion on how to *do things* with texts, rather than how to *teach* texts. The ideology behind this methodology is the belief that the long-standing separation of language teaching and literature teaching, although one could give many good reasons for the separation, has been but one of the *mythologies* that still haunt the teaching profession and therefore need to be carefully *re-thought*. Perhaps it is necessary to re-state that language is an inseparable part of a culture. The values, norms and taboos of a society, and the ideas, feelings, and identities (personal, national, political, sexual, or cultural) of a particular group of people are constructed and communicated through the use of language. For a non-native learner, the most exciting and rewarding way of 'experiencing' them is through reading, tasting and analysing its literary and cultural products, hence *interfacing language and literature in our classroom.* In other words, language learning has to be put back into its cultural context. In the teaching of a British Cultural Studies course in an advanced EFL classroom through literary, cultural and other 'representational texts' (see McRae 1991, pp. 3–4), the enhancement of students' linguistic competence and the acquisition of their literary and cross-cultural pragmatic competence (or '*socio-cultural competence*', see Lavery 1993, p. iv) can and should be integrated. It is also my belief that, in actual classroom management, we should aim at a *balance* between what the communicative approach calls 'student-centredness' and the kind of teacher control that traditional practice (particularly in China) favours (Mao 1993, pp. 82–3). At the centre of our classroom management, I firmly believe, is a *creativity* on the teacher's part, to have at his disposal, and devise whenever possible, a whole range of ways and methods to work with students. By putting imagination, creativity, passion, and fun back into the classroom[2] we can make teaching and learning a joyful business of discoveries, not a painful Sunday service with a boring, babbling priest.

10.2   What's happened to literature

The very term *literature* conjures up a host of contradictions and conflicts. Here let me, first of all, express my deep concern over the *declining* (if not totally marginalised) status of English Literature in university curricula. Since it is impossible to avoid the notoriously big debate over the Canon and Alternative Literature(s) if we want to relate it to British Cultural Studies at all, I feel obliged to pick up that rather hateful topic and then argue that we do need some *redefinitions* of *literature* and re-evaluations of its importance in our everyday life as well as in the language/literature classroom.

At the Graz Conference on English Literature and the University Curriculum (Austria) in 1989, Wolfgang Zach asked a very embarrassing, provocative yet truly fundamental question: 'Are literary scholars today in the situation of dinosaurs on the verge of extinction?' (Zach 1992, p. 11).

As teachers of English language and literature, probably most of us, like scholars all over the world, have strongly felt that there is a fundamental insecurity about the function of literature in our fast-moving (post-?)modern world. Almost every department of English/foreign languages in Chinese universities today, for example, has experienced tremendous pressures for curriculum changes under the powerful impact of what has been called 'Socialist Market Economy with Chinese Characteristics'. Take for instance my own institution, the Guangdong University of Foreign Studies (merged in May 1995 from the former Guangzhou Institute of Foreign Languages and the Guangzhou Institute of Foreign Trade). To meet the needs of mushrooming foreign business enterprises, joint venture companies, hotel and tourism industries in Guangdong and the coastal areas, the former Department of English has split into three departments over the past few years: the International Trade Department, the Foreign Secretarial Department and the English Department, which has been offering 'fashionable' programmes and courses like Marketing, Western Economy, Tourism Management, Economic Information Processing, Strategies in Business Negotiations, Stock Exchange ABC and many others. Our well-established one-year (40–42 weeks) English Literature Course (a history of English literature and selected readings) for the fourth-year undergraduate students has been forced to shrink into a one-semester course. And because of future employment prospects, the number of students who are 'willing' to take the literature course is extremely small. Therefore they automatically regard themselves, not without a touch of the English sense of humour, as an 'endangered species', much less protected than our endangered giant pandas, which can, at least, count on special funds from government and institutions, on the motherly care of environmentalists and also on the awareness of our general public.

What's more, teachers of literature seem to be suffering from an 'identity crisis' brought about by an array of factors: the newly-granted high prestige of natural sciences in our society and the government's tightening of budgets for the humanities and arts (particularly for literary studies); the utilitarian way of thinking and practice of our society with its quasi-American dollar-chasing aesthetics and emphasis on employment prospects among students; and also the socially dominant position of audiovisual mass media. To a certain extent, even the developments of cultural studies, regional studies and media studies have helped in devaluing the long-standing special status accorded to 'the great literary tradition' or the Canon.

In his book entitled *The Western Canon* (1994), Harold Bloom, in an openly contemptuous tone, criticises most of the modern theoretical schools – Marxism, Feminism, New Historicism, Deconstruction, Lacanism and Semioticism – and lumps them together as the *School of Resentment* whose influence, according to Bloom, has made the study of literature an ideological act, in its most fruitful manifestation, or simply a kind of left-wing censorship at its worst. These theorists, if they consider creating a new canon at all, in Bloom's view, will merely choose books by authors who 'offer little but the resentment they've developed as part of their sense of identity'. Bloom's book opens with 'An Elegy for the Canon' and ends with an 'Elegiac Conclusion'. How about the future? Bloom laments (p. 519):

> What are now called 'Departments of English' will be renamed departments of 'Cultural Studies' where *Batman* comics, Mormon theme parks, television, movies, and rock will replace Chaucer, Shakespeare, Milton, Wordsworth and Wallace Stevens. Major, once-elitist universities and colleges will still offer a few courses in Shakespeare, Milton, and their peers, but these will be taught by departments of three or four scholars, equivalent to teachers of ancient Greek and Latin.

In short, scholars like Bloom had decided, clearly with understandable melancholia, that as far as Literature is concerned, the glory is gone, the present wretched, the future bleak. While having every sympathy with Harold Bloom in his love of the Canon, I feel that it would be fitting and proper for us teachers of English language and literature to start exploring what implications the present status of Literature might have for our 'identity crisis', for our ideological positioning, and also for our classroom management.

10.3 Literature vs. literature

However depressing 'the Literature scene' may be, I do not think it would make us feel any better if we go on sentimentalising over these powerful shifts and changes. We may try to defend with traditional arguments the noble, humanistic objectives as well as the established paradigm in the teaching of literature. But the reality is: we have been, more or less, *conditioned* by the moving image over the decades, although we may declare that we have never given up our resistance. It is a fact that our students and, perhaps, most of our young teachers, have been brought up on television, on Hollywood and on hamburgers. We are forced, therefore, to ask some crucial questions such as those asked by Wolfgang Zach (1992, p. 11):

1. How should we react to the ever-increasing impact of the 'new' media in the modern world?
2. Should we simply ignore them in the teaching of literature or should the study of literature be turned into media studies to keep pace with the development in the social environment?
3. Is it justifiable to use them in an ancillary function to literary studies?

Probably, few people would disagree that our world would be extremely impoverished if it were deprived of great masters like Homer, Sophocles, Dante, Shakespeare, Milton, Whitman and T.S. Eliot, who are only part of the accumulated wisdom of humanity stored in the printed word over the centuries. But I personally believe that while we continue to stress the intrinsic value of Literature, its important role in releasing students' linguistic, cultural competence and problem-solving capability, and its 'latent emancipatory, liberating force ... as a residue of complete freedom, of self-realization and human solidarity' (Zach 1992, p. 12), TV, film, cartoon and other forms of representational media just cannot be ignored, precisely because they are central to people's lives today as the most essential source of information and entertainment. In our language/literature classroom, they provide us with an enormous range of texts[3] for comparative studies which can, when *creatively employed*, lead to interesting findings about the different signs and codes, and also to a deeper, more balanced understanding of the texts, literary or non-literary, *referential* (texts that inform) or *representational* (texts that involve) (McRae 1991, pp. 1–7).

What I am suggesting here is that we should get out of the constraints of traditional definitions of Literature with a capital 'L'
and expand it to include other representational texts that open
up, call upon, stimulate and use areas of the mind, from imagination to emotion, from pleasure to pain. This has been termed
literature with a small 'l' (McRae 1991). In other words, 'literature' denotes a rather comprehensive and subdivided field that
neither just means, nor excludes, but *includes* the Canon.

10.4   Topics ⇔ plans ⇔ texts

In my (probably utopian) view, literature with a capital 'L' and
literature with a small 'l' are not necessarily mutually exclusive,
especially in an educational context, because they together provide a wealth of fascinating texts on which we can build up an
infinite number of integrated teaching plans to examine, together
with our students, different topics for linguistic, literary and cultural analyses. In other words, we can set up, in our case, a British
Cultural Studies programme/course through literature as a fully
independent subject, complementary to the existing curriculum,
with courses like Literature, Linguistics, Language Skills,
Translation and Interpretation, Background to Britain, British
History.

In order to help illustrate how we determine the topics, let me
quote Bassnett and Mountford (1993, p. 9) – their beautifully
designed matrix format is displayed along two axes: *identity factors*
(nation, locality, generation, gender, class, race and ethnicity, etc.)
and *institutional contexts* (law, politics, work, education, family, leisure, media, arts, etc.). I totally agree with Bassnett and
Mountford that 'it is the *identity factors* . . . that primarily determine topic, with the institutional context providing a focus for
particular aspects of the topic.' Of course, designing a *workable*
teaching plan for British Cultural Studies through literature will
necessarily take into consideration a host of factors:

– the stock of materials (written, oral, visual, musical) available;
– the type of students; their specific needs in relation to linguistic, literary and cultural competences;
– the time available for such a programme;
– the constraints of teaching/learning habits and approaches.

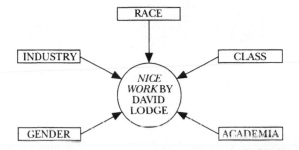

Figure 10.1 One specific work of literature as the main focus

The list can be very long; but once we have come to a fair understanding of the new 'joint venture', we can choose the topics in relation to our different texts. Here we present some illustrations of integrated teaching plans, Figures 10.1 and 10.2 designed by Carlin Dick (1992).

One very important thing to bear in mind is that we may approach the work in terms of enhancing students' linguistic and literary competence, but this should not prevent us from using it *primarily* to explore and understand the nature of Britain, its people, its social institutions and its cultural production. For the reading of *Nice Work* with students, I'd like to draw your attention to the nice work of Andrew Skinner who devised a wonderful teaching plan with *Pre-reading Strategies, While-reading Strategies,* and *Post-reading Strategies,* complete with a list of background texts.[4]

Materials for each text type in Figure 10.2 suggested by Dick were: (1) BBC's *Accents of English*; (2) *Sunday Times* (Oct. 1991) 'Britain's Class Wars'; (3) Kazuo Ishiguro's *The Remains of the Day*; (4) John Braine's *Room at the Top*; (5) Chris Hamnet *et al., The*

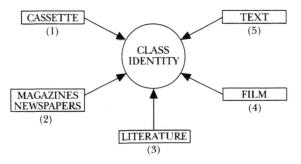

Figure 10.2 One issue/topic as the major focus of study

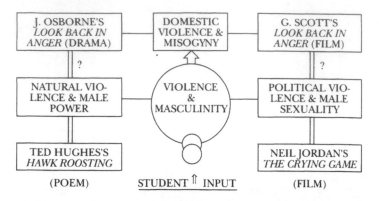

Figure 10.3   Two or more issues with a comparative approach

Changing Social Structure. Again we can use some of the reading strategies designed by Andrew Skinner.

These are just some examples of the unlimited number of ways possible to shuffle various texts around certain topics. Perhaps Figure 10.3 needs some explanation. I believe that teaching British Cultural Studies through literature in a non-British context 'automatically' assumes a comparative approach. I employ the term *'comparative approach'*, basically, to mean three things: (1) Synchronic/Diachronic Comparison; (2) Inter-Genre Comparison; (3) Cross-Cultural Comparison.

10.4.1   *Synchronic/diachronic comparison*

In his discussion on discourse analysis of poetry and the three contexts (the inner and outer context, the intertextual context, the historical context) embedded in texts, Ronald Carter points out,

> To the linguistic analysis must be conjoined an analysis of the poem which attends systematically to the networks the text contracts as part of its place within socio-historical and cultural discourses. This network includes other texts produced at the same historical juncture as well as the poem's antecedents within a literary tradition.
>
> (Carter and Simpson 1989, p. 69)

Following this line of thought, we need to create in the classroom a setting for sharing personal responses, and to help students see how each of these British artists in Figure 10.3 represents, among other issues, violence and masculinity in the texts; then compare the similarities and differences in their representations. A very fundamental task for both the teacher and the students is to explore the intricate relations (definitely beyond what a reflectionist rhetoric promises) between the text and the specific political, economic and cultural context within which the text is produced, and to understand, through comparing texts produced at different social historical moments, how different versions of *reality* are constructed by way of the codes, conventions, myths, and ideologies. I always feel that, no matter how vigorously we argue for *aesthetic* qualities or *formal* features, the production and reception of cultural products are, consciously or unconsciously, framed by *ideological interests*. If analysing a text in a language/literature class only means a systematic and rigorous analysis on a linguistic level, it would be like experiencing the sea only by counting the number of graceful gulls over the sea or colourful shells lying on the beach, without actually plunging into the surging sea itself.

10.4.2   Inter-genre comparison

In contemporary practices of cultural production, a text often retains its existence in more than one genre or form. A novel, for instance, may be adapted through the ages for the stage and also find its way into the cinema and vice versa: a novel ⇔ a play ⇔ a film. Therefore comparing the *original* play *Look Back in Anger* (1956) and Gordon Scott's film version of the play (1958) in cultural terms would shed much light on how differently the issues are treated and how particular effects on the reader/audience are achieved. A classical example is the radically different (even distorted, to some critics) treatment of the themes and the narrative such as the Garden Party and the typically Hollywood romantic ending of George Cukor's *My Fair Lady* (1964), based on Shaw's *Pygmalion* written decades earlier. This kind of comparison would lead not only to explorations of formal peculiarities of different genres (a stage play or a musical, a social drama or a romance) in relation to audiences (middle-class, working-class, youth) but also to debates on authorial intention, originality, function of literature, politics of cultural production and so on.

10.4.3   Cross-cultural comparison

This is where 'Student Input' comes in most prominently. A university course, be it linguistic, literary or cultural, always has a

pretty good chance to collapse without students' active involvement. In an advanced course like British Cultural Studies through
literature, student-centredness should be a priority, not just a
possibility; and students' actual participation in the cross-cultural
(e.g. Sino-British, Anglo-American) comparison with specific texts
from their own culture and other non-British cultures should be
consciously made throughout the learning process. As Susan
Bassnett (1994, p. 68) points out,

> What we are effectively proposing is an approach based on compara-
> tive techniques between cultures that starts with the unknown, the
> believed or misbelieved and the immediately available . . . . If a culture
> is a network of interconnected signs and systems, then global know-
> ledge of all those diverse systems is de facto impossible. What one can
> aspire to . . . is an analysis of the subjective position within a culture in
> terms of language, class, race, ethnicity, gender, age, work, status,
> income, religion, political affiliation and a host of additional factors.

In our EFL classroom, where we use various kinds of texts, a
comparative approach will not only help our students improve
their study skills such as drawing inferences from the linguistic
signs, but also better understand various processes of political,
social and cultural changes within Britain and China, thus
enhancing their cross-cultural awareness, which will reduce cross-
cultural pragmatic failures in real life communication (Mao 1993,
p. 85). Since the social space that the Chinese teachers and
students inhabit is one that is still dominated by different forms of
Confucianism which, more often than not, demand a high degree
of ideological conformity and the subjection of individual will to
the power of the authority, this approach may help them develop
the ability to read texts and hopefully appreciate their social reality more critically and competently, thus leading them on the way
to find a voice of their own.

10.5   Doing things with texts: questions, tasks and games

In an EFL classroom, a crucial part of language teaching is the
gradual acquisition of cross-cultural competence, 'the ability not
only to choose appropriate language to suit a situation but also
awareness of culturally appropriate behaviour' (Lavery 1993,
p. vi). Whether it is an elementary language course, an advanced

literature course or a cultural studies course, the major objective is to train the language learner to become a competent and observant language user, 'sensitive to the linguistic and non-linguistic cues of native-speakers, in order to avoid cross-cultural misunderstandings' (*ibid.*). To achieve this, there are hundreds of ways the teacher can choose in working with texts.

When dealing with texts such as those in Figure 10.3, I believe one of the many possible ways to ensure a fair degree of success with a comparative approach is to ask students linguistic, literary and cultural questions, assign them various tasks and devise games to play with texts. All these questions, tasks and games should be arranged in such a way that they demand an increase in students' overall competence as well as in cognitive complexity. For lack of space, here are only a few samples.

10.5.1   Questions: development of sensitivities

It should be noted that there hardly exists a clear dividing line, for me at least, between what is purely linguistic, literary or cultural, since one is quite often intrinsically related to the other.

In the 'Greenhouse Scene' in Neil Jordan's *The Crying Game*, after Jody's story of 'The Scorpion and the Frog', we have the conversation:

Fergus: So what's that supposed to mean?
Jody: Means what it says. The scorpion does what is in his nature. Take off the hood, man?
Fergus: Why?
Jody: 'Cause you're kind. It's in your nature.
            [Fergus *walks toward him and pulls off the hood.* Jody *smiles up at him.*]
Jody: See? I was right about you.
Fergus: Don't be so sure.
Jody: Jody's always right.

(Jordan 1993, pp. 16–17)

At the end of the film, we have this conversation between Fergus and Dil (who is a transvestite) when s/he visits Fergus in the 'Prison Visiting Room':

Dil: Fergus. Fergus my love, light of my life –
Fergus: Please, Dil.
Dil: Can't help it. You're doing time for me. No greater lover, as the man says. Wish you'd tell me why.

Fergus: As the man said, it's in my nature.
Dil: What's that supposed to mean?
          [*She shakes her head.*]
Fergus: Well, there was this scorpion, you see. And he wants to go
          across the river. But . . .
          [*Camera pulls back, and as* Fergus *tells the story of the scorpion
          and the frog, the music comes up* – 'Stand By Your Man'.]
                                                        (Jordan 1993, p. 69)

These two short conversations are so intelligently constructed that
they not only echo each other in terms of narrative structure but
also contrast and reinforce each other in terms of their exploration of themes such as nature, male bonding, love, and gender
construction. Treat 'nature' as a *key word* and, with the help of dictionaries if needed, relate to fellow students how you understand
nature, its lexical, semantic and pragmatic meanings and how
people struggle under the unshakable forces of *nature*.

Hawk Roosting by Ted Hughes (1957) was written at approxi-
mately the same time as John Osborne's play *Look Back in Anger*
(1956). Can students see any connections between the two texts?
Do both texts seem to express certain 'masculine' states of mind,
emotions and desires? If so, what are they?

Are we justified in saying that Hughes, Osborne and Neil
Jordan are brave and realistic, though brutal, about the horror of
existence and the violent nature of our time? In terms of authorial
attitudes, Hughes seems to commend the predatory vulture's
violent energy to us readers; how about the authors of the other
two texts? Talking about different historical moments (closely
related to the Empire, the welfare state, racial conflicts, class wars,
the profound transformation of Britain from the 1950s to the
Thatcher era), do you think their representations of 'history' and
a modern, multicultural Britain are valid or seriously distorted, or
are they just ways of 'mythologising' the past?

If a critic says that the natural violence in the poem seems to
suggest the essentially possessive spirit of capitalism, and the
violent and very often repulsive behaviour of Jimmy Porter as a
restless, selfish, egoistic and overtly anti-Establishment young man
in the play is rooted in a complex political, cultural and psychological response to a past he cannot escape, a future he would not
accept and a present (the spiritual 'inertia' of 1950s Britain) he
can do nothing to change, the uncompromising visualisation of
violence in *The Crying Game* is, partly at least, a powerful political

critique of contemporary Britain. Do you agree/disagree? And why?

Since plays and films make extensive use of conversations, it is quite necessary for the teacher to be aware of a discourse analysis approach which helps students become more sensitive to the properties, discourse organisation and different kinds of information in the text, such as *ideational information* (the subject, topic or theme), *indexical information* (the speakers' attitudes) and *transaction management information* (how the conversation is controlled, led, dominated, managed or organised (Laver and Hutcheson, quoted in McRae 1985, p. 16). For a detailed example of this approach to dramatic text, see Mick Short's essay 'Discourse Analysis and the Analysis of Drama' (in Carter and Simpson 1989, p. 139–168) in which Short covers topics such as *speech acts, presuppositions, the co-operative principles in conversation* and *terms of address.*

10.5.2   Tasks: a cultural experience

'Texts carry with them cultural baggage . . . [which] becomes evident in the ways texts explore ethical and social concerns, represent characters and customs and negotiate and imply value-systems' (Durant, in Brumfit and Benton 1993, p. 157). Again the following is only a number of the many ways we can employ to make students 'experience' and think about cultural products.[5]

Working in pairs

The misogyny in Porter and his attitude towards Cliff; the almost fascist-like presence of male power and sheer absence of feminine sensitivity in the thinking Hawk; and the conflicting political, moral and sexual forces in Fergus all seem to reveal, one way or another, aspects of masculinity in terms of male sexuality, particularly homo-eroticism and homosexuality. Discuss in pairs how masculinity and homosexuality are socially and culturally constructed and compare the representations of masculinity, if possible, with those of femininity through Jude, the female terrorist, and Alison, the wife victimised by her social environment and her husband. To make your argument convincing, use more evidence from the texts rather than just reporting your intuitions and general impressions. And never stop asking yourself how such themes have been represented in the texts of your own culture.

Working in groups

The mother of Jimmy's friend Hugh Tanner is mentioned a few times but does not appear as a character in Osborne's play; however, in Scott's film version, the mother is transformed into quite an important figure. And also the number of Jimmy's characteristically explosive speeches (usually monologues) is considerably reduced, partly to give a more compassionate, humanistic touch to the character. Divide students into small groups (three or four in each group) and discuss the importance (or significance) of such changes in relation to the thematic lines and artistic effects. In connection with this, discuss how the film *The Crying Game*, through the characterisation of Fergus, can help us re-think and even deconstruct the stereotypes of terrorists generally presented in popular Hollywood cinema (e.g. the *Die Hard* series).

Working on one's own

Feminist discourses have been among the most vigorous driving forces in literary and cultural studies. The statement 'The personal is political' has been a familiar one. Write a short essay comparing the representations of the complex relations between politics and sexuality in Chen Kaige's huge hit *Farewell My Concubine* (1993) and *The Crying Game*. This project can be used later as the basis for individual oral presentations (each, say, within 5 or 8 minutes) in front of the class. If chaired by a student instead of a teacher (remember: *equal footing*), the result could be quite stunning.

10.5.3   Games: texts in action

In this particular situation, I regard 'text' from a post-structuralist position as that defined by Barthes in his short essay 'From Work to Text' (Barthes 1977). For Barthes, *work* is pages with words on them which only have a potentiality for meanings. But *text* exists (that is, springs into life) only while it is being read. Different readers or the same readers at different times would have different responses to and different interpretations of the same work; therefore texts multiply in meanings. Reading is an act of endless exploration, thus 'the pleasure of the text'. Space forbids an extensive exploration of the possibilities one can exploit with the three texts. Here is just an indication of what I mean by 'texts in action' and I shall, for the sake of space and convenience, limit myself only to Hughes's poem *Hawk Roosting*.

Giving a title to the text

In literary or cultural studies, we sometimes forget how powerfully suggestive and definitive the mere name of a book, a painting or an object can be, names or titles such as Milton's *Paradise Lost*, D.H. Lawrence's *Lady Chatterley's Lover*, Caryl Churchill's *Top Girls* almost prescribe their themes. In treating Hughes's poem, the teacher can deliberately hold back the title and, as a 'warming-up' exercise, ask students to read the poem and think up a title for it. In the spring semester 1994, I tried this and my class of 22 students plunged into a heated discussion. They came up with very telling titles such as: *An Ode to Myself, Diary of a Mad Man, The Soliloquy of a Tyrant, The True Face of Nature, My Brave New World, Song of My Law, Fury of a Dragon, The Cry of a Crazed Cow, Vision of a Vicious Vulture, Philosophy of a Bloody Hawk.* Aren't these titles beautifully revealing? These titles are roughly *their* versions of the text's theme.

Drilling students in 'drilling' the text

Even when you deal with a text of classical status, treat it basically as an object of consumption rather than an object of worship. In this poem, there is almost an 'excessive' use of the first person pronouns, both personal and possessive: 'I' (6 times), 'me' (twice), 'my' (12 times), 'mine' (once). This 'extravaganza' undoubtedly goes beyond an exercise of imagining what it would be like to think and speak like a hawk. From the fact that the vulture proudly surveys the world as inferior, and that Creation was put there to serve **him** (strange, one hardly thinks that the hawk can be a **she**), this poem can be *read* as a text about Hitler-like megalomania. Precisely because of the use of pronouns, it would be very interesting to change the first-person 'I', 'me', 'my' and 'mine' to the second-person 'you', 'your', 'yours', and the third-person 's/he', 'her/him', 'her/his' and 'hers/his'. If the poem is read by different readers with different voice quality (loud/soft, raised/creaky, falsetto/bass, male/female), the poem takes on new layers of meaning. To a certain extent, if you change the pronouns, you change the themes; change the voice, change the effect. To quote Durant and Fabb, 'By altering some aspects of a text . . ., you can see what effects a specific change has, and this may help to draw your attention to the properties which create the effect that is altered by the change' (Durant and Fabb 1990, p. 84).

Working against the 'majority'

This is a three D's game (Devise, Debate and Deconstruct), a game for students at a fairly late stage of working creatively with texts. Having studied the text in terms of plot, theme(s), character(s), structure(s) and style(s), the students are now asked to devise a list of words, phrases, or statements that connect with key words such as *Violence, Masculinity*. They will almost certainly agree and disagree with one another; and this is a good point to start debate and learn to recognise that many of the things we habitually associate with certain words, notions and ideologies in a culture cannot be taken for granted after all. For example, when we talk about 'violence', we usually think of it in the form of physical assault, sexual harassment, armed robbery, indiscriminate injuring and killing, but quite often fail to relate it to other forms of violence such as emotional withholding, political oppression, media intrusion of privacy, or human damage to ecological balance.

In working with the poem, we should by all means encourage students to analyse various linguistic and literary aspects such as the seemingly simple verse structure (four lines in each stanza), use of heavy stresses at the end of a line, use of capitalisation of letters ('Creation'), use of alliteration ('my hooked head and hooked feet') and rhyme (only the first stanza), the grouping of sharp images in connection with space. Then they should relate these aspects to the sheer energy, the earthy directness and the quality of brutality that the poem seeks to convey.

Questions, tasks and games are but some of the many ways to help students create for themselves a more challenging space of imagination. By working creatively with different literary and cultural texts, they can develop sharper sensitivities to the formal and material properties of those texts, acquire useful knowledge about the cultural rules of communication (e.g. degrees of politeness, importance of cooperative principles), adopt a more balanced view of both the target culture and home culture, and gradually achieve a true cross-cultural competence.

10.6 Conclusion

In his essay 'Linguistic Models, Language and Literariness: Study Strategies in the Teaching of Literature to Foreign Students', Ronald Carter writes, 'It is clear that . . . any adequate teaching of a literary text goes beyond language teaching techniques, however widely used and principled they may be' (Brumfit and Carter 1986, p. 111). To a certain extent, this has been a guiding notion behind my methodology and treatment of texts. In the first part of this paper, I attempted to deal with several issues that confront us when we teach British Cultural Studies through literary and cultural texts in an EFL classroom: our anxieties over the marginalised status of *Literature* in the classroom as well as in our everyday life, the necessity and possibility of redefining *literature* with a small 'l'. Then I explored how we could, in determining topics, selecting texts and making teaching plans, use a comparative approach to the teaching of a British Cultural Studies course in our non-native context. Finally, I demonstrated some of the ways we could choose to '*interface*' our teaching of language and that of literature through activities such as questions, tasks and games. Of course, the acquisition of literary and cultural competences in the way described above *presupposes* a quite fluent capacity in students to read English and a certain amount of general knowledge about English culture and society.

To conclude, let me give an analogy: teaching language, literature and culture in an EFL classroom is very much like getting to understand an English stately home. You need to know the shape, the structure, the physical and cultural properties, and the functions of different parts of the house; you need to see the gardens, the lawns, the various plants and of course the fences (never forget, 'Good fences make good neighbours'); what's more, you need to talk and get to understand the people who inhabit the house. Reading literary and cultural texts is never just a matter of knowing the language, because those texts encode knowledge of history, culture and society. Divorcing language and literature from their cultural contexts is something like visiting the house but refusing to see its people, the soul of the inhabited space.

Notes

1. I would like to thank Susan Bassnett, John McRae, Ronald Carter, Jeremy Hunter, and Gill Westaway for their valuable comments on an earlier version of this paper, originally presented at the seminar on the Teaching of British Studies, held in Bandungan, Indonesia, 2–5 May 1995, and co-sponsored by the University of Diponegoro and the British Council. The responsibility for whatever flaws that still exist is entirely mine.

2. Here I tend to favour Louise M. Rosenblatt's view of 'literature as exploration' (Rosenblatt 1968) and value the significance of the imaginative education of young people living in an increasingly audio-visual machine age.

3. There are, according to Bassnett and Mountford (1993, p. 14), three major text types: A) Visual Texts (film, TV, cartoon, photographs, drawings, advertisements, etc.); B) Verbal (Spoken and Written) Texts (interviews, spoken drama, film/TV commentaries, radio pro-grammes, poetry, novels, play scripts, journalism, newspapers, academic writings, brochures, pamphlets, etc.); C) Musical Texts (vocal/instrumental records, CDs, LDs, etc.). For a fuller discussion of texts in relation to text-types, text-tokens, formal and material proper-ties of texts, effects of texts on the reader, and texts, contexts and circumstances, see especially Chapter 3 of Durant and Fabb 1990, pp. 49–65.

4. Andrew Skinner (University of Innsbruck, Austria) provides over thirty reading strategies such as questioning, marking and annotating in the book margin, note-taking, comparing different texts and views, draw-ing diagrams of narrative structures, relationships and developments, group and cross-group work, listening to and viewing documen-tary/fictional programmes. (Skinner presented his paper at the British Studies Conference, *Britain 2000*, held at the University of Vienna, 10–12 April 1995, co-sponsored by the British Council.)

5. In the book *Widening Horizons: Teaching the Language/Literature Interface in South Asia* (Orient Longman, Madras, forthcoming) being edited by John McRae, Pushpinder Syal and Robert Bellarmine, I propose in my article 'Language, Culture, and Film as Text' an input-fermentation-output model for an advanced EFL classroom, using Martin Scorsese's *Taxi Driver* (1976) as text.

11

'Viewer, I married him': literature on video

ANTHONY JENNINGS

The author suggests that theme-linking of concepts common to works of literature and films available on video for classroom exploitation has a likely pay-off in encouraging students to bridge the gap between 'classic' novels and popular culture.

He draws many cultural conclusions initially from a consideration of the Disney cartoon *The Lion King*. Then his theme moves towards a consideration of the 'madwoman' theme, from the mid-nineteenth century to the 1980s. Using the myth of the 'monster woman', he shows how cultural assumptions concerning the role of passionate women are shown from Brontë's *Jane Eyre* to the 1987 film *Fatal Attraction*, and are shared or subverted in such novels as *Great Expectations* and *Rebecca* when they become 'films of the book'.

He argues against a formalist approach to the use of video in the language/literature classroom, demonstrating how the use of video material with comparable themes (or meanings) to the 'classics' which remain on syllabuses can be made rewarding for students and not over-demanding for teachers, and how this can lead to a broader frame of critical awareness and appreciation. This paper complements the previous chapter in productive ways.

11.1 Introduction

The use of feature films in the language and literature classroom is becoming more widespread as more facilities become available, and teachers are obviously keen to take advantage of a resource which promises to make the study of literature more stimulating. Despite this enthusiasm, however, the difficulties of exploiting video in the literature classroom can prove daunting. What is the teacher to do beyond showing 'the film of the book'? The answer has tended to involve some kind of focus on technique. Common activities include 'translation' from one medium to another (e.g. preparing a screenplay from a text, then comparing your version with the filmmaker's); discussion of viewpoint (e.g. how can a film approximate to a first-person narration?) or of plot (what is omitted or altered in the transference of a novel's plot to the screen?). This formalist approach pervades other aspects of literature teaching, of course, but it tends to dominate film studies in the language and literature classroom because it offers a justification for doing something (watching a film instead of reading a book) which might otherwise seem an irrelevant form of relaxation.

The rationale for the formalist approach in general is summed up by Moffett and McElheny in a highly successful pedagogic anthology of short stories, *Points of View* (1995):

> Someone who has become acquainted with all the forms will naturally be a more perceptive and sophisticated reader.
>   What a story is about is partly a question of how it is told. You cannot separate the tale from the telling. . . . Heeding form will tell the reader more about what an author is doing or saying than will direct analysis of meaning, which may break the spell and spoil the pleasure.
>   (Moffett and McElheny 1995, p. 587)

In practice, I think the opposite is the case, perhaps especially where film is concerned. Talking about form and technique will 'break the spell and spoil the pleasure', and all too often render arid and tedious what might be enjoyable. In this paper I want to outline a different approach, based on the analysis of theme in literature and film, which does not rely on technical distinctions between the two media, but simply lumps them together as 'stories'. After presenting a couple of illustrations, I will discuss the pros and cons of my approach and of the formalist alternative as ways of creating a 'perceptive and sophisticated reader'.

A substantial part of my paper will be devoted to critical rather than methodological questions. This is partly because my point will not be clear unless I illustrate in some detail the kind of analysis and comparison I have in mind, but it is also the result of my conviction that teachers and teacher-trainers tend to think too much in terms of means and too little of ends. Every conference, every handbook, every new development in methodology, gives us more techniques to use in presenting language and literature in interesting and student-centred ways, while questions of course content and overall objectives tend to take second place. A good reader is not only a reader skilled in techniques of analysis, but above all one who sees the relation of literature to life. A well-honed methodology can produce the first kind of reader, but not the second. Though I recognise the need of all sorts of carefully chosen methodological tactics to communicate the ideas I will outline, I feel that their development constitutes a second and subsidiary phase. The overall strategy – the question of *what* we are teaching and *why* – seems to me often to get lost among questions concerned with the *how*. To redress this imbalance, and for reasons of space, I will leave it to my readers to decide how the topics I describe could be presented to their classes. Though I recognise that the problem exists, and is an important one, I do not see it as in any way insoluble – indeed I believe that a sensible adaptation of well-known techniques would be enough.

11.2   The Lion King

A common problem for teachers of literature who use video is inherent in the 'film of the book' approach. With a few exceptions (*A Room with a View*, for example), great literature makes mediocre cinema and vice versa. The teacher who wants to exploit the best films available, irrespective of their literary provenance, would be well advised, I think, to focus on thematic links between film and literature. Let's assume, for the sake of argument, that a teacher wants to show the Disney cartoon *The Lion King*. A comparison with the written version (yes, there is a book of the cartoon) in terms of form and technique holds out very little prospect of firing the class's enthusiasm. Rather, it is likely to kill the interest even of hardened Disneyphiles. What about a thematic approach? What are the dominant themes of this story?

Clearly the film is concerned with authority: the just authority of the Lion King and its usurpation by the tyrannical Scar. The film opens with the pilgrimage of the animals to pay homage to the new-born prince Simba, son of Mufasa, the Lion King. Mufasa rules by a universally recognised divine right: even the zebras and the antelopes pay their homage willingly, with no suggestion of fear for the predator. When Scar, Simba's uncle, kills his brother Mufasa and usurps the crown, a reign of terror is introduced in which the hyenas act as a kind of Gestapo (even to the extent of parading in neat military rows before their leader). The land suffers a drought, and despite the urging of the hyenas, the lionesses are unable to kill enough meat to feed themselves. Meanwhile Simba grows up in exile in a kind of prelapsarian paradise, in which he learns to live exclusively on larvae and bugs and to dance musical numbers with a warthog and a raccoon. Finally the ghost of his dead father Mufasa appears to him, urging him to resume his dynastic respons-ibilities, and he returns to his homeland to do battle with Scar and restore the principle of legitimacy. A thunderstorm bursts over him as he roars out his triumph, and the drought is ended.

The conscious literary antecedents of the film include, of course, *Hamlet* and *The Waste Land*. But the link with Shakespeare's history plays is perhaps more interesting. The film is a classic example of the way in which art can give life to a myth of origins, transposing a relation based on naked power into one of traditional authority with roots in the long-forgotten past. Never in the film is a lion seen to kill or eat another animal: rather than devour his friends, Simba learns to live on bugs. In reality, the lion is king of the jungle by reason of his strength and speed: antelopes and zebras are not known for their interest in dynastic questions. In this film, Simba and Mufasa rule through the author-ity of tradition: usurpation, on the other hand, brings divine retribution. The myth of Mufasa's divine right is thus similar to the Tudor myth (the idea, sedulously fostered by the Tudor kings, that Henry VII was acting as the instrument of Providence in deposing Richard III and 'restoring legitimacy'), and Shakespeare's history plays, written out of deference to this myth but embodying some trenchant criticisms of it too, are in fact a similar but more complex analysis of the relation of power to authority. Simba's exile with the fat and jovial warthog Pumba can be compared to Prince Hal's dalliance with his fat and jovial friend Falstaff: a period of innocence and irresponsibility with a loving and anarchic father-figure before the weight of destiny settles on his shoulders. Unlike Disney, however, Shakespeare reminds us that law and order on the one hand, and careless ease on the other, can only be bought at a price. The price of orderly rule is the ruthless suppression of dissent; the price of Falstaff's misrule is the triumph of anarchy and the destruction of the weak (such as the invalids and beggars whom Falstaff sends to their deaths through his corrupt recruiting practices). *The Lion King*, on the other hand, embodies a less ambiguous, more obviously authoritarian ideology, encouraging unthinking obedience to the king, without questioning (indeed doing all it can to disguise) the source of his authority.

But Disney's studios gloss the brutality of this message with a veneer of democracy and political correctness. They are perhaps worried about an accusation of racism, possibly in reaction to the storm that greeted early versions of *Aladdin* (they were forced to rewrite the lyrics of one song, which had praised the brutal, primitive and culturally deprived nature of Aladdin's Middle Eastern home). So in token homage to Africa, where the film is set, and to the American negro, Mufasa speaks in the deep, throaty tones of an Afro-American. The freedom-loving Simba, inevitably, has a north-American whine, while the evil Scar is dubbed in a refined British upper-class voice. The opposition between British culture (interpreted as tyranny) and American nature (seen as a love of liberty) can be traced back to the War of Independence, and is obvious in popular films like *Spartacus*, where the all-American Kirk Douglas plays the rough, uncomplicated rebel while the parts of the cruel and sophisticated Romans are taken by the British actors Laurence Olivier and Charles Laughton. In its choice of accents, then, the film is following a long-established Hollywood tradition of associating the British with cruel tyrants and sus piciously intellectual aesthetes. Scar's superior intelligence in this film is merely a sign of the moral degeneracy implicit in this accent, and is contrasted unfavourably with the simple-mindedness of the good lions. Thus Simba is cast in the role of Spartacus and George Washington: the straightforward man of the people who champions freedom and democracy against a corrupt and tyrannical authority. It is ironic that he should also represent the purest and most uncompromising form of absolute monarchy.

11.3   Madwomen: introduction

I now want to look at another set of films and books, in order to illustrate a thematic linking of literature and film in rather more detail. The theme is the presentation of the madwomen in *Jane Eyre*[1] and a number of other works of literature and cinema. I hope to show that works as different as *Jane Eyre* and *Fatal Attraction* have enough in common to make a comparison between them both feasible and rewarding in the classroom. An exploration of this kind combines the study of literature and film in a way that students will find stimulating, and puts into practice the often-expressed aim of bridging the gap between literary classics and works of popular culture without devaluing the former or reducing the discussion to a collection of banalities.

Apart from *Jane Eyre* and its by-product *Wide Sargasso Sea* (Jean Rhys's novel has recently been filmed, and is available on video), I am interested in *Great Expectations, Rebecca* (both du Maurier's novel and Hitchcock's film), and the films *Psycho* and *Fatal Attraction*. (Though I do not deal with them for reasons of space, both the film and the novel of *The French Lieutenant's Woman* also fit very well into the pattern I describe.) I will first look at the relation between these works, in order to show that this relation is the product not only of conscious imitation (though there is certainly some of that) but also of unconscious shared assumptions about the role of women in life and society. I will then look at the different ways in which the authors and filmmakers I am discussing approach the 'madwoman' theme, and what these differences tell us about their different attitudes.[2]

11.3.1   *The myth: monster women*

The works I have selected all contain at least one madwoman whose presence impinges on the heroine in a mysterious and threatening way. The mad wife in *Jane Eyre* is well-known; Bertha Mason's descendants include Rebecca and her sinister alter-ego Mrs Danvers in du Maurier's novel, Mrs Bates in *Psycho* and the rabbit-boiling Alex in *Fatal Attraction*. Slightly different, but nevertheless comparable (cousins, perhaps, rather than direct descendants), are Estella's real and surrogate mothers, Molly and Miss Havisham, in *Great Expectations*. All these women are mad, and all but Miss Havisham are murderous in intention, if not in fact. In each case (with the partial exception of *Great Expectations*) they are contrasted with a gentle and unassuming heroine, with whom they struggle for possession of the hero.

Maxim de Winter, the hero of Daphne du Maurier's *Rebecca*, finds himself in a predicament very similar to Rochester's in *Jane Eyre*. Like Rochester, he is a wealthy man who has married a beautiful and glamorous wife, and the marriage has gone wrong. His wife (the Rebecca of the title) dies, and, like Rochester, he marries a timid, unglamorous girl much younger than himself. Further parallels between the two novels emerge when we meet Mrs

Danvers, the sinister housekeeper at Manderley, de Winter's country seat. Charlotte Brontë's mad wife seems to have been split in two in this novel. On the one hand, there is the splendid and corrupt Rebecca, now dead, who has so much in common with the young Bertha Mason, the West Indian beauty. On the other, there is the ghost-like virago Mrs Danvers, who glides noiselessly about, jealous of the heroine's happiness, tries to frighten her to death, and eventually sets fire to the house, like Bertha Mason in her decadence.

Dickens's Miss Havisham is another Gothic madwoman who lives imprisoned (by choice, this time) in a dark, windowless upper room. Like Bertha Mason and Rebecca, she is a highly passionate woman crazed by disappointment in love, and determined to revenge herself on the man who has failed her. Interestingly, Dickens plays a variation on this theme in a minor key in the figure of Molly, Estella's real mother, another passionate woman driven by jealousy to murder and madness.

Both *Psycho* and *Fatal Attraction* follow these novels in using the motif of the monstrous woman driven mad by jealousy. In the latter film, Alex resorts to a series of unappetising stratagems to terrorise her recalcitrant lover back to her, and eventually ends up attempting to murder him and his wife. In *Psycho*, the monster woman is Mrs Bates who, according to the account given by her son, murdered her lover when she discovered that he was betraying her. Sexual jealousy – this time of the woman her son meets – also seems to lie behind her subsequent atrocities. Like *Jane Eyre*, then, this film features a monstrous female, confined by day and never seen, who escapes at night to commit unspeakable crimes born of jealousy.

11.3.2 Alternative readings

Though the savage lunatic and the gentle heroine of *Jane Eyre* look very different at first sight, the similarities lie close to the surface, and several critics have commented on the hidden links between heroine and virago. In *The Madwoman in the Attic* (1979), Sandra Gilbert and Susan Gubar talk of Bertha Mason as 'the sedate heroine's double' who 'not only acts for Jane, but also acts like Jane' (pp. 314, 361). In this interpretation, Mrs Rochester represents not merely a macabre obstacle in Jane's path to happiness, but a victim who has succumbed to forces that threaten all women, Jane included. Gilbert and Gubar see in Bertha Mason an image of the predicament of women in a patriarchal society: the madwoman imprisoned in the attic as a warning to others, an illustration of the dangers of rebelling against social restraints that all women must accept. These implications are made explicit in Jean Rhys's short novel *Wide Sargasso Sea* (1966), which tells how Rochester's coldness and suspicion gradually plunge his passionately loving wife into despair – a despair which Rochester takes for the first signs of madness. Isolated from her home and her family, and mistrusted by her husband, she becomes increasingly hysterical, until he transports her to a foreign country, a cold climate, and imprisonment in the attic of Thornfield Hall. Here solitude, homesickness and confinement ensure that she soon becomes as crazy as her husband believes her to be.

When Jean Rhys rewrote the story of Edward Rochester and Bertha Mason, she cast Rochester as the villain, reversing the assumptions that Charlotte Brontë had made. But this reversal is to some extent prepared for in the original novel, and a close reading of some passages makes it clear that – whether Brontë was aware of it or not – Bertha Mason is a victim of her husband's and her society's double standards as much as and more than Jane. This becomes clear if we look at Rochester's apologia, the speech in which he explains to Jane how he came to find himself in the role of attempted bigamist. Shocked by his first wife's 'giant propens-ities' for drink and sex, he says that he looked into the question of divorce (by appeal to the House of Lords, presumably – divorce in other courts did not become a possibility until ten years after the publication of *Jane Eyre*). But he found to his disappointment that 'I could not rid myself of it (i.e. her) by any legal proceedings: for the doctors now discovered that my wife was mad.' He attributes the madness not only to heredity but essentially to Bertha Mason's taste for extra-marital relations: 'her excesses', he explains with nicely scientific detachment, 'had prematurely developed the germs of her insanity.' By an unfortunate irony, the very adultery which might have constituted grounds for divorce has driven her insane – and thus made divorce impossible, for if she is insane she is not responsible for her actions.

But Rochester's apologia hides another irony which tells against himself. His case against Bertha Mason is that she drinks and sleeps around – 'excesses' which drive her mad and force him to lock her up in the attic at Thornfield Hall. Distraught, he wanders around Europe trying to forget. 'I tried dissipation,' he says,

'– never debauchery: that I hated, and hate.' He admits, that is, that he is not averse to drinking like his wife (he calls it 'dissipation'), but denies that he fell into her other favourite vice. Yet a few lines later he glibly remarks that 'I could not live alone; so I tried the companionship of mistresses.'

Drink and sex drive Mrs Rochester mad; Rochester is forced to lock her up and wander forlornly about the continent, consoling himself with sex and drink. Women who take lovers go mad, he implies; men find it soothes their nerves. Though *Jane Eyre* is in other ways a novel of feminist protest, the double standard is operating at full force here, and apparently with the author's approval, for Brontë seems to expect the reader's pity and sympathy for Rochester to equal Jane's. We will find the pattern repeated in the other works I have singled out.

Du Maurier's nameless narrator in *Rebecca* devotes most of the novel to explaining how the shadow of Rebecca hangs over her, making her painfully aware of the contrast between her brilliant predecessor and her humble self. Rebecca, it seems, had all the joie de vivre that she lacks, and that Bertha Mason had before insanity claimed her. As she listens to her husband's account of his previous marriage, she says, 'the real Rebecca took shape and form before me. Rebecca triumphant.' But then her husband startles her: 'I found her out at once,' he was saying, 'five days after we were married. . . . She sat there laughing, her hair blowing in the wind; she told me things about herself, told me things that I shall never repeat to a living soul.'

The exact content of this frightful confession is never revealed, but it is enough to make the marriage a marriage in name only from that moment on. Eventually it becomes de Winter's principal justification for killing his wife, just as sexual misconduct – Bertha Mason's 'giant propensities' – had originally induced Rochester to lock her up. Presumably Rebecca's unspeakable offences date from before the wedding, since the confession is made only five days after it; we wonder what form of perversion could have put so sudden an end to her husband's devotion. The very implausibility makes us suspect that de Winter's reaction is out of all proportion to the offence confessed, and he begins to look rather a cold (or wintery) fish. For him as for Rochester, it seems, a woman who betrays a liking for sex is beyond the pale. Double standards lie behind his repudiation of Rebecca just as they had lain behind Rochester's repudiation of Bertha.

- They can also be seen behind the figure of Mrs Danvers. Like Bertha Mason, Mrs Danvers is insane, and again the insanity is cause and consequence of sexual misconduct. Du Maurier hints (and Hitchcock more than hints) that a lesbian passion for the dead Rebecca is the cause of Mrs Danvers's resentment – a resentment that turns into madness. Irregular passions in women lead to insanity, here as in *Jane Eyre.*

The subversive reading of *Jane Eyre* that Jean Rhys applied in *Wide Sargasso Sea* thus fits almost equally well to *Rebecca.* In each case a beautiful, passionate woman marries a rather cold and uncomprehending man, who very soon begins to suspect her sanity. Sexual misconduct confirms this diagnosis in the husband's eyes, until the wife is utterly repudiated, and either imprisoned or killed. In each novel a ghost-like figure (Bertha Mason or Mrs Danvers), maddened by jealousy, patrols the house in secret, spying on the heroine and obstructing her attempts to construct a happy relationship with the hero.

The parallels between Mrs Rochester and Mrs Danvers are reinforced by their deaths, and link them in turn to Miss Havisham of *Great Expectations,* for all three are burnt in fires of their own making. Fire is an important symbol in each of these novels, in fact, pointing to the unsatisfied and destructive passions which are consuming these women: Mrs Rochester sets fire to her husband's bed; Miss Havisham to her own bridal dress and wedding banquet; Mrs Danvers, like Mrs Rochester, to the house, and (in Hitchcock's film) to Rebecca's bed, with the lovingly embroidered 'R' – the sign of their illicit passion – being consumed by flames in the last images of the film.

The idea that female passion leads to madness is evoked in a small way in the depiction of the heroine in *Psycho,* for Marion Crane too has been driven, not to full-scale lunacy, but to a moment of insanity by her inability to contain her desires. Because she is not prepared to wait two years or so for Sam to free himself from his financial commitments and marry her, she steals the $40,000 that sets the plot in motion, and leads to her watery death beneath the shower.

The close similarities between these works are not, I believe, the results only of coincidence or a shared taste for Gothic melodrama. Surface similarities reveal an underlying theme common to all of them, which can be summarised as a cautionary tale aimed at women who challenge the double standard and attempt to break out of the mould that confines them to passive, subservient roles. The unspoken premise of *Jane Eyre*, made explicit in *Wide Sargasso Sea*, is that Victorian society cannot accommodate female passion, and that women who are burdened with a passionate nature must either repress it or go mad. The same message can be found in the more recent productions. Each of these works involves a woman driven towards murder by excesses of passion and jealousy, who is shown to be mad and usually punished with death. The apparent premise of each work – the simple Gothic motif of the spectral, ghoulish female who stands between the nice girl and a happy marriage – can be read as a warning to all women to accept their subordinate position and keep their passions well under control on pain of insanity, imprisonment and possibly death.

What differentiates these works from each other is the degree to which the author or filmmaker seems either to endorse or to criticise this 'cautionary-tale' element in his or her story, and this, I suggest, should constitute the ultimate object of study in a course based on this theme.

11.3.3   Degrees of endorsement

It is convenient to begin with *Fatal Attraction*, for the film reveals a fairly simple and uncritical endorsement of the repressive message. As Joan Smith (1989, pp. 24–28) points out, the film is a vicious attack on 'liberated' working women: Alex, the heroine with a male name, the working woman who aspires to equality on a professional and sexual level, is revealed to be a dangerous lunatic, given more to boiling children's pets than filling a responsible position in a publishing company (we see her at work only once). In the end she is revealed as a kind of modern-day witch: she lives above a sinister meat market, turns water into blood, penetrates well-protected premises without difficulty, and returns from the dead, surviving the traditional test of witchhood – ordeal by drowning. She is in every way different from the gentle, loving wife whom she tries to murder. The film, then, is based on an opposition between the two stereotypes of virago and innocent, and scarcely stops to question this opposition. The other works under consideration seem to rely on the same opposition, but a closer analysis shows that the more the author is aware of the repressive message inherent in the myth of the madwoman, the more this opposition is undermined, and it is suggested that virago and heroine are not after all related by opposition as guilty villain and innocent victim, but by equivalence as victims of a third party, the man. Let us look at each of these works in turn, to see this procedure in action.

Again and again in *Jane Eyre*, Jane speaks of herself in terms that the mad Bertha Mason might have used to describe her own descent into insanity. As a rebellious child, she is imprisoned by her aunt, just as her 'double' will later be imprisoned by Rochester and Grace Poole, and the terror of confinement produces 'a species of fit', comparable – though on a smaller scale – to Bertha's madness. After the discovery of Bertha Mason's existence, she insists on leaving Rochester, saying 'I will hold to the law given by God when I was sane, and not mad – as I am now. . . . I am insane, quite insane, with my veins running fire, and my heart beating faster than I can count its throbs.'

These and similar extracts prove that Jane is very close to the kind of hysteria which led to Bertha's imprisonment, and that she knows it. The description of her pacing 'backwards and forwards' in frustration along the third-storey corridor is especially interesting, for, only a few feet away from Jane, Bertha Mason is also pacing up and down in her cell. (Brontë actually uses the same phrase 'backwards and forwards' for both of them.) Again and again in the novel, Jane speaks of herself as hysterical and close to insanity because of the way she finds her emotions and desires blocked. The novel makes it clear that the only alternatives before passionate women are those of repression and madness. Unlike her rival, Jane is strong-willed enough to repress her desires, and she remains just on the right side of the border of sanity.

What these links show is that Brontë was to some extent aware of the subversive reading later applied to her novel by Jean Rhys. Her intuition suggested that both women – the monstrous villain and the innocent heroine – are victims of the same pressures, and that the madness of the former is not the result of personal delinquency so much as a surrender to these pressures. Though she might not have been happy to admit it, she realised that on one level the villain of *Jane Eyre* is Rochester and not Bertha.

Du Maurier seems to have woven the same subversive message into her repressive story with more conscious deliberation. 'I wish I was a woman of about thirty-six dressed in black satin with a string of pearls,' says the nameless heroine, uncomfortably conscious of her lack of a well-defined personality. De Winter reassures her that he is attracted to her precisely 'because you are not dressed in black satin, with a string of pearls, nor are you thirty-six.' Though much of this novel is concerned with the difference between de Winter's two wives, it presents not so much the contrast between the two women, as the failure of the heroine to construct an independent identity of her own. Marriage seems to offer her the chance to assume an adult personality, to become like Rebecca, to use her personalised stationery and to copy her costume for the masked ball, yet she is always conscious of her own shortcomings, and in the end she admits her failure. Maxim had loved her for what she was not: not thirty-six, not dressed in black satin, not sexually experienced and threatening like Rebecca. But when she loses these negative attractions, what will be left? This question hangs over the conventional romanticism of both the novel and film of *Rebecca*, and conflicts with the lushly romantic treatment that the film's producer David Selznick insisted on. The novel shows the heroine refusing the variously unwelcome roles offered her by society, and failing to find an alternative. Neither a *femme fatale* like Rebecca nor a virago like Mrs Danvers – nor any longer a childish innocent – she fails to fit into any female role and becomes, literally, a nobody, living in exile with her husband, with no home, no occupation, no company, no friends, no children, and no name.

In this sense, the book, like the other works in discussion, is concerned not with the contrast between heroine and villain, but with their common predicament, with the pressures which force women to adopt 'villainous' roles, simply because no alternative is available. Rebecca acts on her desires and is killed for it; the narrator suppresses (or never discovers) hers, and ceases to exist as a person. *Rebecca* is not only the novelettish story of a young girl who found her identity through love, but a more complex tale of the impossibility of creating a female identity outside the models imposed by society.

Great Expectations is too complex a novel to do more than scratch its surface, but I think that the approach I suggest can do a lot to provide a key to some of the interpretative problems that the book presents. Why is Estella so insistently cold? Why does she marry the sadistic Bentley Drummle, whom she claims to despise? In a society which offers passionate women the choice of repression and insanity, repression is obviously the better alternative,

even repression of so fierce a kind that the subject is led to
declare, like Estella, 'I have no heart.' With Molly for a mother
and Miss Havisham for a stepmother, Estella is no stranger, either
genetically or by education, to the ravages of female passion, so
that her ice-cold indifference to Pip can be seen as a considered
reaction to a society which leaves her no better alternative.
Marriage to a sadist like Bentley Drummle is the extreme expression of a nature traumatised into masochistic passivity.

These readings suggest that Brontë, du Maurier and Dickens
were all at least partially aware of the alternative readings outlined
above, as Adrian Lyne was not. Heroine and villain are presented
in their novels not only as opposites but also as twins, caught in
the same trap. *Psycho* is the most self-conscious of all these works,
for it explicitly rather than implicitly demolishes the myth on
which it feeds. The film reveals that Mrs Bates is not a monstrous
lunatic, but an ordinary woman who dared take a lover long after
her husband's death, and was killed for it. Norman is the villain
not only in the suppressed sense of the novels, but because he
really is a murderous psychopath, killing women who attempt to
find scope for their feelings. What is more, the monster woman is
his creation, not metaphorically but actually: where the unspoken
assumptions of Rochester and his heirs turned passionate women
into monstrous criminals, Norman creates a monster with his own
hands (by embalming his mother's corpse) and then attributes his
atrocities to this creation. And he recreates this monster woman
each time he puts on his mother's clothes and assumes her voice.
Psycho can thus be read as a literal rendering of the process by
which men make monsters out of women, and then accuse them
of their own crimes. Like Brontë and du Maurier, Hitchcock
stresses the links between heroine and monster. Marion defies the
law, Mrs Bates her son, for the men they love, and both are victims
of the same man, who punishes their presumption with death.
Viragos or innocents, women must be repressed into conformity.

All of these works raise questions about the role of women in
society, and about the extent to which a woman should curb her
own nature in order to fit in with social preconceptions of what
women should be. All use the stereotype figure of the lunatic
virago to delineate the alternative to repression. What differentiates them is the attitude of the writer/filmmaker; the extent to
which the values of society are upheld or criticised. Adrian Lyne
comes out badly here: his film seems unaware of the complexities

of the problem, while Hitchcock comes out surprisingly well, given his reputation for misogyny. I would suggest that 'degrees of endorsement' of the repressive message can give at least a provisional index of the value of these novels and films.

11.4 Formalism in the classroom

It may be objected that my proposal has little to do with films as such, but only with 'texts', or stories. This is part, in fact, of the more general objection that I imagine will be made by my readers of formalist tendencies: that I ignore form in order to concentrate on meaning. Because I think this is the fundamental issue in literature teaching, I will dedicate the rest of this paper to answering this kind of objection. First, however, it is worth pointing out that my approach, though it does not deal with 'film' in the sense of film technique, nevertheless opens up one or two new prospects for the teacher with video facilities. It makes it possible to use classic films like David Lean's *Great Expectations* or Hitchcock's *Rebecca* in the classroom, even where the topic of study is *Jane Eyre*, so that the teacher whose main focus is on Brontë's novel is no longer compelled between doing without the video and showing the rather feeble films that have been made of this novel.

A formalist would claim that the varying attitudes to women revealed in these works can only be understood through an analysis of form and technique. I am convinced, instead, that teachers would do better to make their starting point 'what happens', rather than the way it is presented. First of all, this has the obvious practical advantage of relating directly to students' interests (they all go to the cinema, but few of them spontaneously discuss technique). But it is also defensible on a more theoretical plane. It is a commonplace that meaning is inseparable from form; what is often forgotten is that this argument, which the formalists use to justify them in ignoring meaning, can equally logically justify us in ignoring form. Instead of trying to understand meaning by talking about form, why not do the opposite?

Nigel Ross's article 'Literature and film' (1991) is a fairly typical example of the formalist approach in practice. Ross gives details of a course which concentrated on a comparison of the prose and screen versions of *Nineteen Eighty-four*, *A Passage to India*, *Sophie's Choice* and so on. To make this feasible, more than half the time available (sixteen weeks out of a total of twenty-eight) was devoted to a preliminary examination of literary and cinematic techniques. There is certainly a lot to be gained from this, but there is a price to pay too.

The heavy emphasis on technique, both in cinema and prose fiction, will tend to have the alienating effect which all formalist approaches to art produce in the classroom. Readers and filmgoers think naturally in terms of a story to be told, rather than of the means used in telling it. Do we really need to suggest that sixteen weeks' preliminary study is needed, not to understand but merely to lay the groundwork for understanding the films that everyone watches on television and in the cinema? When the teacher destroys the fictional illusion by pointing out the technical dexterity of writer or filmmaker, the students' emotional involvement in the story for its own sake is transformed into a detached intellectual curiosity about the artist's skill. In this way we risk transmitting the nihilistic message that all meanings are equivalent, and only style is valuable. If *Psycho* is a pernicious film, as many critics believe (see for example Smith 1989, p. 20), its stylistic accomplishment only makes it more so. The crucial question is not how many separate takes are spliced together in the shower murder sequence, nor how Hitchcock managed to give so convincing an impression of nudity without ever showing a nipple or a buttock (moleskin patches), but whether the spectator is invited to participate in the murder as knife-wielding maniac, as victim, or as witness. Of course this is also a stylistic question, involving camera angles and identification techniques, but it is above all a question which involves our total response to the story as it has unfolded so far.

Too often, film versions of well-known novels simply transpose a successful story to another medium. What is the teacher to do, for example, with Jack Gold's excellent version of Graham Greene's *The Tenth Man*? Some of the hiccups in the novel are smoothed out, and Anthony Hopkins is moving in his role, but the message of the film remains the same as that of the book. Comparison therefore is forced to concentrate on the trivia of technique, and to lose sight of the meaning. In this case, it would be more logical to study the film or the story on its own. Sometimes, of course, a film makes changes to the plot which are so significant that comparison becomes worthwhile, as in the case of *Great Expectations*. In the light of my discussion of madwomen above, there is a lot to be said for David Lean's image (which has no counterpart in the novel) of Estella widowed and alone, sitting in darkness in Miss Havisham's chair, succumbing to the madness which, it seems, is every woman's birthright in Victorian England. More often, the film is like the BBC version of *Jane Eyre*: faithful but uninspiring; too close to the original to make comparison stimulating, too far to be anything but a poor substitute for the 'real thing'.

The major practical advantage of approaches which concentrate on style and technique is that they can be generalised: an activity devised for dealing with the film of *Pride and Prejudice* will work equally well with anything else, from *My Fair Lady* to *The Dead*. If we talk about meaning, on the other hand, every story is different, so that every theme-based approach has to be worked out from scratch. Thus it may seem that there is a serious problem of feasibility. It must look as if I am asking teachers to do an enormous, unmanageable amount of research before they are ready to attempt a thematic approach at all. I have two answers to this.

First of all, if the validity of the approach were accepted by syllabus designers, textbook writers and teacher-trainers, then it would become their task to take the weight off the practising teacher's shoulders by developing a range of topic-based units for teachers to experiment with. Secondly, the approach can be considerably 'diluted', and developed bit by bit over a long period. Thus a teacher might begin with a simple comparison of *Rebecca* and *Jane Eyre*, used principally as a starting point for discussion and language development. As new ideas emerge, they can be grafted onto this simple base, and integrated into the unit next time around, with another class.

Another disadvantage of my kind of thematic approach will be immediately apparent: a lot of time is going to be spent on books and films which probably don't appear on the syllabus. If the teacher has to prepare a class for an examination on *Jane Eyre* or the Victorian novel, it may seem hard to justify spending time on *Rebecca*, *Psycho* and *Fatal Attraction*. Equally, it may seem that everything in *Jane Eyre* and *Great Expectations* which is not concerned with madwomen gets ignored, so that students will emerge from a course of this kind with an unbalanced and partial view of the novels. I am not very worried by these objections, partly because I think that any teacher who takes literature seriously must be prepared to go into depth somewhere, even at the expense of breadth of coverage, and partly because I think that the issue I have discussed throws light on all parts of the works in question in a way that a more superficial analysis could never do. In any case, I offer the approach not as a solution to the problems of literature teaching through video, but as one possible itinerary among many, which teachers are welcome to use and adapt as they think fit. I do believe, however, that its advantages far outweigh these disadvantages.

What are these advantages? Above all, this thematic and comparative approach breaks down the barrier that normally separates novels like *Jane Eyre* and *Great Expectations* from the popular culture that is part of our students' daily lives. This principle is frequently stated, but it is difficult to put it into practice in a convincing way without either trivialising the classics or giving inflated significance to contemporary ephemera. The analysis outlined above would, I think, not only encourage students to look at the classics with fresh and unprejudiced eyes, but also to reflect on the meaning of things that happen around them every day.

To do this it might be enough to find points of similarity between the works on the syllabus and the films at the cinema. But the teacher who has made it clear that *Fatal Attraction* deserves the same kind of attention as *Great Expectations* ought then to be able to convince the class that it is worth spending more time on the latter. In other words, it should become clear that though the two products do not differ in kind, they do in quality. Having shown what Brontë and Dickens have in common with Hitchcock, du Maurier and Adrian Lyne, we should give some explanation for the difference in the amount of critical respect that is generally accorded to them. Otherwise the literature syllabus will seem a fraud – an arbitrary imposition of works which are canonical only because their authors have been dead long enough to be canonised. A further advantage of my approach, therefore, is that it provides some kind of framework for evaluation, by allowing us to compare the subtlety with which different authors and directors handle the same topic.

The rather sterile debate about the place of the 'canon' in literature teaching continues to flicker on. Do authors earn a place on the syllabus because they've always been on it, as traditionalists argue, or because they are considered politically correct? Both schools practise opposing forms of indoctrination, denying students the privilege of an open mind. Yet it is only by keeping an open mind, by asking the same questions of a classic novel and a popular film, of a canonical and uncanonical text, that our students will learn to achieve an accurate appreciation of both. *Fatal Attraction* and *The Lion King* are neither canonical nor politically correct, but they can both be discussed intelligently in relation to 'classics' like *Jane Eyre* or *Henry IV*. Once this is clear, then the controversy evaporates and literature becomes relevant to life again.

Notes

1. Charlotte Brontë's novel *Jane Eyre* was first published in 1847, and has been filmed many times. Charles Dickens's *Great Expectations* dates from 1860/61, and was the basis of David Lean's highly successful film in the 1940s. Daphne du Maurier's *Rebecca* was published by Gollancz, London, in 1938, and filmed by Alfred Hitchcock in 1940. Hitchcock's film *Psycho* was released in 1960. Jean Rhys's *Wide Sargasso Sea* was published by Deutsch, London, in 1966, and filmed by John Duigan in 1992. John Fowles's *The French Lieutenant's Woman* was published by Cape, London, in 1969, and filmed, with a screenplay by Harold Pinter, in the 1970s. The film *Fatal Attraction*, directed by Adrian Lyne, was released in 1987. The cartoon film *The Lion King* was released by Disney Studios in 1994.
2. Readers may like to note that the theme of 'madness' is also treated in the paper by McCarthy and in section 1.5 of the paper by Carter. [Eds.]

12

Common ground: incorporating new literatures in English in language and literature teaching

MALACHI EDWIN VETHAMANI

In this concluding paper, the author presents teaching approaches to five texts drawn from a range of 'new literatures in English' – from Malaysia, Singapore, Thailand, and the Philippines. Language-based activities and stylistic analysis are used for tasks before, during, and after reading.

Given that the same approach with the same objectives is equally valid in the study of south-east Asian texts as those deriving from the western canon, Vethamani argues that new literatures are unjustly overlooked in most teaching contexts, and that their inclusion can broaden students' perceptions of the use of English in wider cultural contexts. This is a deliberately practical, classroom-focused paper underlining that texts from all literatures in English can be given similar classroom treatment; implicitly, the paper reinforces the theoretical issues raised in the papers by McRae, Cook and Mao Sihui, in particular, concerning canonical and non-canonical text.

Teachers are often quite happy using the safe and tried texts that they have used over the years with their students. It is also not uncommon that these were the very same texts that they had studied as students. Consequently, selections of texts limited to English and American literary works have become their traditional source for teaching, and other invaluable resources which are readily available in new literary traditions in English are neglected.

It was MacCabe (1982, p. 18) who said that 'English literature is dead – long live writing in English.' What he was talking about was the emergence of new Englishes and their attendant literatures. Zach (1991, p. 15) acknowledges this and adds that 'we cannot but widen our field of study from "English (and American) Literature" into "Literature(s) in English".'

In the ESL/EFL teaching context, even in countries which are rich in new literatures in English, there is an almost wilful denial of locally produced writing in favour of the more fashionable new literatures in English, according to the fashion of the moment. In view of this, in this paper, I want to introduce some unfamiliar texts which can be used to discuss a few shared universal themes. All readings of the texts will be organised into pre-reading, while-reading and post-reading stages (see McRae 1991; Wallace 1992), using language-based activities and stylistic analysis (see Carter and Long 1991; McRae 1991). The title and name of the writer are revealed only at the end of the reading activity.[1]

Text 1

Pre-reading tasks

Read the extract given below and answer the following questions.

1. How many people are mentioned in this passage?
2. Who is Shirley?

> The next day I visit my parents. I am always gratified by mother's fuss. Father is gruff, as usual. He hardly speaks. No doubt he resents the impotence of old age, the dependency into which my success has thrust him. Looking at those tough hands that once wielded ever so readily a stout bamboo cane I cannot resist a certain satisfaction. This quickly passes however, for I want his approval more than his resentment. I know he is disdainful of the fact that Shirley has not accompanied me, that she would never tend me as mother does him. He cannot understand that it is a different world, that no woman, at least no worthwhile woman, can devote herself to a man in the way that was once universal. They want their own lives, their own identities, and Shirley does a lot of good in the community, with charities and women's groups, though sometimes I wish she'd spend more time with Weixian (but who of course am I to talk?).

While-reading tasks

1. (a) Fill in the blanks in Column B with the persons with whom the words in Column A are associated.

Column A	Column B
gratified	. . . .
impotence	. . . .
dependency	. . . .
success	. . . .
resentment	. . . .
disdainful	. . . .

(b) Who do you think chose these words? What could suggest this?

2. Describe the father and son's attitudes towards each other.
3. Why does the son observe that 'it is a different world'? Does he seem happy with the change? How can you tell?
4. What is the son's view of a 'worthwhile woman'? Do you agree with his view?
5. What can you infer about the father and son's perceptions of the roles of the wife? Is there any difference? If there is, how do they differ? Which is closer to your own opinion?
6. What does the line '(but who of course am I to talk)' tell the reader about the son? Why is this in brackets?

Post-reading tasks

- A question which might be opened up for class discussion: Is the change in the traditional role of women as universal as the speaker in this extract claims?
- Show and Tell session: Students find articles on the topic – 'Today's Woman'.
- Debate the motion: 'A Woman's Place is Where She Feels at Home'.

Summary

The treatment of man–woman relationships as with other forms of inter-personal relationships is a cornerstone in literature. The extract from this short story presents a perception of husband–wife roles. As societies have varying perceptions of the roles of husbands and wives, it will be interesting to see how students react to a Singaporean character's views. This extract is from Singaporean writer Philip Jeyaretnam's short story entitled *Making Coffee*.

Text 2

Pre-reading task

1. (a) Complete the first line of each stanza with a word.

I came to you at _____
With silvery dew on sleeping lotus
Sparkling in my gay hands;
You put my flowers in the sun.

I danced to you at _____
With bright raintree blooms
Flaming in my ardent arms;
You dropped my blossoms in the pond.

I crept to you at _____
With pale lilac orchids
Trembling on my uncertain lips;
You shredded my petals in the sand.

I strode to you at _____
With gravel hard and cold
Clenched in my bitter fists;
You offered me your hybrid orchids,
And I _____

   (b) Teacher and students discuss students' choice of words.
   (c) Teacher provides the poet's choice of words (see Appendix) and class discussion follows: do students prefer their own choices to the poet's?

While-reading tasks

1. Sentence completion.
   (a) Students read the poem again and provide a final line.
   (b) Teacher asks students to study their line and see if the lines are positive or negative in tone.
   (c) Class discussion on students' answers follows.
   (d) Teacher provides the original sentence from the poem; students compare the poet's sentence with their own and comment.
2. Examining relationships.
   Teacher asks students to speculate on the relationship between the 'I' and the 'you' in the poem. Students give reasons for their answers.

3. Exploring conflict.
   (a) Teacher asks students to pick out the words used to describe the speaker's movement in each stanza.
   (b) Students are asked to comment on the significance of the words and also the time references in relation to the speaker's attempts to present his/her 'gifts'.
   (c) Students are asked if they approve of the speaker's action in the final stanza.
4. Interpreting images.
   Students are asked if there is any difference in the flowers which the speaker brought and the flowers that were given to the speaker. What could this tell us?

Post-reading tasks

1. Inferring voice.
   Teacher asks students if the speaker is male or female. Does knowing the sex of the speaker make any difference in the interpretation of the poem?
2. Giving a title.
   (a) Teacher asks students to give an appropriate title for the poem. Students could be asked to think of a one-word title or this could be left open-ended.
   (b) Teacher provides the original title (see Appendix) and students compare the poet's title with their own, and comment.

Summary

Rejection is another human predicament which is universal and experienced by people of all ages. The Malaysian poet, Hilary Tham's *Offerings* (see Appendix) highlights this theme, and reading this text provides a lot of opportunities for students to discover how writers from various cultural backgrounds could depict it.

Text 3

Pre-reading task

Answer the following questions as you read the extract given below.

- What do you think Dan's religious faith is? Which words in the extract suggest this?

The blazing sun kept beating on him, yet he prayed on. 'Oh lords have mercy on Grandma and all the old people. Grandma eats nothing; she is so old and bony. Her clothes are also old and tattered. Have pity on old people for they cannot dig for yams or taro or chase grasshoppers and catch lizards for food.'

His endurance was that of a child's. Curiosity forced him to open his eyes to see the effect of his rite. But to his dismay the skies remained cloudless; there was no cool breeze to herald the approach of rain.

Heavy with disappointment, the boy sighed and shifted. Perhaps his suffering was seen as a child's fancy, a mockery of the solemn and sacred rite reserved for monks and old men.

'My lords;' Dan made another attempt, but no more words came.

The dehydrating heat of the sun was immense. He trembled at the thought that he would be punished consequently by the spirits for his fanciful action.

There seemed to be so much of the cynicism in life, the universal suffering, sorrow, the primeval bitterness and the futility of all things.

Now it was his own seriousness that frightened him so that he shuddered. But there was no way out now except to prove his sacrifice to the lords.

The knife taken from his father's toolbox flashed in the noon sun.

Only then was he convinced that he would not fail, for the sacrifice would be so immense that the lords would take pity on him and yield rain.

But the sharp metal opened the wound deeper than intended on his wrist.

Dan winced with pain, throwing the instrument away. The flow of blood made him giddy. Still he lifted the wounded hand towards the sun for the lords to see, till he fell.

Lying flat on his back, Dan tried to call out for help but could not. His throat was dry, and he trembled, seeing that darkness was descending quickly on him.

Yet he strained in sheer effort to hear any rumble of thunder that would mean rain.

While-reading tasks

1. Understanding character.
   (a) What does paragraph 1 tell the reader about Dan? Try to suggest a word to describe his attitude in his prayer.
   (b) Why does Dan doubt the power of his prayer? Do you think he is sincere?

   (c) Why does Dan think the lords might think his action as a 'child's fancy'? What does the word 'fancy' mean in this context? What are some of the other meanings of this word?

   (d) Why did Dan eventually cut his wrist? Do you think he meant the cut to be fatal?

2. Examining viewpoints.

   (a) Explain what you think the following expressions from the extract mean. Do you agree with the view of life presented in these expressions? Comment.

     (i) cynicism in life

     (ii) universal suffering and sorrow

     (iii) the primeval bitterness

     (iv) the futility of all things

   (b) Would you consider Dan's act as suicide or it is sacrifice? Is there any difference in the context of this story? Do you approve of Dan's cutting his wrist?

   (c) The extract is the final part of the story. It is rather ambiguous about what will happen to Dan. Do you consider the ending positive or negative?

Post-reading tasks

1. Write two or three paragraphs about the events which could have happened before the beginning of this extract.
2. Imagine that the story does not end as it does in this extract. Write your own ending for this story.

Summary

The notion of sacrifice varies according to cultures, and discussion on this theme could arouse students' concern for different viewpoints on this subject and also give students the opportunity to present their perceptions of character in the text. This extract is from Thai writer Pira Sudham's short story, *Rains*.

Text 4

Pre-reading task

Students are asked to make five words from the words in the poem below.

While-reading tasks

1. Reading the poem aloud.
   Due to the nature of concrete poems, readers tend to look at the visual representation and not attempt to read them aloud. It would be interesting if students are asked to study the poem and consider how the poem could be read aloud. This can be done individually or in groups. Students could give reasons for the ways in which they choose to read the poem. Students can be informed that this poem has been 'performed' by its writer.
2. Interpreting.
   (a) Students are asked to give their interpretation of the line: 'I cannot escape'.
       Students could be asked to provide a context and draw relationships between controlling forces and those who are subjected to that control.
   (b) Students are asked to consider who or what they would describe as 'walls' in their lives.
3. Word association.
   Students are asked to list words which they associate with being kept in a restricted area. Students give reasons for their choice of words. Students can look at their list of words for the pre-reading task and see if they have repeated any of the words.
4. Translation.
   The poem *The Wall* is an English translation of a Malay (the official language in Malaysia) poem. Students are asked to consider what word in their own language would be suitable to present the same idea. Students can consider how they could present it as a concrete poem.

Post-reading task

Teacher gives the following words and asks students what or who could be 'walls' for these people:

- parents
- teachers
- an employee
- a king/president/prime minister

Summary

No one enjoys being controlled or restricted. *The Wall* by Malaysian poet Abdul Ghafar Ibrahim provides a rather unusual way of looking at people's need for freedom. The poem can be exploited in a number of ways depending on the students' age and maturity. Discussing restriction and external control is often appealing to adolescents; teachers could use this poem as it is subject to numerous interpretations.

Text 5

Pre-reading task

Below is a popular verse which people may recite with the hope of finding their future lovers or life partners.

> Mirror, mirror
> show to me
> her whose lover
> I will be.

Can you think of other verses like this?

Do you think it safe to dabble with spirits to find out even about a future loved one?

While-reading task

Read the following extract:

'Oh, Grandpa, how you frightened me!'

Don Badoy had turned very pale. 'So it was you, you young bandit! And what is all this, hey? What are you doing down here at this hour?'

'Nothing, Grandpa. I was only . . . I am only . . .'

'Yes, you are the great Senor Only and how delighted I am to make your acquaintance, Senor Only! But if I break this cane on your head you may wish you were someone else, sir!'

'It was just foolishness, Grandpa. They told me I would see my wife.'

'Wife? What wife?'

'Mine. The boys at school said I would see her if I looked in a mirror tonight and said:

> Mirror, mirror
> show to me
> her whose lover
> I will be.'

Don Badoy cackled ruefully. He took the boy by the hair, pulled him along into the room, sat down on a chair, and drew the boy between his knees. 'Now, put your candle down on the floor, son, and let us talk this over. So you want your wife already, hey? You want to see her in advance, hey? But do you know that these are wicked games and that wicked boys who play them are in danger of seeing horrors?'

'Well, the boys did warn me I might see a witch instead.'

'Exactly! A witch so horrible you may die of fright. And she will bewitch you, she will eat your heart and drink your blood!'

'Oh, come now, Grandpa. This is 1890. There are no witches anymore.'

'Oh-no, my young Voltaire! And what if I tell you that I . . . .'

What do you think Don Badoy's grandfather is going to tell him? Now read on and see if your prediction was correct.

'Oh-no, my young Voltaire! And what if I tell you that I myself have seen a witch?'

'You? Where?'

'Right in this room and right in that mirror,' said the old man, and his playful voice had turned savage.

'When, Grandpa?'

'Not so long ago. When I was a bit older than you. Oh, I was a vain fellow and though I was feeling very sick that night and merely wanted to lie down somewhere and die, I could not pass that doorway of course without stopping to see in the mirror what I looked like when dying. But when I poked my head in what should I see in the mirror but . . . but . . .'

'The witch?'

'Exactly!'

'And did she bewitch you Grandpa?'

'She bewitched me and she tortured me. She ate my heart and drank my blood,' said the old man bitterly.

'Oh, my poor little Grandpa! Why have you never told me! And was she very horrible?'

Describe what you think the 'witch' looked like.

Continue reading the extract. Is the description in any way similar to yours?

'Horrible? God, no – she was beautiful! She was the most beautiful creature I have ever seen! Her eyes were somewhat like yours but her hair was like black waters and her golden shoulders were bare. My God, she was enchanting! But I should have known – I should have even known then – the dark and fatal creature she was!'

A silence. Then: 'What a horrid mirror this is, Grandpa,' whispered the boy.

'What makes you say that, hey?'

'Well, you saw this witch in it. And Mama once told me that Grandma once told her that Grandma once saw . . .'

What do you think 'Grandma once saw'? Now read on and find out what the grandmother saw.

'Well, you saw this witch in it. And Mama once told me that Grandma once told her that Grandma once saw the devil in this mirror. Was it of the scare that Grandma died?'

What would your answer be to Don Badoy's last question to his grandfather?

Now read the whole text again. Why do you think Don Badoy's grandfather says this of his wife:

'She bewitched me and she tortured me. She ate my heart and drank my blood.'

Did she really do this? What does he mean? How did the grandmother perceive her husband, in your opinion?

Post-reading tasks

Students answer the following questions and class discussion follows.

1. Is this an effective story?
2. Is the most important thing horror, surprise, mystery or something else?

Summary

Supernatural elements and people's reactions to them and involvement with them are common in most cultures around the world. In this story, Filipino writer Nick Joaquin effectively exploits this element. Teachers can draw upon students' own superstitions and knowledge of the supernatural to motivate them to read the extract.

Conclusion

The five themes dealt with in this article are obviously not peculiar to the new literary traditions in English. The setting and treatment of the themes may be different but their relevance to all readers of literatures in English cannot be denied. Many texts with similar themes can be found in other literary traditions – they will make excellent points of contrast and comparison. The various writers in all the English-language literary traditions have used the English language in their own distinct ways and they offer an expansion of the usual range; these texts integrate and expand the English-language literary canon geographically and culturally.

Thus a thematic approach can be expanded in almost any direction, including geographically. If we expand our concept of canons to encompass literatures in any of the new Englishes, we must be careful not to ignore the possibilities of cross-references which work across time as well as across physical distances. The Malaysian poet Shirley Lim (1986) in an article entitled 'The Dispossessing Eye: Reading Wordsworth on the Equatorial Line' speaks vividly of her own experience in reading across cultural, geographical, and period differences.

Joaquin's use of the supernatural might easily be used as a cross-reference into the opening scene of *Macbeth*; the 'mirror mirror' idea could relate to Tennyson's *The Lady of Shalott*, and equally well to fable (*Snow White and the Seven Dwarfs*).

What is required is a flexibility of reference, a building-up of what McRae earlier in this volume (p. 21) calls 'the wider language frame of reference' which combines the familiar and the unfamiliar, the local and the foreign, old and new: all samples of text will benefit from the broadening of the horizons this will bring about in both individual and experiential readings of literary texts.

Appendix

The full text of the Hilary Tham poem (Text 2) is as follows:

Offerings
I came to you at sunrise
With silvery dew on sleeping lotus
Sparkling in my gay hands;
You put my flowers in the sun.

I danced to you at midday
With bright raintree blooms
Flaming in my ardent arms;
You dropped my blossoms in the pond.

I crept to you at sunset
With pale lilac orchids
Trembling on my uncertain lips;
You shredded my petals in the sand.

I strode to you at midnight
With gravel hard and cold
Clenched in my bitter fists;
You offered me your hybrid orchids,
And I crushed them in my despair.

Note

1. Sources for quotations in this paper are as follows:
    Text 1: Philip Jeyaretnam 1993 *Making Coffee*. In Loh, C. Y. and Ong, I. K. (eds.) *Skoob Pacifica Anthology no. 1: South-East Asia Writes Back*. Skoob Books, London.
    Text 2: Hilary Tham 1976 *Offerings*. In Thumboo, E. (ed.) *The Second Tongue*. Heinemann, Singapore.
    Text 3: Pira Sudham 1983 *Rains*. In *Pira Sudham's Best*. Shire Books, Bangkok.
    Text 4: Abdul Ghafar Ibrahim 1990 *The Wall*. In *Yang Yang: That's That*. Dewan Bahasa dan Pustaka, Kuala Lumpur.
    Text 5: Nick Joaquin 1970 *May Day Eve*. In David-Maramba, A. (ed.) *Philippine Contemporary Literature*. Bookmark, Manila.

Bibliography

A composite bibliography of all academic works referred to in these papers – and a few other significant works besides – follows.

The brief preliminary reading list which precedes the full bibliography is offered as a (less daunting) selection of introductory works for students and teachers with little or no experience in the field of the interfacing of language and literature studies.

Reading list

BASSNETT, S. and GRUNDY, P. 1993. *Language through Literature: Creative Language Teaching through Literature.* Longman, London.

BENTON, M. *et al.* 1988. *Young Readers Responding to Poems.* Routledge, London.

CARTER, R. and LONG, M.N. 1991. *Teaching Literature.* Longman, London.

COLLIE, J. and SLATER, S. 1987. *Literature in the Language Classroom.* Cambridge University Press, Cambridge.

DAVIES, F. 1995. *Introducing Reading.* Penguin, London.

DUFF, A. and MALEY, A. 1990. *Literature.* Oxford University Press, Oxford.

DURANT, A. and FABB, N. 1990. *Literary Studies in Action.* Routledge, London.

LAZAR, G. 1993. *Literature and Language Teaching.* Cambridge University Press, Cambridge.

MCRAE, J. 1991. *Literature with a Small l.* MEP/Macmillan, Basingstoke.

POPE, R. 1995. *Textual Intervention: Critical and Creative Strategies in English Studies.* Routledge, London.

SHORT, M. (ed.) 1989. *Reading, Analysing and Teaching Literature.* Longman, London.

VAN LIER, L. 1995. *Introducing Language Awareness.* Penguin, London.

Composite bibliography

ABORN, M., RUBENSTEIN, H. and STERLING, T.D. 1959. Sources of contextual constraint upon words in sentences. *Journal of Experimental Psychology* 57 (3): 171–80.

ALDERSON, C. and URQUHART, A.H. 1984. *Reading in a Foreign Language*. Longman, London.

APPLE, M.W. 1982. Curricular form and the logic of technical control: building the possessive individual. In Apple, M.W. (ed.) *Cultural and Economic Reproduction in Education*. Routledge, London.

BARTHES, R. 1968/1977. The death of the author *and* From work to text. In Barthes, R. *Image – Music – Text*: 142–8, 155–64. Fontana, London.

BASSNETT, S. 1994. Teaching British cultural studies: reflections on the why and the how. *Journal for the Study of British Cultures* 1 (1): 63–74.

BASSNETT, S. and GRUNDY, P. 1993. *Language through Literature: Creative Language Teaching through Literature*. Longman, London.

BASSNETT, S. and MOUNTFORD, A. 1993. *British Studies: Designing and Developing Programmes Outside Britain*. The British Council, London.

BEAUGRANDE, R. de 1987. Schemas for literary communication. In Halasz, L. (ed.) *Literary Discourse: Aspects of Cognitive and Social Psychological Approaches*: 49–100. Walter de Gruyter, Berlin.

BELLARD-THOMSON, C. 1992. *The Literary Stylistics of French*. Manchester University Press, Manchester.

BENNISON, N. 1993. Discourse analysis, pragmatics and the dramatic 'character': Tom Stoppard's *Professional Foul*. *Language and Literature* 2 (2): 79–99.

BENSON, E. and CONOLLY, L.W. (eds.) 1994. *Encyclopedia of Post-Colonial Literatures in English*. Routledge, London.

BENTON, M. and BENTON, P. 1990. *Double Vision: Reading Paintings . . . Reading Poems . . . Reading Paintings . . .* Hodder and Stoughton, London.

BENTON, M. *et al.* 1988. *Young Readers Responding to Poems*. Routledge, London.

BICKLEY, V. (ed.) 1990. *Language Use, Language Teaching and the Curriculum*. Hong Kong Education Department, Institute of Language in Education, Hong Kong.

BILLINGTON, M. 1990. *Alan Ayckbourn*. Macmillan, Basingstoke.

BIRCH, D. 1989. *Language, Literature and Critical Practice: Ways of Analysing Text*. Routledge, London.

BIRCH, D. 1991. *The Language of Drama: Critical Theory and Practice*. Macmillan, Basingstoke.

BLOOM, H. 1994. *The Western Canon*. Harcourt Brace, New York.

BREEN, M.P. and SHORT, M. 1988. Alternative approaches in teaching stylistics to beginners. *Parlance* 1 (2): 29–48.

BROWN, G. 1990. Cultural values: the interpretation of discourse. *English Language Teaching Journal* 44 (2): 11–17.

BRUMFIT, C.J. (ed.) 1991. *Assessment in Literature Teaching*. Modern English Publications/The British Council, Basingstoke/London.

BRUMFIT, C.J. and BENTON, M. (eds.) 1993. *Teaching Literature: A World Perspective*. Modern English Publications/The British Council, Basingstoke/London.

BRUMFIT, C.J. and CARTER, R.A. (eds.) 1986. *Literature and Language Teaching*. Oxford University Press, Oxford.

BRUNER, J. 1966. *Towards a Theory of Instruction*. Harvard University Press, Cambridge, Massachusetts.

BURTON, D. 1980. *Dialogue and Discourse: A Sociolinguistic Approach to Modern Drama Dialogue and Naturally Occurring Conversation.* Routledge, London.

CANDLIN, C. 1981. *The Communicative Teaching of English Principles and an Exercise Typology.* Longman, London.

CARLSON, S. 1991. Ayckbourn's *Woman in Mind*: contemporary despair and the comic woman. In Carlson, S. *Women and Comedy: Rewriting the British Theatrical Tradition*: 113–26. Michigan University Press, Ann Arbor.

CARTER, R. 1986. Linguistic models, language and literariness: study strategies in the teaching of literature to foreign students. In Brumfit, C.J. and Carter, R.A. (eds.) *Literature and Language Teaching*: 110–32. Oxford University Press, Oxford.

CARTER, R. 1987. *Vocabulary: Applied Linguistic Perspectives.* Routledge, London.

CARTER, R. 1988. Vocabulary, cloze and discourse. In Carter, R. and McCarthy, M. (eds.) *Vocabulary and Language Teaching*: 161–80. Longman, London.

CARTER, R. 1995. *Keywords in Language and Literacy.* Routledge, London.

CARTER, R. and LONG, M.N. 1987. *The Web of Words: Exploring Literature through Language.* Cambridge University Press, Cambridge.

CARTER, R. and LONG, M.N. 1991. *Teaching Literature.* Longman, London.

CARTER, R. and MCCARTHY, M. (eds.) 1988. *Vocabulary and Language Teaching.* Longman, London.

CARTER, R. and MCCARTHY, M. 1988. Lexis and structure. In Carter, R. and McCarthy, M. (eds.) *Vocabulary and Language Teaching*: 18–38. Longman, London.

CARTER, R. and MCCARTHY, M. 1995. Discourse and creativity: bridging the gap between language and literature. In Cook, G. and Seidlhofer, B. (eds.) *Principles and Practice in Applied Linguistics: Studies in Honour of H.G. Widdowson.* Oxford University Press, Oxford.

CARTER, R. and MCRAE, J. 1996. *The Penguin Guide to English Literature.* Penguin, London.

CARTER, R. and MCRAE, J. 1997. *The Routledge History of Literature in English: Britain and Eire.* Routledge, London.

CARTER, R. and NASH, W. 1990. *Seeing Through Language: A Guide to Styles of English Writing.* Blackwell, Oxford.

CARTER, R. and SIMPSON, P. (eds.) 1989. *Language, Discourse and Literature.* Unwin Hyman/Routledge, London.

CARTER, R., WALKER, R. and BRUMFIT, C.J. (eds.) 1989. *Literature and the Learner: Methodological Approaches.* Modern English Publications/The British Council, Basingstoke/London.

CHAN, M. and HARRIS, R. (eds.) 1991. *Asian Voices in English.* Hong Kong University Press, Hong Kong.

CHIARO, D. 1991. *The Language of Jokes.* Routledge, London.

COLE, P. and MORGAN, J. (eds.) 1975. *Syntax and Semantics III: Speech Acts.* Academic Press, New York.

COLLIE, J. and SLATER, S. 1987. *Literature in the Language Classroom.* Cambridge University Press, Cambridge.

COOK, G. 1986. Texts, extracts and stylistic texture. In Brumfit, C.J. and Carter, R.A. (eds.). *Literature and Language Teaching.* Oxford University Press, Oxford.

COOK, G. 1992. *The Discourse of Advertising.* Routledge, London.

COOK, G. 1994. *Discourse and Literature.* Oxford University Press, Oxford.

COOK, G. 1995. Language art. In Maybin, J. and Mercer, N. (eds.) *Using English: From Conversation to Canon.* Routledge, London.

COOK, G. and SEIDLHOFER, B. (eds.) 1995. *Principles and Practice in Applied Linguistics: Studies in Honour of H.G. Widdowson.* Oxford University Press, Oxford.

CULLER, J. 1975. *Structuralist Poetics.* Routledge, London.

CULLER, J. 1977. Structuralism and literature. In Schiff, H. (ed.) *Contemporary Approaches to English Studies:* 59–76. Heinemann, London.

CULLER, J. 1981. *The Pursuit of Signs.* Routledge, London.

CULLER, J. 1983. *On Deconstruction.* Routledge, London.

DAVIES, F. 1995. *Introducing Reading.* Penguin, London.

DICK, C. 1992. British cultural studies as a multi-dimensional subject. *British Studies:* pp 17–20. The British Council, London.

DICKINSON, L. 1987. *Self-Instruction in Language Learning.* Cambridge University Press, Cambridge.

DICKINSON, L. and CARVER, D. 1980. Learning how to learn: steps towards self-direction in foreign language learning in schools. *English Language Teaching Journal* **35** (1).

DOUGILL, J. 1987. *Drama Activities for Language Learning.* Macmillan, London.

DUFF, A. and MALEY, A. 1990. *Literature.* Oxford University Press, Oxford.

DURANT, A. 1993. Interactive approaches to teaching literature in Hong Kong. In Brumfit, C.J. and Benton, M. (eds.) *Teaching Literature: A World Perspective:* 150–71. Modern English Publications/The British Council, Basingstoke/London.

DURANT, A. and FABB, N. 1987. New courses in the linguistics of writing. In Fabb, N. *et al.* (eds.) *The Linguistics of Writing: Arguments Between Language and Literature.* Manchester University Press, Manchester.

DURANT, A. and FABB, N. 1990. *Literary Studies in Action.* Routledge, London.

EIKHENBAUM, B.M. 1927/1978. The theory of the formal method. In Matejka, L. and Pomorska, K. (eds.) *Readings in Russian Poetics.* Michigan University Press, Ann Arbor.

ELLIS, G. and BREWSTER, J. 1991. *The Storytelling Handbook for Primary Teachers.* Penguin, London.

ELLIS, G. and MCRAE, J. 1991. *The Extensive Reading Handbook for Secondary Teachers.* Penguin, London.

ELLIS, G. and SINCLAIR, B. 1989a. *Learning to Learn English: a Course in Learner Training.* Cambridge University Press, Cambridge.

ELLIS, G. and SINCLAIR, B. 1989b. *DTE Package 2: Learner Training.* The British Council, London.

EVANS, G. 1977. *The Language of Modern Drama.* Dent, London.

FABB, N. *et al.* (eds.) 1987. *The Linguistics of Writing: Arguments Between Language and Literature.* Manchester University Press, Manchester.

FAIRCLOUGH, N. 1989. *Language and Power.* Longman, London.

FAIRCLOUGH, N. 1992. *Discourse and Social Change.* Polity Press, Cambridge.

FEARON-JONES, J., LAWRENCE, R. and MEDD, H. 1990/1994. *British Studies Files.* Guangdong University of Foreign Studies, Guangzhou.

FEIST, A. and HUTCHISON, R. 1990. *Cultural Trends.* Policy Studies Institute, London.

FISH, S. 1980. *Is There a Text in This Class?* Harvard University Press, Cambridge, Massachusetts.

FOWLER, R. 1986. *Linguistic Criticism.* Oxford University Press, Oxford.

GADJUSEK, L. 1988. Toward wider use of literature in ESL: why and how? *TESOL Quarterly* **22** (2): 227–57.

GAUTAM, K. 1987. Pinter's *The Caretaker:* a study in conversational analysis. *Journal of Pragmatics* 11:49–59.

GAUTAM, K. and SHARMA, M. 1986. Dialogue in *Waiting for Godot* and Grice's concept of implicature. *Modern Drama* 29 (4): 580–6.

GENETTE, G. *Figures II.* Quoted in Culler, J. 1975 *Structuralist Poetics:* 160. Routledge, London.

GILBERT, S. and GUBAR, S. 1979. *The Madwoman in the Attic.* Yale University Press, New Haven.

GOWER, R. 1986. Can stylistic analysis help the EFL learner to read literature? *English Language Teaching Journal* 40 (2).

GRADDOL, D., SWANN, J. and LEITH, D. (eds.) 1996. *English History: Diversity and Change.* Routledge, London.

GRICE, H.P. 1975. Logic and conversation. In Cole, P. and Morgan, J. (eds.) *Syntax and Semantics III: Speech Acts:* 41–58. Academic Press, New York.

HALASZ, L. (ed.) 1987. *Literary Discourse: Aspects of Cognitive and Social Psychological Approaches.* Walter de Gruyter, Berlin.

HAYES, S. 1984. *Drama as a Second Language* National Extension College, Cambridge.

HE ZIRAN 1987. *A Survey of Pragmatics.* Hunan Educational Press, Changsha.

HERMAN, V. 1991. Drama dialogue and the systematics of turn-taking. *Semiotica* 83 (1/2): 97–121.

HILL,. C. and PARRY, K. (eds.) 1994. *From Testing to Assessment: English as an International Language.* Longman, London.

HOLEC, H. 1981. *Autonomy and Foreign Language Learning.* Pergamon, Oxford.

HYLAND, P. (ed.) 1986. *Discharging the Canon.* Singapore University Press, Singapore.

JAMES, C. and GARRET, P. (eds.) 1992. *Language Awareness in the Classroom.* Longman, London.

JORDAN, N. 1993. *The Crying Game.* Vintage, London.

KACHRU, B.B. 1986. Non-native literatures in English as a resource for language teaching. In Brumfit, C.J. and Carter, R.A. (eds.) *Literature and Language Teaching:* 140–9. Oxford University Press, Oxford.

KACHRU, B.B. 1990. Cultural contact and literary creativity in a multilingual society. In Toyama, J. and Ochner, N. (eds.) *Literary Relations East and West: Selected Essays:* 194–203. University of Hawaii at Manoa and the East–West Center, College of Languages, Linguistics and Literature, Honolulu.

KORPIMIES, L. 1983. *A Linguistic Approach to the Analysis of a Dramatic Text.* University of Jyvaskila, Jyvaskila (Finland).

KRAMSCH, C.J. 1993. *Context and Culture in Language Teaching.* Oxford University Press, Oxford.

LABOV, W. 1969. The logic of non-standard English. *Georgetown Monographs on Language and Linguistics* 22: 1–31.

LABOV, W. and FANSHEL, D. 1977. *Therapeutic Discourse.* Academic Press, New York.

LAKOFF, R. and TANNEN, D. 1984. Conversational strategy and metastrategy in a pragmatic theory: the example of *Scenes from a Marriage. Semiotica* 49 (3/4): 323–46.

LAVER, J. and HUTCHESON, S. 1972. *Communication Face to Face.* Penguin, London.

LAVERY, C. 1993. *Focus on Britain Today.* Macmillan, Basingstoke.

LAZAR, G. 1990. Using novels in the language-learning classroom. *English Language Teaching Journal* **44** (3): 204–14.

LAZAR, G. 1993. *Literature and Language Teaching.* Cambridge University Press, Cambridge.

LAZAR, G. 1994. Using literature at lower levels. *English Language Teaching Journal* **48** (2): 115–24.

LECERCLE, J.-J. 1993. The current state of stylistics. *European English Messenger* **2** (1): 14–18.

LEECH, G.N. 1969. *A Linguistic Guide to English Poetry.* Longman, London.

LEECH, G.N. and SHORT, M.H. 1981. *Style in Fiction: A Linguistic Introduction to Fictional Prose.* Longman, London.

LI XIAOJU 1986. *Communicative English for Chinese Learners* (*CECL*; 4 vols.). Shanghai Foreign Language Press, Shanghai.

LIM, S. 1986. The dispossessing eye: reading Wordsworth on the equatorial line. In Hyland, P. (ed.) *Discharging the Canon.* Singapore University Press, Singapore.

LODGE, D. 1977. *The Modes of Modern Writing.* Edward Arnold, London.

LOTT, S.W., HAWKINS, M.S.G. and MCMILLAN, N. (eds.) 1993. *Global Perspectives on Teaching Literature: Shared Visions and Distinctive Visions.* National Council of Teachers of English, Urbana, Illinois.

MACCABE, C. 1982. *Towards a Modern Trivium: English Studies Today. The Inaugural Lecture of Professor Colin MacCabe.* University of Strathclyde, Glasgow.

MACKAY, R. 1992. Lexicide and goblin-spotting in the language/literature classroom. *English Language Teaching Journal* **46** (2).

MALEY, A. 1982. *Drama Techniques in Language Learning.* Cambridge University Press, Cambridge.

MALEY, A. 1989. Down from the pedestal: literature as resource. In Carter, R., Walker, R. and Brumfit, C.J. (eds.) *Literature and the Learner: Methodological Approaches*: 10–24. Modern English Publications/The British Council, Basingstoke/London.

MALEY, A. 1994. *Short and Sweet.* Penguin, London.

MALEY, A. and MOULDING, S. 1985. *Poem into Poem: Reading and Writing Poems with Students of English.* Cambridge University Press, Cambridge.

MAO SIHUI 1992a. 'To Kill a Mockingbird' called uncritical thinking in the Chinese classroom of English literature. Paper delivered at the National Conference on the Teaching of Foreign Literatures, Guilin.

MAO SIHUI 1992b. Designing and teaching an MA modern British and American drama course in the Chinese context. *ELT in China.* The British Council, Beijing.

MAO SIHUI 1993. Creativity and the CECL classroom. In *Research on Foreign Languages Higher Education* **2**: 79–93 (Guangzhou).

MATEJKA, L. and POMORSKA, K. (eds.) 1978. *Readings in Russian Poetics.* Michigan University Press, Ann Arbor.

MATTHEW, H. and MORGAN, K. 1992. *The Oxford History of Britain. Vol. 5: The Modern Age.* Oxford University Press, Oxford.

MAYBIN, J. and MERCER, N. (eds.) 1995. *Using English: From Conversation to Canon.* Routledge, London.

MCCARTHY, M. 1990. *Vocabulary.* Oxford University Press, Oxford.

MCCARTHY, M. 1991. *Discourse Analysis for Language Teachers.* Cambridge University Press, Cambridge.

MCCARTHY, M. and CARTER, R. 1994. *Language as Discourse: Perspectives for Language Teaching.* Longman, London.

MCRAE, J. 1985. *Using Drama in the Classroom.* Pergamon, Oxford.

MCRAE, J. 1991. *Literature with a Small l.* MEP/Macmillan, Basingstoke.
MCRAE, J. 1992. *Wordsplay.* Macmillan, Basingstoke.
MCRAE, J. and BOARDMAN, R. 1984. *Reading Between the Lines.* Cambridge University Press, Cambridge.
MCRAE, J. and PANTALEONI, L. 1985/1986. *Words on the Page.* La Nuova Italia/Oxford University Press, Florence/Oxford.
MCRAE, J., SYAL, P. and BELLARMINE, R. (eds.) forthcoming. *Widening Horizons: Teaching the Language/Literature Interface in South Asia.* Orient Longman, Madras.
MOFFETT, J. and MCELHENY, K.R. 1995. *Points of View.* Signet, New York.
MONTGOMERY, M. *et al.* 1992. *Ways of Reading: Advanced Reading Skills for Students of Literature.* Routledge, London.
MONTGOMERY, M 1995 (2nd edn.). *An Introduction to Language and Society.* Routledge, London.
NASH, W. 1989. Changing the guard at Elsinore. In Carter, R. and Simpson, P. (eds.) *Language, Discourse and Literature:* 23–41. Unwin Hyman/Routledge, London.
NATION, P. and COADY, J. 1988. Vocabulary and reading. In Carter, R. and McCarthy, M. (eds.) *Vocabulary and Language Teaching:* 97–110. Longman, London.
NEO, V. 1990. Using literature to extend language awareness and skills in the classroom: a language-based technique. In Bickley, V. (ed.) *Language Use, Language Teaching and the Curriculum:* 689–701. Hong Kong Education Department, Institute of Language in Education, Hong Kong.
NUNAN, D. 1994. *Introducing Discourse Analysis.* Penguin, London.
O'MALLEY, J.M. *et al.* 1985. Learning strategies used by beginning and intermediate students. *Language Learning* **35** (1).
OXFORD, R. 1989. *Language Learning Strategies: What Every Teacher Should Know.* Newbury House, New York.
PHILLIPSON, R. 1992. *Linguistic Imperialism.* Oxford University Press, Oxford.
PINKER, S. 1994. *The Language Instinct.* Penguin, London.
POPE, R. 1995. *Textual Intervention: Critical and Creative Strategies in English Studies.* Routledge, London.
RICHARDS, I.A. 1929. *Practical Criticism.* Routledge and Kegan Paul, London.
RONNQVIST, L. and SELL, R.D. 1994. Teenage books for teenagers: reflections on literature in language education. *English Language Teaching Journal* **48** (2): 125–32.
ROSENBLATT, L.M. 1968. *Literature as Exploration.* Noble and Noble, New York.
ROSS, N. 1991. Literature and film. *English Language Teaching Journal* **45** (2).
ROSSITER, P. 1991. At cloze quarters: the use of gapfill in teaching poetry. *Essays and Studies in British and American Literature* **37**: 73–96 (Tokyo).
RUBIN, J. 1975. What the good language learner can teach us. *TESOL Quarterly* **9** (1).
RUSHDIE, S. 1983/1991. 'Commonwealth literature' does not exist. In Rushdie, S. *Imaginary Homelands.* Granta, London.
SACKS, H., SCHEGLOFF, E. and JEFFERSON, G. 1974. A simplest systematics for the organisation of turn-taking for conversation. *Language* **50** (4): 696–735.
SAGE, H. 1987. *Incorporating Literature in ESL Instruction.* Prentice-Hall, Englewood Cliffs, New Jersey.

SANDERS, D. 1990. *Losing an Empire, Finding a Role: British Foreign Policy since 1945*. Macmillan, Basingstoke.

SCHIFF, H. (ed.) 1977. *Contemporary Approaches to English Studies*. Heinemann, London.

SEVIER, M. 1991. Notes to *The Twits* by Roald Dahl. In Ellis, G. and McRae, J. *The Extensive Reading Handbook for Secondary Teachers*: 60–74. Penguin, London.

SHEPHERD, V. 1994. *Literature about Language*. Routledge, London.

SHKLOVSKY, V. *Art as Technique*. Quoted in Lodge, D. 1977. *The Modes of Modern Writing*: 13. Edward Arnold, London.

SHORT, M. 1981. Discourse analysis and the analysis of drama. *Applied Linguistics* 111 (2): 180–202.

SHORT, M. 1986. Speech presentation, the novel and the press. In van Peer, W. (ed.) *The Taming of the Text*: 61–81. Routledge, London.

SHORT, M. (ed.) 1989. *Reading, Analysing and Teaching Literature*. Longman, London.

SHORT, M. 1989. Discourse analysis and the analysis of drama. In Carter, R. and Simpson, P. (eds.) *Language, Discourse and Literature*: 139–68. Unwin Hyman/Routledge, London.

SHORT, M. and BREEN, M.P. 1988. Innovations in the teaching of literature: putting stylistics in its place. *Critical Quarterly* 30 (2): 1–8.

SIMPSON, P. 1989. Politeness phenomena in Ionesco's *The Lesson*. In Carter, R. and Simpson, P. (eds.) *Language, Discourse and Literature*: 171–93. Unwin Hyman/Routledge, London.

SIMPSON, P. 1993. *Language, Ideology and Point of View*. Routledge, London.

SMITH, J. 1989. *Misogynies*. Faber and Faber, London.

SOUDEK, M. and SOUDEK, L.I. 1983. Cloze after thirty years: new uses in language teaching. *English Language Teaching Journal* 37 (4): 335–9.

TALIB, I.S. 1992. Why not teach non-native English literature? *English Language Teaching Journal* 46 (1): 51–5.

TANNEN, D. 1989. *Talking Voices: Repetition, Dialogue and Imagery in Conversational Discourse*. Cambridge University Press, Cambridge.

TATLOW, A. (ed.) 1982. *The Teaching of Literature in ASAIHL Universities: Proceedings of the Seminar of the Association of South-East Asian Institutes of Higher Learning*. Hong Kong University Press, Hong Kong.

TAYLOR, J.R. (ed.) 1968. *John Osborne, 'Look Back in Anger': A Casebook*. Macmillan, Basingstoke.

TOYAMA, J. and OCHNER, N. (eds.) 1990. *Literary Relations East and West: Selected Essays*. University of Hawaii at Manoa and the East–West Center, College of Languages, Linguistics and Literature, Honolulu, Hawaii.

TRAUGOTT, E.C. and PRATT, M.L. 1980. *Linguistics for Students of Literature*. Harcourt Brace Jovanovitch, New York.

TURNER, G. 1993. *Film as Social Practice*. Routledge, London.

VAN LIER, L. 1995. *Introducing Language Awareness*. Penguin, London.

VAN PEER, W. (ed.) 1986. *The Taming of the Text*. Routledge, London.

VAN PEER, W. 1989. How to do things with texts: towards a pragmatic foundation for the teaching of texts. In Short, M. (ed.) *Reading, Analysing and Teaching Literature*: 267–97. Longman, London.

WALLACE, C. 1992. *Reading*. Oxford University Press, Oxford.

WATT, I. 1957/1963. *The Rise of the Novel*. Peregrine, London.

WENDEN, A. 1986. Incorporating learner training in the classroom. *System* 14 (3): 315–25.

WENDEN, A. 1991. *Learner Strategies for Learner Autonomy*. Prentice Hall, Hemel Hempstead.

WENDEN, A. and RUBIN, J. 1987. *Learner Strategies in Language Learning.* Prentice Hall, Hemel Hempstead.

WESTON, A. 1989. Poetic viciousness: translation virtues. *Le Lingue nel Mondo* 4/5: 268–75 (Florence).

WIDDOWSON, H.G. 1975. *Stylistics and the Teaching of Literature.* Longman, London.

WIDDOWSON, H.G. 1984. *Explorations in Applied Linguistics 2.* Oxford University Press, Oxford.

WIDDOWSON, H.G. 1992. *Practical Stylistics.* Oxford University Press, Oxford.

WILKINSON, J. 1994. *Introducing Standard English.* Penguin, London.

WILLIAMS, R. 1976/1983. *Keywords.* Fontana, London.

WILLIAMS, R. 1977. *Marxism and Literature.* Oxford University Press, Oxford.

WILLING, K. 1989. *Teaching How to Learn: Learning Strategies in ESL.* Macquarie University, Sydney.

WITTGENSTEIN, L. 1967. *Zettel.* Oxford University Press, Oxford.

ZACH, W. (ed.) 1990. *Literature in English: New Perspectives.* P. Lang, Frankfurt.

ZACH, W. 1991. The study of 'new literatures in English' at university level. In Chan, M. and Harris, R. (eds.) *Asian Voices in English.* Hong Kong University Press, Hong Kong.

ZACH, W. (ed.) 1992. *English Literature and the University Curriculum.* P. Lang, Frankfurt.

ZYNGIER, S. 1994a. *Literary Awareness.* Federal University, Department of English, Rio de Janeiro.

ZYNGIER, S. 1994b. Introducing literary awareness. *Language Awareness* 3 (2): 95–108.

Index

The following index is primarily a subject index and refers the reader to sections of the book where there is substantial discussion of the topics concerned. Names of authors of primary literary and film texts are also included but secondary critical and biographical sources are not indicated.

Guildford College
Learning Resource Centre

Please return on or before the last date shown.
No further issues or renewals if any items are overdue.
"7 Day" loans are **NOT** renewable.

0 9 NOV 2007

1 8 JUN 2008

Class: 420. 7 CAR

Title: Language, Literature and the Learner

Author: CARTER, Ronald